"I REFUSE TO HAVE A BAD DAY"

- Don Tyson

Foreword by Don Tyson
Written by Paul Whitley

Publisher: PBWINSIGHTS LLC
Email: appliedleaderwshipprinciples@gmail.com
Publishing, Writing, Consulting

ISBN: 1-4196-9422-7
ISBN-13: 9781419694226
LCCN #: 2008906309

Visit www.booksurge.com to order additional copies.
Visit www.amazon.com.

DON TYSON HONORS FUTURE FARMERS OF AMERICA

As a high school boy Don Tyson was an active member of the Future Farmers of America at Springdale, Arkansas High School. His experience with FFA gave him a good introduction to production agriculture that has served him will ever since.

Five years later, in April of 1995, at the age of 65, Don retired as Chairman of the Board of Tyson Foods, Inc., at the time the world's largest poultry based food company. Today, his son John Tyson is Chairman of the Borad of the company, now the largest beef, pork and chicken processor on the planet.

This book honors the millions of past and present high school FFA teachers and students whose motto is: *"Learning to Do; Doing to Learn; Earning to Live; Living to Serve."*

TABLE OF CONTENTS

Foreword by Don Tyson   4

Introduction   12

Dedication   9

Acknowledgements   10

Chapter Titles

1.   LEARNING TO LEARN, WORK
   AND LEAD   22

2.   THE TRIUMVIRATE   57
   Don Tyson, Leland Tollett, Donald "Buddy" Wray

3.   PROFITABILITY, THE SWEET MUSIC OF
   CUSTOMER SATISFACTION   83

4.   A WORK ENVIRONMENT BUILT ON TRUST,
   INDIVIDUAL RESPONSIBILITY AND
   ACCOUNTABILITY   143

5.   SEGMENT, CONCENTRATE, DOMINATE 199
   Tyson's Growth Strategy, Odyssey of Acquisitions

6.   1989 HOLLY ACQUISITION   247
   Reaching the Goal to Be Number One in the
   Poultry Industry

7. INVESTING IN SCIENCE AND
    TECHNOLOGY TO ACHIEVE A
    COMPETITIVE ADVANTAGE.   287
    "By the way, Lord, thanks for chicken!"

8. POLITICS, GOVERNMENT, AND THE
    MEDIA   313

9. PACKAGING AND TRANSMITTING THE
    SPIRIT OF DON TYSON   329
    Training and Development

    London, Arkansas, 1985–A Place for People to Grow

10. DON TYSON RETIRES   369

Endnotes   376

FOREWORD by Don Tyson

I was studying poultry science at the University of Arkansas at Fayetteville, when my dad had an opportunity to sell Tyson Feed and Hatchery in 1952 to Swanson. He called and asked me what my plans were when I finished my studies. I told him I had always wanted to come into the family business. He did not sell the company. I left the university in 1952 and from that day until 1963, the year I took the company public, I worked in the business six days a week and on Dad's farm on the seventh day.

I learned early on that when my fellow team members and I were having fun at work, we were productive. I also learned the power of mutual trust. The more I trusted them, the more they trusted me. That mutual trust began small but grew, as together we had successful experiences. Out of those relationships of trust came a growing sense of confidence, and as we worked together our company did well.

We learned to take risks and manage them based on the confidence we had in ourselves and our company. When we went public in 1963 our stockholders and our workers began to reap the rewards of investing their time and money in the business. Share values began to rise. We made it easy for our workers to buy stock. Today, thousands of our early hourly workers, now in retirement, are sharing in the success of ownership. That sense of ownership by our people has been one of the keys to our becoming number one in the chicken-based food industry.

Our company's rapid growth in the 1960s, 1970s, and 1980s created opportunities for our people to grow and prosper as they took on more responsibility. I encouraged my folks to train their replacements so they would be ready when opportunity knocked. We believed we should grow our own and rarely went outside for talent. We made a bunch of acquisitions that proved to be a rich source of new talent.

Sales grew from a million dollars in 1952 to eleven million in 1959. That year (1959) was the year we built our first processing plant. I realized I needed help managing the business. I recruited Leland Tollett in 1959 and Buddy

Wray about a year later. Both had recently completed their education at the University of Arkansas. Leland's job was to manage the live chickens, and Buddy's job was to manage processing and sales. They had skills and abilities I didn't have, but knew we needed to grow the business. My work was more about the future, and I got out of their way as they managed the present. Much of the credit for Tyson's success belongs to Leland and Buddy and their management skills, which Whitley writes about in this book.

Paul Whitley came to Tyson when we acquired Tastybird/Valmac in 1984. He had initiated a sales training program that was producing good results for his company. In 1985, he was chosen to create a management development program including building Tyson's Management Development Center in a resort setting on Lake Dardanelle on the Arkansas River near Russellville, Arkansas. In that job he was charged with the responsibility of understanding our work culture or belief system and training our people accordingly. My philosophy was simple—satisfied workers satisfy customers and satisfied customers satisfy shareholders.

Whitley retired in 1997 at age 65. He came to me in November 2004 and said he had an "itch that only I could scratch." His itch was a need to write about what he had experienced during his time as our training guru. The book title came from a comment I made to him as he was leaving my office after one of his many visits, when I reminded him that "I REFUSE TO HAVE A BAD DAY."

Don Tyson, October 2006
Springdale, Arkansas

DEDICATION

A leader's greatest need is for followers. I dedicate this book to the thousands of followers who did the work of making Tyson Foods number one in the poultry base food business.

Paul Whitley

ACKNOWLEDGMENTS

*"We have friends, or we are friends, in order that we
do not get killed."*
Martin Marty, On Friendship. Argus Communications

Barbara Berry Whitley, whose patience and long-suffering
loved the writer through cycles of perspiration, inspiration,
depression, frustration, writer's block, five a.m. coffee, eleven
p.m. coffee and the tortoise pace of a seventy-five-year-old
unpublished author!

Don Tyson, Leland Tollett, Buddy Wray, Johnny Tyson,
Mary Rush, Leta Bell, Annabel Claypool, Harry Erwin,
James Blair, Dick and Mary Stockland, Bob Womack,
Gerald Johnston, Dr. John Hardiman, James Bell, Aubrey
Cuzick, Bill Ray, Don Tharp, Dr. James Tollett, David
Whitmore, Howard Baird, Bill Jaycox, Senator David Pryor,
Senator Dale Bumpers, Col. John Torres, Charles Wyche,
Pete Lovette, Bill Lovette, Herman Tuck, Shelby Massey,
Reynolds Skinner, Sue White, Bob Justice, Gwen Baskin,
Suzanne Graham, Marilyn Seymour, Neil Carey, Mike
Hudlow, Jim Cate, Lois Bottomley Keller, Mitch Newton,
Clark Irwin, Greg Lee, Dr. Neal Apple, Hal Carper, Bob
Keyser, Lyle Sparkman, Dr. Andre Guerrero, Dr. Ursula
Chandler, Joe and Geri Williams, Dr. John Farrell, Roland
Goicoechea, Dr. E.L. Stephenson, Dr. James Denton, Dr.
Ellis Brunton, Dr. Rick Roop, Dr. Lionel Barton, Dr. Diana
Bisbee, Jim Thilmont, Brad Johnson, Pastor Jim Anderson,
Charles Fichthorn, Henry Covillo and George Whitley, my
big brother.

Professor John Jorstad of Sioux City, Iowa, leader of the Top-of-the-Summit-Street-Think-Tank– Shannon, Sarah, Lynne, Guy, Richard.

Bob Keyser III, connoisseur of the good life whose guidance, friendship and a Rocky Mountain High which he inspired as we rode our motorcycles to the top of Mount Evans, Colorado, altitude 14,264 feet.

Drs. Burton and Beverly Elliott, whose sustaining friendship over many years has made all the difference in the world!

Archie Schaffer, whose understanding and knowledge of the leadership strengths at Tyson Foods coordinated interviews and communication with interviewees. Archie is a truth teller, the epitome of professionalism, integrity and friendship.

To my book editors who demonstrated extraordinary empathy by editing a chaotic manuscript, I am forever grateful.

Judge Google, my four year old Boston Terrier whose humorous antics brightened every day with his refusal to take life too seriously.

I have tried diligently to give credit to all the sources I write about. If I have erred in this vital task, I regret the errors and will correct in later editions.

INTRODUCTION

Tyson Foods was named the largest food processor in the United States by *Food Processing Magazine* published in August 2005

ALL FIGURES IN MILLIONS OF DOLLARS—add six zeros.

1.	Tyson Foods $24,086	11. General Mills $9,519
2.	Kraft Foods 22,060	12. H.J. Heinz Co. 8,012
3.	PepsiCo 19,399	13. Swift & Co. 8,000
4.	Nestlé (US & Can) 13,775	14. Campbell Soup 7,109
5.	ConAgra 11,396	15. Coca-Cola Co. 6,643
6.	Anheuser-Busch Cos. 11,351	16. Kellogg Co. 6,369
7.	Dean Foods 10,822	17. Unilever N.A. 6,136
8.	Sara Lee Corp. 10,743	18. Cargill, Inc. 5,500
9.	Mars, Inc. 10,600	19. Pilgrim's Pride 5,364
10.	Smithfield Foods 10,332	20. Dole Foods 5,316

The Tyson name properly belongs to a class of unique business leaders who led transformational change in food processing and marketing. Names like: Phillip Danforth Armour in meat processing, Clarence Birdseye in frozen vegetables and juices; Jack Simplot in potatoes, George A. Hormel in meat, Henry John Heinz in food condiments, "Gussie" Busch in beer, Robert Rich Sr. in non-diary toppings and desserts, Dr. John Harvey Kellogg in cereal, and James Harvey Kraft in milk and cheese.

Don Tyson, the entrepreneurial son of company founder Mr. John Tyson, recruited two Arkansas native sons, Leland Tollett and Buddy Wray, students at the University of Arkansas at Fayetteville, to create the leadership team—"the triumvirate"—that worked together for most of forty years to build the world's largest food processor.

These men wore no masks; they were comfortable in their own skin. They were transparent; deceit had no place in their living—professional or personal. They rarely socialized with each other. They gave each other space to be unique; cloning was neither desired nor practiced. Their religious connections, political preferences, social styles, community interests, and lifestyles were diverse. They were men with a sense of spirituality, i.e., the nonphysical reality of wholeness, personhood, respect, and dignity for their fellow travelers, spirituality derived from their knowledge of the human spirit. Organizational integrity was the result of leader behaviors that created a work environment of trust. Trust has its basis in integrity.

They understood that personal power flowed from the bottom up. Position power flowed from the top down. They developed the skill of balancing position power with personal power—the integration of head and heart, and used power wisely.

In the beginning Mr. John Tyson bought and sold fresh produce. Later he designed a system to transport live chickens to Chicago. He learned Chicago consumers would pay more for chicken that was fresh—live was really fresh! When he formed Tyson Feed & Hatchery, the company was a local supplier of feed and baby chicks to local farmers who subsidized their farm income by raising chickens. In 1958, Don Tyson built Tyson's first processing plants to process and market fresh chickens. Tyson Foods grew organically and by making thirty-six acquisitions from 1962 to 1997.

This book is a collection of research-based stories of leader and follower behaviors and responses I observed during my years at Tyson Foods, 1984-1997. Prior to that time I was a competitor. In addition to observing behaviors as VP, Training & Development, based at Tyson's Management Development Center in Russellville, Arkansas, I listened to hundreds of leadership and management stories told by Tyson folks who came to the Center for training and development. The Center orchestrated and/or hosted meetings and seminars for virtually all senior and middle managers during that time. Those events provided opportunities to listen and learn about Tyson's rich cultural history. My work placed me in close proximity to the triumvirate to observe their behaviors "up close and personal."

Writing Intentions

Following retirement at sixty-five, I learned to ride motorcycles and pursued the "airstream-of-consciousness—wind-in-your-face" (old men dreams men and all that metaphysical stuff) to experience the land that I had seen from the air, having traveled by air for thirty years. At truck stops, biker hangouts and visitor centers in Montana, Wyoming, Colorado, Nebraska, New Mexico, and North and South Dakota, I met other biker retirees. Our conversations turned frequently to how and where we had earned our bread. When I told my newfound friends that I had retired from Tyson Foods, their responses indicated they knew the Tyson brand as consumers. As I listened, I learned their perceptions of Tyson Foods were very different from the reality I had experienced during my tenure as VP, Training & Development. Their perceptions were based on a barrage of stories in the media that followed the 1992 election of Arkansas Governor Bill Clinton as the forty-second president of the United States. The stories ranged from tabloid sensationalism of misinformation, disinformation, innuendos, and lies to an occasional story based on sound principles of journalism in search of truth, supported by multisource verification.

Don Tyson was a lifelong Democrat as was his dad. Also like his dad, he worked all sides of the political spectrum supporting or opposing legislation that had an impact on his company. Until the election of the Southern Baptist preacher Reverend Mike Huckabee—a Republican from Hope, Arkansas, in the 1996 gubernatorial race, Arkansas had been Democratic. Reverend Huckabee was only the third Republican governor since Reconstruction.

Retired bikers tend not to be in a hurry. They listened. I shared my knowledge and experience at Tyson Foods. Some were especially interested in the relationship Don Tyson had with Bill Clinton. The population of the State of Arkansas at the time was similar to the population of Chicago, Houston, or metro Denver. In a state with such a small population and limited resources, politics, state government, and business frequently coalesced around the common interests of education, taxes, and regulation. As the personal and private business lives of President and Mrs. Clinton became grist for the media mill, many in the media reported and/or speculated that President Clinton and Don Tyson had a quid-quo-pro relationship. They did not. Details are in chapter eight. In Clinton's autobiography, My Life, he described his loss in 1981 to Republican Frank White on page 281: "[Frank White] had strong support from all the interest groups I'd taken on, including utility, poultry, trucking and timber companies, and the medical associations." The major companies headquartered in northwest Arkansas, Tyson Foods, J.B.Hunt Transportation, and Wal-Mart, would have suffered from Clinton's policies. He was defeated by Frank

White, only the second Republican governor in Arkansas since Reconstruction. Bill Clinton, the "come-back kid," defeated Frank White in the next election.

Another writing intention was to scratch an intellectual "itch" to elaborate on and correlate the leadership behaviors of the Triumvirate—Don Tyson, Leland Tollett, and Buddy Wray with the growing body of research that began in the late fifties and early sixties. Prior to that period empirical research in the field was limited.

The work of one of my mentors, Dr. Paul Hersey--educator, behavioral scientist, and practitioner of applied leadership principles as a leader/manager in the trenches of corporate life, was determinative in my business career. My first contact with him was in the mid-seventies when as a national sales manager I desperately needed his help and attended one of his seminars in Houston. Using two large reversible chalk boards (before white boards) an overhead projector, four flip charts and the Academy Award winning motion picture, "Twelve O'Clock High", he presented the essence of the best empirical research that was the framework supporting his "Situational Leadership Model". The 1972 edition of "Managing Organizational Behavior" has been a constant influence in my work and personal life.

On two or three other occasions I caught up with him at the University Associates conferences in San Francisco created by J. William Pfeiffer. At one of those events in the early eighties, Dr. Hersey described an early connection with Tyson Foods when he was an associate professor at the University of Arkansas at Fayetteville, Arkansas .In the early fifties Mr. John Tyson, Don's dad and founder of Tyson Feed & Hatchery, hired him to do training for Tyson. Don was a student at the University and learned that Professor Hersey's sports roadster had broken down. On leaving class Hersey was given the keys to Don's automobile with a note telling him he could use Don's car until the roadster was repaired. Don was not in any of Hersey's classes but had been looking for an opportunity to meet the man his dad had hired for training. Some fifty years after their first meeting Hersey's work continues to influence the training and development of Tyson's people.

Dr. Hersey, with post-graduate degrees in education, the behavioral sciences, and business administration, is a teacher's teacher. He told this writer that his first love had always been the classroom but believed that to be most effective as a teacher he needed to validate what he was teaching by practicing the behavioral principles and theories he had learned as a student and researcher. He made a commitment to himself that he would spend ten years in corporate management before going back to the classroom. In an interview with Dr. John Schermerhorn, Jr., at Ohio University at Athens, Hersey talks about his experience in business. "I spent ten years in a variety of different types of business settings. The last position I had been in was a huge technical laboratory (Sandia National Laboratories). The company had a unique problem They had seven thousand of the brightest scientists and engineers in the country, perhaps in the world. Most came in with graduate degrees in engineering, physics, or mathematics. They had tremendous technical skills. But when it came time to become a manager in this company, basically you got promoted based on your technical skills. So the company would often lose a super researcher and gain a very mediocre to poor manager. This was actually Peter's Principle working getting promoted to your level of incompetence. We weren't using then what I call today the anti Peter Principle vaccine: training and development prior to being promoted, the opportunity to try the job on a part-time basis before you get promoted to it full time." Dr. Hersey corrected this human resource mess by designing and implementing a training program where people not only learned leadership skills as concepts and knowledge but practiced them before going into their new assignments.

In 1969, working with Ken Blanchard, Hersey's landmark work was published by Prentice Hall—"Management of Organizational Behavior: Utilizing Human Resources.

The value and or genius of Hersey's work are that he didn't fall into the trap of researchers, business scholars and consultants who were searching for the Golden Fleece. He built on the works of Likert, Merrill and Reid, Blake and Mouton, Argyris, Maslow, Herzberg, Carl Rogers, Elton Mayo, Schien, Odiorne and others.

His work continues at The Center for Leadership Studies headquartered at Escondido, California. Dr. Hersey, Founder and "god father at MOB, President Ron Campbell and their staff do business with a global client list. They have offices around the world. Their work has been translated in nine languages.

All organizations of human beings, from families to giant organizations, are messy by nature. Some are messier than others. I could have written a "gotcha" about messes and human weakness but I chose to write bout individual and organizational strengths and leader behaviors that affirmed persons, building on their unique strengths. Building a life or an organization on weakness is the strategy used by the Malevolent One who seeks to tear down and destroy.

Don Tyson is the most positive and affirming person I have worked for.

An Expression of Gratitude

I never applied for a job at Tyson Foods. They found me and gave me an opportunity to have more fun at work and more freedom to be productive than I ever thought possible. My spirit is filled with gratitude to Tyson Foods,

Buddy Wray, Leland Tollett, Don Tyson and thousands of Tyson folks who lived Don Tyson's dictum that "if you are not having fun at work, change yourself or change jobs."

Leadership Defined

Leaders are people who influence the behaviors of others and contribute to the success of those they lead.

On some occasion or another I heard Dr. Hersey say, "I can only influence the behavior of another by my own behavior."

Peter Drucker, the grand old man of business consulting, wrote in The Effective Executive, [1]

There seems to be little correlation between a man's effectiveness and his intelligence, his imagination, or his knowledge. Brilliant men are often strikingly ineffectual; they fail to realize that the brilliant insight is not by itself achievement. They never have learned that insights become effectiveness only through hard systematic work. Conversely, in every organization there are some highly effective plodders. While others rush around in the frenzy and busyness which very bright people so often confuse with "creativity," the plodder puts one foot in front of the other and gets there first, like the tortoise in the old fable.

Respectfully,
Paul Whitley
Carrollton, Texas 75010

CHAPTER 1

Learning to Learn—Learning to Work—

Learning to Lead

The quest for leadership is first an inner quest to discover who you are. Through self-development comes the confidence needed to lead. Self-confidence is really awareness of and faith in your own powers. These powers become clear and strong only as you work to identify and develop them. As you begin this quest, you must wrestle with some difficult questions: How much do I understand about what is going on in the organization and the world in which it operates? How prepared am I to handle the complex problems that now confront my organization? Where do I think the organization ought to be headed over the next ten years? What are my beliefs about how people ought to conduct the affairs of our organization? How certain am I of my own conviction as to stated vision and values? What are my strengths and weaknesses? What do I need to do to improve my abilities to move the organization forward? How solid is my relationship with my constituents? Am I the right one to be leading at this very moment? The questions continue…While scholars may disagree on the origins of leadership, there is a strong consensus that leaders must be interpersonally competent. You must be able to listen, take advice, lose arguments, and follow. Unless you can develop the trust and respect of others, you cannot lead. Kouzes and Posner[2]

Don Tyson, son of the founder of what would become the world's largest protein-based food company, built Tyson's first chicken processing plant. The year was 1958, six years after he came into the business as general manager. The entire first day's production of four thousand chickens was condemned by the in-plant inspectors of the U.S. Department of Agriculture. His response to this challenge was quick, decisive, and effective. He identified the causes of the failure, made a decision and removed the causes of failure from the system—all in a few hours.

When he built the plant, he and his dad agreed to spend $75,000. In fact, the cost was $95,000. He went to his dad for more money, and Dad said, "No, you said it would cost $75,000. You find the money." Don raised the money from a local car dealer and others he knew. This experience was a precursor of Don's ability to grow the business using a wide variety of financial resources, including debt. His ability to raise capital and exploit opportunities would become one of his most vital leadership skills.

Don's road to success, wealth, and power, was not a freeway of inherited wealth or years of postgraduate work at one of America's premier business schools. His was a gifted person who learned experientially and by a lifelong pursuit of knowledge. He became one of the foremost effective and results-driven transformation leaders in the food industry.

LEARNING TO WORK

Don's learning began as a boy doing various jobs in the business. As kids tend to do, he was easily distracted and allowed to be the rambunctious boy he was. He was known in the community as a boisterous young fellow whose sense of adventure was the driving force in his young life. His entrepreneurial skills surfaced early as a high school student who launched a number of money-making ventures at school. His marketing antennae were always up searching for opportunities. Don's youthful entrepreneurial successes weren't always congruous with school policy, but as is characteristic of the entrepreneurial mind, a failure or two didn't derail the pursuit of his goals. When this goal confusion could not be resolved, his dad enrolled him in the Kemper Military Academy in Kansas City.

About the same time, Herman Tuck, another young high school boy from northwest Arkansas, was enrolled at Kemper by his dad for similar reasons—entrepreneurialism run amuck! They became friends, bound together by their entrepreneurial spirits, and their friendship continues to this day. Herman went on to open an iconic restaurant in northwest Arkansas. Herman's restaurant is a five-minute drive from Tyson's world headquarters. When Don took the company public, he encouraged Herman to buy as many shares as possible. Herman bought stock, even though at the time he said he couldn't afford to own an automobile.

Herman's became the place for Tyson folks to entertain and enhance relationships with customers and others. Dick Stockland, senior vice president of international sales, called Herman and made reservations for several Japanese customers. Dick ordered Herman's two-pound porterhouse steaks for his guests. When the Japanese customers arrived, their tables were set with steaks in place; they all left in a big hurry! Herman was shocked, wondering if he had violated some cultural custom. Before his anxiety passed, they returned as quickly as they had left, with cameras in hand. Don Tyson and Herman Tuck were blessed with a "fun gene" in their DNA.

Mr. John Tyson started the business in 1935 hauling live chickens to markets in the Midwest. He had devised a transport system to provide water, feed, warmth, and cooling during transit. This system was a precursor to his mindset of doing inventive and creative things to satisfy customers. In those days fresh, young chicken was not available all year. He hoped customers would pay more for fresh and for a reliable supply. He was right. "Customering," John Tyson style, was underway.

As his trucking business prospered and generated capital, he added to his asset base a system to buy baby chicks, feed, and other raw materials. Customer demand grew, creating demand for larger volumes of raw material. His suppliers couldn't keep up, thus limiting Mr. Tyson's ability to grow the business and take care of his customers. His relationship with customers was a sacred pact. It was about personal integrity. Take care of the customer—no excuses accepted.

The $235 profit he earned on his first load of live chickens sold in Chicago was rock-solid evidence that he was on the right track. In those days he didn't have the capital to buy gasoline for his trucks going to markets in the Midwest. To solve the problem he stopped along the way and worked out deals with local gas stations to charge the purchase. He sold his product in cash and used that cash to pay the gas merchants on the return trip. In the 1930s, cash was scarce. It was a win-win partnership that proved to be a sound basis for building supplier relationships.

He continued to invest in assets to expand and control raw materials. He developed his own hatchery and expanded his ability to mix feed. It was a strategic decision as it marked the beginning of vertical integration in the poultry industry. To avoid any interruption of service to customers and to assure high quality products, he knew he had to control all the processes in the business from genetics to product quality on consumers' plates.

FIVE DECADES OF STABLE LEADERSHIP ASSURED

The business was profitable and growing rapidly. In fact, growth was beginning to exceed the ability to raise cash for expansion. Mr. Tyson reached a decision point about the company's future. He needed capital for expansion. Like numerous other businesspeople who survived the deplorable poverty of the Great Depression of 1929, he abhorred the idea of going into debt. His comfort level was directly proportionate to cash on hand and equity.

When John Tyson bestowed the mantle of leadership on Don in 1952, it marked the beginning of Don's leadership for five decades, now moving into the sixth. Don stepped down as chairman of the board in 1995 to become the senior chairman. He continued as senior chairman until 2001 when he retired. He continues to serve on Tyson's board and maintains an office there where he is seen frequently. Ownership has its influence.

In 1952, annual sales were about a million dollars. No chickens were processed by Tyson at the time. The work of Tyson Feed & Hatchery was to produce and sell feed, hatch and sell baby chicks, grow chickens and sell them to those companies that were processing chickens. At about the same time Don's dad, Mr. John, was considering an offer from Swanson Foods to buy Tyson Feed & Hatchery. Don was at the University of Arkansas studying agriculture and had expressed little interest in the business. It was time for father and son to have a meeting of minds. It was one of those determinative, Robert Frost fork-in-the-road moments when two human beings reached understanding through communication. Both men were gifted with the unique skill to "communicate for understanding." Is there a better definition for effective communication?

The conversation was brief. As John Tyson reported, "I called Don and asked him if he wanted to come back and go into the business with me. Don replied, 'All I ever wanted to do was to work with you.'" Later Mr. John said, "I don't know why it took a little thing like that to make us understand each other, but I didn't sell to Swanson." [3] Don left his academic pursuits and entered the hard-nosed learning environment in which final exam results were prepared by accountants reporting test scores on cash flows, profit and loss, returns on assets, equity and sales.

Paul Whitley

THE FRONT OFFICE STAFF CREATES MENTAL MODELS

Mental models are pictures created in the minds of people of patterns of work, behaviors—how things get done. The original office staff at Tyson headquarters on Emma Street in Springdale created the mental models that influenced how work was done in the front office. Those mental models became a vital part of Tyson work culture.

ANNABEL CLAYPOOL, one of the key people in the office, began her forty-one years of service in 1947. She retired the first time in 1953, returning in 1963 to finally retire in 1998. At the time Don was seventeen years old. ANNABEL remembers Don's bubbly enthusiasm when he came to the office to see his folks or just hang out. In the Founder's Room there is a note describing the work week for ANNABEL.

ANNABEL worked six days a week; 8:00 a.m. to 5:30 p.m. She was paid $33.84 per week; 51 hours at 66¢ per hour. She audited feed tickets, worked with growers who came into the office and handled accounts receivable. ANNABEL described Mr. John's insistence that things be kept neat, orderly, tidy and well organized. When she retired she had experienced the dramatic technological revolution in office work that occurred in the years following the end of WWII—from hand posting the general ledger to nanosecond fast computers. She remembers Don coming to her office in the 1980s asking how it was that before computers he could come to her office and get the numbers he needed. Now he

29

had to wait until the next morning. Her reply, "Progress, sir, progress."

She retired in 1998, a fulfilled, professional Tyson employee."

LETA BELL signed on during the first year of the new processing plant operations in 1959. She was trained by Mr. John and his wife Helen, who taught her the importance of keeping chicken growers happy. In those days, growers came to the office to pick up their settlement checks. Managing grower relationships was unique, as growers weren't employees. They were farmers who contracted with Tyson. The management task was to find a power balance that was productive for both. It was a learning process for growers, Tyson Foods, and other buyers of live chickens. A weekly chicken auction was used for some time in an effort to prevent either party gaining an advantage and to bring some order into a process that didn't allow either party to do proper planning. LETA BELL retired in 1994 after thirty-five years of service becoming a role model for the young folks who worked in the office: how to dress, how to work, how to behave, and how to grow a successful career at Tyson Foods.

MARY RUSH joined the company's finance and accounting group in 1972. The three of women worked together for most of the great growth years. When Mary retired in 1998 as corporate secretary and director of investor relations, she had completed twenty-six years of service. Mary's work was the "satisfying shareholders" piece of Don's "satisfying customers with satisfied workers." Mary felt responsible for shareholders' money. When a shareholder called with questions, she was prepared with straight, no-spin answers. The shareholder could be a Tyson hourly plant worker or a large institutional investor. She was highly respected in the financial markets by analysts and investment firms. She traveled with Don, Leland, Buddy, and Gerald Johnston, CFO, as they participated in guidance meetings on Wall Street and other financial centers.

The work of these three executive women and others like them was the work of data collection, production and sales reports, payables, receivables—all the daily stuff—and most of the work was without the benefit of modern office systems. As good communicators, they met the business needs of Tyson for two generations of leaders and managers. They believed in the company and had fun at work. They were the beneficiaries of a work climate that provided immediate feedback on job performance, good or otherwise. As shareholders they participated in the wealth creation of Tyson's rewarding stock purchase plan.

A SERENDIPITIOUS MOMENT

Over lunch at the Springdale Holiday Inn, ANNABEL and LETA talked about their work in the early days of Tyson. MARY RUSH provided continuity, covering her tenure from 1972 to 1998. They described a work environment that was the cradle in which Tyson's work culture was born and nourished, growing to full fruition in the 1960s.

During our lunch Buddy Wray and Leland Tollett came by our table. For several minutes I was the outsider, transported back and forth in time as these five Tyson people demonstrated their respect and love (contributing to the personhood of another) for each other. Neither Tollett nor Wray were known to exude their emotions. On this occasion they did and it was very good!

SYNCHRONICITY

Carl Jung, writing on synchronicity, said, "We like to think we may be the protagonists for our own lives; we are the extras or spear carriers in some larger drama." The larger drama was unfolding. Their work was vital to the continuity of the work-life principles of John and Helen Tyson. Cultural continuity, beliefs, behaviors, and assumptions that determined how work was to be done—work that was productive—work that created—work endowed with social responsibility.

DON TAKES THE COMPANY PUBLIC TO FINANCE HIS VISION FOR GROWTH

Tyson went public in 1963, selling one hundred thousand shares at $10.50 per share on the NASDAQ. In October 1997, Tyson moved to the New York Stock Exchange. In 2005, they were included in Standard & Poor's 500 index.

The Arkansas poultry story is a story of feed mill hands with discolored faces; sun-bronzed farmers who gained a new life from poultry when fruit crops failed year after year; mothers who worked on eviscerating lines to secure their children's college education; and white-clad agricultural scientists who labored tirelessly to breed better stock, develop more nutritious feed and promote poultry health. It includes bold business executives; internationally known companies and world-renowned scientists. The epic of the Arkansas poultry industry is a profoundly human narrative, forged by an economic struggle in which small price swings meant the difference between success and failure, wealth and bankruptcy. [4]

There was no silver spoon at this young man's place setting. For the first eleven years he didn't have a day off. He worked in the business six days and on the seventh day he worked on the farm. As a teen, his dad taught him how to work by mixing chicken feed using a #10 scoop shovel. He learned how to catch chickens by hand, which, for the uninformed, is real work. At age fourteen, he was driving a truck.

His new work was the work of learning to learn; learning to work; learning to lead the company in pursuit of one of his goals to become a fully integrated chicken-based food company. He demonstrated early on what behavioral psychologist E.L. Deci at Carnegie Mellon University called "intrinsically motivated behavior conceptualized as a continuous process of seeking and overcoming challenges." [5]

After many years of studying human behavior and a bunch of motivational theories, we still cannot accurately predict or measure this driving, motivating force in people. Psychologists, anthropologists, neuroscientists, motivational speakers, head hunters, clergy, teachers, corporate trainers, parents, and coaches search for a key that will unlock human potential. Could it be that the motivational door is unlocked from the inside? The source of Don's motive power was internal. He believed his employees had the same internal motivational forces, and he instilled that expectation throughout his young organization. It was his intrinsic motivation that enabled him to take risks driven by a powerful internal goal-seeking mechanism. I recall the influential psychologist Carl Rogers using the term "actualizing tendency." Don never permitted a failure to dilute his strength of purpose. In fact, he learned to analyze and trust the process. The task was not to fix blame but to fix processes that caused failures.

Warren Buffet, the Omaha genius investor, wrote, "I've often felt that there might be more to be gained by studying business failures than business successes. In my business, we try to study where people go astray, and why things don't work." [6]

A few months before I retired in 1997, Don gave me a copy of Frederick Reichheld's The Loyalty Effect. It is an analytical study of corporations with long histories of success. Reichheld's study showed that companies that had learned how to create value for shareholders, employees and customers, consistently outperformed companies that chose other strategies. Reichheld's book, copyright 1996, describes Tyson's strategic thinking. Reichheld's research gives us another clue about how Don learned. He learned how to process failure, learning from the process. His ego didn't need the protection of hiding from failure or blaming others—major time wasters in some organizations. Reichheld writes:

> There are two principal reasons why organizations do not study their own failures. The first is bureaucracy, which is almost perfectly designed to conceal mistakes and utterly disinclined to seek them out and lay them bare. The second is an almost universal fixation with success. In a bureaucratic organization, the key to a great career— pay raises, promotions, funding for projects—is

the boss. Bureaucrats can often succeed by pleasing their superiors in ways that have little to do with value creation, but with feeding the boss's starving ego. Some people make a game of disguising their failures or cleverly fixing them before the boss finds out.[7]

Some bureaucratic individuals have massive files for the sole purpose of CYA behaviors. Bureaucratic behaviors are as common in business, churches, marriages, and universities as they are in government.

Bob Justice, Tyson's public relations man for many years, told me that when he traveled with Don, Don always had his "face in a book." On a trip to China, Bob said Don read most of the way, pausing only for few minutes to describe the purpose of the trip. At the conclusion of one of the meetings with Chinese officials and business leaders, Don excused himself, saying he had to leave to catch his next flight. Bob was left to his own devices to conclude the meeting.

Others have described similar moments of delegation. During one of our interviews Don said that one of the early influences in his business life was Alford Sloan's book, My Years with General Motors. Sloan's book was published in 1963, the same year Don took Tyson Foods public. After reading Sloan's book, Don applied the ideas from Sloan's successful management career at General Motors. For example, on the subject of being a growth company, Sloan writes, "Growth, or striving for it, is, I believe, essential to the good health of an enterprise. Deliberately to stop growing is to suffocate; growth and progress are related, for there is no resting place for an enterprise in a competitive economy. Obstacles, conflict, new problems in various shapes, and new horizons arise to stir the imagination and continue the progress of industry. Success, however, may bring self-satisfaction. In that event, the urge for competitive survival, the strongest of all economic incentives, is dulled. The spirit of venture is lost in the inertia of the mind against change." On the subject of intuition Sloan writes, "The final act of business judgment is of course intuitive." [8]

To expand on the significance of Sloan's work, General Motors was formed by William Durant in 1908. "Durant [was] the grandson of a Michigan governor and a self-made millionaire in the horse-drawn carriage manufacturing business." [9]

Durant was a super salesman with highly developed visionary skills whose ego addiction and hubris had blinded him to the need for bringing into his inner circle trusted leaders with veto power to balance his entrepreneurial skills. He was forced to step aside in 1910. He regained control in 1916 and led the business until November 30, 1920, when he was forced to resign. When he retired to a New York apartment with his wife, he was dependent for income on four old friends: C.S. Mott, R.S. McLaughlin, John Thomas Smith, and Alfred P. Sloan. He died March 18, 1947.

Sloan's involvement with the automobile industry was that of a supplier of roller bearings. His company, Hyatt Roller Bearing Company, was enjoying success when, in the spring of 1916, prior to Durant's gaining control of General Motors the second time, Durant called Sloan and said he would like to buy Hyatt. A deal was struck. Sloan's early work at General Motors was with the accessory group and as a member of the Executive Committee.

APPLYING THE KNOWLEDGE DON LEARNED AND THE MISTAKES HE DIDN'T MAKE

—He never lost control of the company by issuing two classes of stock.

—He was never blinded by ego addiction or hubris.

—He never cloned himself or his style.

—He was never vindictive in his business dealings.

—He did not micromanage; he empowered his people to do the work for which they were hired.

—He never isolated himself, but stayed close to his people, all of them, not just the executive group.

—He never behaved with arrogance or pomposity.

—He rejected the traditional trappings of status.

—He never stopped learning.

—He never betrayed the trust of his people.

In the 1990 edition of Sloan's book, there is a quote on the front cover by Bill Gates: "I think Alfred Sloan's *My Years with General Motors* is probably the best book to read if you want to read only one book about business. The issues dealt with in organizing and measuring, in keeping [other executives] happy, dealing with risk, understanding model years and the effect of used vehicles, and modeling his competition all in a very rational, positive way is inspiring."

Peter Drucker writes in the preface and concludes his remarks about Sloan, "Finally—and perhaps the most important lesson—the professional manager is a servant. Rank does not confer privilege. It does not give power. It imposes responsibility." Peter Block said it this way: "When you are responsible, you push accountability and authority to the limit." [10]

Don learned a vital leadership principle from his dad that became one of his mantras, proving to be a sound basis for doing the work required for customer satisfaction: "If you see a job that needs to be done, do it! It is your responsibility, and you are accountable!"

Job descriptions and organization charts, if they existed at all, never offered easy escape for not doing all the work necessary to satisfy a customer. Translated, it meant you were responsible for customer satisfaction; if you see the task—do it! Don successfully attached personal and social responsibility and accountability to employees' work. It was reminiscent of medieval times when shoemakers and other craftsmen did their work directly for their neighbor/ customers. Don included a written, personal guarantee with his products and reminded his people it was their job to do the work of customer satisfaction.

A word about the word *employee* and Don's attitude and behavior related thereto. It has become popular to use phrases like associates, team members, employee owners, or whatever corporate word crafters create in an effort to suggest an organization is behaving in a superior way toward its workforce. We consumers of products and services are supposed to feel better about an organization we do business with based on words—duh! Words you hear after holding on the phone too, too long: "Your call is important"—words, words, words! This is an example of cognitive dissonance caused by the business misusing a phone system that negates their words, "We care."

These new descriptors are about as effective as vision and core value statements written by public relations departments who learned them from consultants who don't have to hang around to deal with employee and customer dissatisfaction. These statements have value to the degree the words are transformed into behaviors. The words, though well intended, are like a sign in a chicken house on an egg farm that reads, "Grade A Eggs Only." The hen laying the eggs does the best she can with the work environment she is in. She knows that when her productivity begins to decline she will be sold to a soup company. So, why sweat the Grade A stuff? Just keep the foxes out of my nest and I will do the best I can!

"HOW TO WIN FRIENDS AND INFLUENCE PEOPLE"

[11]Don and others participated in the training based on Carnegie's research and observations of human behavior. Years before the heyday of behavioral scientists, Dale Carnegie wrote and taught principles that met the learning needs of millions of folks whose lives had been shattered by the depression of 1929. He never claimed to create anything new. He simply observed behaviors and actions that "won friends and influenced people." He taught that it was possible to change other people's behavior by changing one's reaction to them. He was an early proponent of what we now call *responsibility assumption*, which assumes that high human productivity is enhanced when a person takes total responsibility for his or her actions. His concept was so imbedded in Tyson's work culture that we included a "100 percent responsibility" component in Tyson's training and development curricula. It is perhaps one of the most difficult concepts to teach and to learn, as some folks in our culture have accepted blaming behaviors and avoidance of responsibility and accountability as best practices. Office files and computers are filled to overflowing with CYA memos. Politicians and other high-profile, thin-skinned folks have lost the courage to say, "I was wrong"; churches and other institutions are paying exorbitant prices trying to hide their

failures and the failures of their leaders. When some folks reach celebrity status they suffer from the malignancy of narcissism—assumed entitlement!

INTUITIVE STRENGTHS

Don's intuitive skills became a strength on which he and others came to rely. We used to think women had better intuitive skills than men. Researchers are now telling us that men have intuitive skills similar to women, but women trust and use their intuition more effectively. Someone has said that intuition is a mental muscle that needs to be exercised and put to work. As Don exercised his mental muscle and dad John applied his rational thinking skills, the young company made its way through turbulent economic times in the industry. "By 1950, poultry was the second-most-important source of agricultural income in Arkansas, with cotton at number one. An estimated 90 percent of all Arkansas farmers had chickens, and over ten thousand farmers were involved in commercial production."[12] The industry was fragmented, poorly financed, undisciplined, and hamstrung by retail price manipulators.

LEARNING ACCOUNTING FROM HARRY ERWIN, LONGTIME CPA FOR TYSON FOODS

Don processed data quickly, discarding extraneous stuff without wasting time in circuitous thinking. When Harry Erwin of Tyson's longtime CPA firm, Russell Brown & Co., was asked if he was one of Don's mentors on fiscal matters, he answered, "Well, I don't know if he would give me credit as his mentor. I did a lot of hand-holding with Don in those early days." Mr. Erwin worked on the Tyson account from 1954, when he did the Tyson audit, until his retirement in 1983. Mr. Erwin remembers Mr. John saying to his young managers more than once, "Don't screw up this business. When I lock up at night I want to go home and relax." Russell Brown & Co. merged with Arthur Young, which became Ernst & Young. Harry Erwin described Mr. John as being active in the political process in Arkansas when legislation had a negative impact on his company. In the Arkansas gubernatorial campaign of 1954, incumbent Governor Francis Cherry was opposed by Orval Faubus, a former schoolteacher from Greasy Creek in Madison County. The legislature had imposed a 2 percent tax on seed, feed, and fertilizer, which Cherry had criticized as unfair. This endeared him to poultry growers. However, when the legislature sent a bill repealing the tax to the governor, he vetoed it! John Tyson and the young poultry industry worked to defeat Francis Cherry, making him a one-term governor, and elected Orval Faubus, who occupied the office for twelve years—1955–1967. Governor Cherry wore virtue and morality on his sleeve and went into the reelection campaign of 1954 "confident that virtue would reward him…but he was unskilled in the art of not antagonizing people." [13] Don learned from his dad his responsibility to protect his company's interests in the political arena. One of Harry Erwin's most interesting assignments from Don was to accompany him to Las Vegas to evaluate the closed Bonanza Casino and Hotel as a possible acquisition. Harry's story goes something like this, During the early 1900's, especially the 20's and 30's, Hot Springs, Arkansas was a popular destination for the rich and famous attracting the likes of Andrew Carnegie, F.W. Woolworth, Gangster Al Capone. Capone's mob occupied the entire fourth floor of the popular Arlington Hotel. There is a brass plate on suite 442 which his mob occupied when in town. Illegal, but allowed, gambling thrived in Hot Springs during the 40's and 50's, even into the 60's. In 1967 Governor Winthrop Rockefeller closed the casinos.

Don had heard that the Bonanza was closed and for sale. His entrepreneurial mind suggested there were a bunch of trained, unemployed casino workers in Hot Springs who needed work. If he could make the right kind of deal for the Bonanza it could be staffed immediately by folks from Hot Springs.

After their do-diligence, they passed on the opportunity.

SELF-UNDERSTANDING

A young Don Tyson was developing a sense of self-understanding following the ancient Greek admonition, "Know Thyself." This inscription appeared on the sun god Apollo's Oracle of Delphi temple. Apollo, son of Zeus, was a creative, handsome, charismatic, and charming leader. Young Don and the Greek sun god Apollo share more than one attribute in common. Don knew who he was and was very comfortable in his own skin. He didn't hide behind masks, nor did he try to squeeze himself into someone else's mold. His authenticity as a person was evidenced by the trust he inspired among his people—from hourly new hires to senior managers. Perhaps one of the most valuable lessons Don learned was that no one individual is endowed with all the strengths and skills required to build a great company. The grand old man of management consulting, Peter Drucker, in his landmark work, *The Effective Executive* writes:

> The effective executive makes strength productive. He knows that one cannot build on weakness. To achieve results, one has to use all the available **strengths**—the strengths of associates, the strengths of superiors, and one's own strengths.

These strengths are the true opportunities. To make strength productive is the unique purpose of organization. It cannot, of course, overcome the weaknesses with which each of us is abundantly endowed. But it can make them irrelevant. Its task is to use the strength of each man as a building block for joint performance. [14]

One of Don's strengths was selecting people on the basis of their unique strengths and empowering them to utilize those strengths fully, without the encumbrance of micromanagement, as evidenced by Tyson's ability to outperform competitors. The writer heard him say, "When my people and I agree to skin a cat, they can skin the cat any way they choose."

HAVING FUN AT WORK

Writing in Studs Terkel's book, *Working*, [15] Nora Watson says in the introduction, "Most of us, like assembly line workers, have jobs that are too small for our spirits." Don and his people found ways to make what could have been dull, monotonous, and routine work, something more. One of the actions they took was to give workers the right to have fun at work. No longer did one have to subscribe to the puritanical belief that work was punishment for some distant sin that condemned the created to toil and earning their bread by the sweat of the brow. Could it be that having fun at work and having a corporate sense of humor might make the workplace more productive? The definition that came out of this process of fun: Having fun at work is not the absence of all the daily stuff of monotony, repetition, cold, wet processing plants, working shifts, sitting day after day peering into a computer screen. Having fun at work was having confidence in oneself and having confidence in the future. We now know after years of research on kinds of intelligence that "not only are emotions very much a part of the work experience, but to a large degree they set the course that a company follows." [16] Following that idea, "Laughter is good medicine and good policy, and it irritates the Theory Xers!" [17]

Another action they took to make ordinary jobs extraordinary was allowing ownership of company stock. Today, there are a number of retirees, including hourly workers, enjoying the multiplication and rising prices of Tyson stock over time. Having fun at work! Don taught it. He behaved it and is still doing it today.

THE COMPLEXITY OF VERTICAL INTEGRATION

In 1952 the chicken industry was mostly a conglomeration of independent suppliers of raw materials and services. Competition was composed of several independent and regional companies. There were a few national competitors such as Swift, Armour, and Wilson, that had divisions that were selling what was known as ice-pack chicken. Whole chickens were packed in ice in wire-bound crates made of cottonwood. It was a sell-it-or-smell-it process. If a processor didn't have his week's production sold early, his sales department got on the phones and conducted an auction, selling to the highest bidder. Supermarket buyers capitalized on these auctions to offer consumers what they called loss leaders designed to get customers in their stores.

There are at least two stories I know about the origins of the chicken industry. There is the Maryland version that goes like this. In 1923 Cecile Steele received five hundred baby chicks from the Dagsboro, Maryland hatchery. It was a fateful mistake as she had ordered only fifty! What was one to do? She raised the chicks and sold them for a hefty profit and hatched the modern broiler industry. The Arkansas version: In 1916, J.J. Glover's daughter Edith raised 20 broilers that Glover sold for $1 a bird. Glover called his birds the Arkansas Broilers and maintained that they were distinguished by both their tender flesh and large size.

The work of producing and marketing chicken-based food products, compared to the work of producing and marketing most hard goods, was complicated by a staggering number of disparate variables. For example, the raw material is alive, growing, and consuming high-priced feed. The raw material is subject to disease, extreme heat and cold, improper housing and handling, and of course there are the foxes to worry about. The raw material has to be caught by hand, transported, harvested humanely, inspected by the federal government one bird at a time, disassembled, and processed into desirable consumer products that are safe and low cost. And the product is perishable. There was the further complicating factor of managing a live inventory of millions of these little protein-conversion machines in that they keep consuming high-priced feed and keep coming even when the market goes south and consumers stop buying! Understanding all these variables and being able to reduce variations in minute increments is a complex process. Despite this, Don said over and over again, "Don't let your work get complicated. Keep it simple." Keep it simple by knowing what's going on in all the process variables that were measured in mills—down to one-tenth of a cent.

FROM SIMPLICITY TO COMPLEXITY TO SIMPLICITY

Young Don found himself in a complex business that was becoming more complex as consumers and foodservice operators wanted more than chicken. They wanted it sized raw, cooked, sauced, marinated, flavored, fried, baked, smoked, grilled, and high quality at a low price. He worked diligently to simplify the work of complexity. He said often,

"Folks, don't let your work get too complicated. Keep it simple. It isn't easy, but we must keep it simple." I asked him to tell me how he measured the success of the company. "It's real simple. I count the marbles in the morning. When I count them in the evening, if I have more marbles in the evening, the day has been successful." He could have given me a lesson in business economics. He could have impressed me with his brilliance. He simply chose to communicate a principle. Having played a lot of marbles growing up in the Texas Panhandle, I understood.

His belief that a mind-set of complexity could interfere with work was demonstrated in the work of theoretical physicist and Nobel Prize winner Murray Gell-Mann who writes, "It is interesting to note, therefore, that the two words, [simplicity and complexity], are related. The Indo-European root plex gives rise to the Latin verb plicare, to fold, which yields simplex, literally once folded from which our English word simple derives. But plex likewise gives the Latin past participle plexis, braided or entwined, from which is derived complexus, literally braided together, responsible for the English word, symplectic." [18]

Chief Justice Oliver Wendell Holmes, Jr., weighed in on the subject when he wrote, "I would not give a fig for the simplicity this side of complexity; but I would give my life for the simplicity on the other side of complexity." [19] Commenting on Justice Holmes's quote, James O'Toole writes, "The leadership challenge is to get to the other side of complexity. But how does one get there? Only one sure route has been identified: the enhancement of understanding. To move beyond the confusion of complexity, executives must abandon their constant search for the immediately practical and, paradoxically seek to understand the underlying ideas and values that have shaped the world they work in." [20]

SEX IN THE CHICKEN HOUSE

My mentor on this subject was John Pledger at the Clarksville, Arkansas Hatchery. Before a broiler chicken, a young, not-sexually-active chicken is placed in a contract farmer's chicken house, a fertile egg is required. Since the reader may not have firsthand knowledge of the sex life of chickens, this is how it works. In a breeder house where all this stuff happens, a ratio of ten hens to one rooster creates fertile eggs by means of rudimentary copulatory organs. The fertile eggs are gathered and transported to hatcheries with machines that replicate the work of mother hens, warming and turning the eggs until the baby chicks peck their way out of their shells. Hatching takes twenty-one days and is one constant the poultry scientists have not yet been able to speed up. Through genetics, improved nutrition and grow-out practices, the time required today to produce a marketable broiler is five to seven weeks, depending on the size desired. And the reader needs to know that no growth hormones are used; chicken a la natural! Over the last several years the industry has reduced the time to grow a broiler about one day each year. Poultry scientists tell us this trend will continue. Meanwhile as these processes are going on, corn, soybean meal, and other ingredients are being purchased, scheduled for delivery, hauled to feed mills and formulated to meet specific nutritional needs. The finished feed is delivered to contract farmers who provide housing, heat, cooling, water, and labor. The company provides technical assistance and animal health support. On the science side of the business was the work of geneticists, veterinary research, animal nutritionists, food scientists, a cadre of engineers with varying specialties, food safety scientists, and an ever-growing number of staffers who ensure compliance with federal, state, and local regulations.

EXPLOITING THE SOFT UNDERBELLY OF THE INDUSTRY

The industry was suffering from what Dr. John Hardiman, Tyson geneticist, called "inbreeding depression" in animal genetics. He explained, "If no new genes are added to the gene pool, significant change is not probable. If new genes are added to the gene pool, change is certain to happen, although it is not possible to always predict what the change will be."

The writer has appropriated Dr. Hardiman's idea as a proper metaphor to think about how change or resistance to change impacts organizations and persons. Change is one of those experiences most of us want to happen to someone else. Personal and organizational change is frequently caused by pain and suffering or a powerful personal vision. Cardinal John Henry Newman's quote hangs on the writer's office wall: "In a higher world it is otherwise; but here below, to live is to change, and to be perfect is to have changed often"— an impossible, but worthy goal. One of the primary causes for ongoing change at Tyson Foods was listening to and responding to customer needs—a source of Tyson's hybrid vigor!

The customer may not always have been right, but the customer was always the customer—the primary source of growth and profit. Therefore, deliver satisfaction or an enlightened competitor will! There were times when satisfying customers created significant risks. Risk is inherent in the change process and Don had an uncanny ability to measure and to manage the risk-reward process. In a later chapter you will read about million-dollar risks that over the short term were costly, but over the long term very profitable.

ENCOUNTER WITH ANOMALY [21]

In the 1969 annual report Don wrote, "We plan our future in ways that *break tradition* with the poultry industry." Describing how scientific revolutions or paradigms occur in science, Thomas Kuhn describes the "set of beliefs that form the foundation of a scientific community." Scientists defend these beliefs with vigor to avoid straying into error. In this rigid, scientific community, change or a new paradigm results from an "encounter with anomaly." Kuhn's description explains Don's attitude toward the industry. The industry was generally resistant to paradigm changes while Don's company was forming the "critical mass" leading to changes in the industry.

Don was asked how it was that he was able to acquire so many poultry companies. He said some of the acquired companies got into financial trouble and couldn't figure out the future. How then, was he able to figure out their future? What did he know about them that they didn't know about themselves? He was a bit reluctant to say much more than some of the acquired companies had leadership problems. Some competitors suffered from the complacency born of success, put their cash in the bank, retired in place and resisted fundamental change—and Don bought a bunch of them!

LEADERSHIP INSIGHTS

- Leaders transform the basic human instinct for learning into a lifelong, aggressive pursuit for knowledge, understanding and skills.
- "Learning is a basic, adaptive function of humans, More than any other species; people are designed to be flexible learners and active agents of acquiring knowledge, understanding and skills.
- Much of what people learn occurs without formal instruction, but highly systematic and organized systems; reading, math, the sciences, literature, and the history of society require formal training, usually in schools." [22]

CHAPTER 2
THE TRIUMVIRATE
Don Tyson, Leland Tollett, Buddy Wray

I shall call them the triumvirate. For most of forty years, these three men from Arkansas merged their unique and diverse leadership and management skills to grow a small chicken company into a global giant. This is rare in that the average life of corporations in the Fortune 500 is thirty years. The triumvirate's behaviors influenced the behaviors of thousands of Tyson folks who made the company successful.

Each man brought different skills and attributes to their leadership roles. Their strengths were synergistic and triumphed over whatever weaknesses or flaws they had. One of their critical qualities was the ability to keep their healthy egos healthy by keeping their egos subservient to rational thinking. Working partnerships fail most from the toxins of egocentric behaviors.

To reach their goal to become a fully integrated poultry company, Tyson Feed & Hatchery needed more folks trained in the animal sciences. They turned to the University of Arkansas at Fayetteville just a few miles south of Springdale. Two early recruits were Leland Tollett and Buddy Wray.

LELAND TOLLETT'S ROOTS IN SOUTHWESTERN ARKANSAS

Leland grew up in Nashville, Arkansas. He did his freshman and sophomore work at Southern State College in Magnolia. The name was changed in 1975 to Southern Arkansas University.[23] He transferred to the University of Arkansas at Fayetteville to complete his undergraduate work and a master's in poultry nutrition.

His boyhood home Nashville, Arkansas is in the southwest corner of the state, about thirty miles north of Hope, President Bill Clinton's boyhood home. Leland's dad owned a meat market across the street from William Dillard Sr.'s first department store, T.J. Dillard & Company. Mr. Dillard was one of those out-of-the-Depression Arkansas visionaries like John Tyson, Sam Walton, J.B. Hunt and W.R. "Witt" Stephens who went on to build great Arkansas-based companies: Sam Walton and William Dillard Sr. in retailing, J.B. Hunt in transportation, "Witt" Stephens in investment banking, and John Tyson in chicken. Leland remembers his dad worrying about Mr. Dillard when he announced the opening of his second store. Was he expanding too fast?

Dr. James Tollett, Leland's older brother, told me that Mr. Dillard gave him and Leland their high school graduation suits. Today Dr. James Tollett occupies the chair and is a professor in the Department of Agriculture at Southern Arkansas University.

There were four boys and four girls in the Tollett family in Nashville. Dr. Tollett described growing up in Nashville as a time of hard work, little money, and demanding teachers at school. He said money was so scarce that when Leland followed him to college at Magnolia, Leland arrived on campus with his clothes in a cardboard box, as James was using the family suitcase. James and Leland both worked in their dad's meat market. One of their jobs was to sit on top of the grinder and push large chunks of meat into the grinding machine.

The school mascot was and still is THE SCRAPPERS. These SCRAPPERS broke through the roadblocks placed in their way by the limited resources of the Great Depression—no loans, grants, scholarships, or other student aid.

Dr. E.L. Stephenson, [24] former head of the Department of Poultry Science at the University of Arkansas (1964–1982), Leland's major professor, called Mr. John and recommended Leland as a good thinker, problem solver, risk taker and nutritionist. In 1959 he was offered and accepted $80 a week for the first six months; $90 for the second six months and $100 after one year. When he reported for work, Mr. John told him to clean up the storage warehouse that housed poultry meds and other assorted supplies. Leland remembers, "I picked up the big industrial-size broom and leaned on it, wondering if I had made the right decision. Did I get an education to do this kind of work?" Then he remembered his dad's instructions as he dropped him off for his first job as a boy: "If you take a man's money to work for him, give the man a full day's work for a full day's pay." Twenty-five years later, the writer heard Leland, who was then the COO, tell a group of churchmen, "It doesn't matter how high you are in the company, you always have a higher authority. For me it is my boss, Don Tyson, the board of directors, my customers and ultimately the authority of God."

Leland's sense of humility, power under control, was reflected in his answer to a question asked as we walked out of the plush Pinnacle Country Club dining room in Rogers, Arkansas. The question: "When you were thinking about a job as a student at the University of Arkansas in the late fifties, could you have imagined living and enjoying this lifestyle?" His response: "No, all I thought about was getting a job with a regular paycheck and maybe, someday, owning a new car."

As a five-year-old, Leland injured his right eye with a pocket knife, which, in his words, "made me a lefty." This injury impaired his sight but was manageable for many years. In 1980 he developed cancer in his good left eye, which made him a "righty." With a lens implant in the right eye and radiation and surgery on his left eye, he was able to do his work as CEO. However, his vision continued to deteriorate and was one of the factors prompting his early retirement at age sixty-one in 1998. In Leland's retirement statement to the board of directors, he said, "I am stepping down from the helm of this great company at this time simply because I think the timing is right. As many people know, I have had vision problems for a number of years. These problems are not improving with age, and have become more than an inconvenience in trying to carry on my daily responsibilities. This concern, coupled with the fact that the Hudson acquisition is now behind us, and many of the outside issues that have distracted us for the past five years have been resolved, makes it a good time for me to retire." Leland remained on the Tyson board following his retirement and serves in that capacity today and is a major stockholder.

He learned early on growing up in Nashville to be a "Scrapper." Whatever the challenge, he never backed away. Leland and a few of his friends became avid bird hunters using their well-trained bird dogs to hunt pheasant and ducks. When asked recently if he could see well enough to hunt pheasant, he said yes. Was he going pheasant hunting this fall? He said, "Yes, and as long I can walk, I will hunt!"

BUDDY WRAY AND LELAND TOLLETT CONNECT

The year was 1955. The place was Southern State College, Magnolia, Arkansas, home of the Muleriders. Southern State operated a college farm on which the major motive power was mules. In 1922 their mascot was changed from Aggie to Mulerider, and the student paper was named *The Bray.*

Ag student Leland Tollett of Nashville, Arkansas and a few of his buddies watched as a newly arrived freshman walked on campus. Leland asked one of his buddies, "Who is that big boy?" His buddy answered, "He's the new football player on the Mulerider football team, and he has a new car." Leland responded, "We've got to meet that big boy and be his friend." Leland, being a sophisticated sophomore and more experienced in campus life, recognized in this big boy an opportunity. This big boy from Des Arc, Arkansas was Donald "Buddy" Wray. Leland seized this moment as he and Buddy would seize many moments over the next forty years.

DONALD "BUDDY" WRAY'S ROOTS IN THE ARKANSAS DELTA

Buddy was raised on the eastern side of the state in the delta river town of Des Arc, located on the White River. Des Arc was one of the oldest river ports in Arkansas, about fifty-five miles east of Little Rock. Des Arc owes its beginning to the White

River as it became an important stop for steamboats transporting lumber and cotton. Fishing, boat building, eight lumber mills, and button making formed a vibrant economy in the mid-1800s. Buttons were made from mussel shells. The 1850 census of Prairie County counted 2,097 white citizens and 257 slaves. The Civil War took a huge toll on the county. Des Arc's population was reduced to 400. Today this rich, fertile soil produces cotton, rice, soybeans, and wheat.

Buddy's daddy owned the Chevrolet dealership in Des Arc, a farm, and had partnership interests with his brother, which included a bus service that carried workers from the surrounding area to work in the munitions plant in Jacksonville supporting the World War II effort. Of all the kinds of work he did as a boy, he loved working on the farm making hay and taking care of livestock. His boyhood connection to WWII was the source of his deep feelings of patriotism and gratitude for the sacrifices of those who went to war. He spoke fondly of Tom Brokaw's *The Greatest Generation.*

Buddy's dad had a sixth-grade education and insisted that his children go to college and prepare themselves for their futures. His mother, a teacher, inspired the love of learning in her son and his sister. Buddy's sister went on to complete her education and had a long and successful career with Arkansas Power & Light, forerunner of Entergy, which became a major player in the energy business in the South. Buddy also had a brother who died at age six. At Des Arc High School Buddy developed his big, athletic body playing all sports. He was a bull rider until a bull threw him over the bull's head and stepped on his neck, breaking it! His football prowess influenced his choice of colleges. It was the college connection that brought Buddy and Leland together.

Buddy believes the constancy of his lifelong relationship with Leland had its origins in the work he and Leland did the year they managed the college dairy at Southern State College at Magnolia. Milking cows before and after classes seven days a week, managing the nutrition of the cows, cleaning the milking barn, plus doing college class work proved to be a human lab in managing relationships at work and prioritizing time. For the uninformed reader, to procrastinate the milking of cows, on the *cows'* schedule, would cause serious consequences, as would neglecting class work. Their work managing the college dairy was foundational to the process of learning how to manage relationships and served both men well to this day. Buddy signed on in February 1, 1961. He was a year behind Leland as a result of military service. His first job was enlisting growers and providing growers with technical support. In 1964 he was named manager of processing. Buddy was responsible for processing the chickens that Leland was responsible for growing. There were times, according to Buddy, when the quality of chickens Leland was sending to Buddy's processing plants was "terrible." He would call Leland and complain, sometimes vociferously. They would rag on each other to a certain point, but never beyond it. That point was the bond of trust that they never severed.

Two other students at Southern State College would play a role in the future of Tyson Foods: James Whitmore and Lionel Barton. Lionel Barton grew up on a "two-mule" cotton farm near Magnolia. He said "two mule" indicated they couldn't afford a tractor. As a cotton picker, he said about the best he could pick was two hundred pounds a day because the rocky soil was so poor. As the chicken industry moved toward vertical integration, those "two-mule" farmers began to grow chickens that produced chicken litter that improved pasture grasses that produced cattle. That cycle was a major factor in improving economic opportunities for farmers. The chicken industry transformed those dirt-poor farms into productive farms with tractors and a new source of stable income. When Lionel completed his PhD in poultry nutrition in Michigan, he received a call from Leland Tollett who wanted to hire him as the company nutritionist. He gave it serious consideration but declined the offer. He didn't want to do anything to endanger the friendship he had with Leland, and he said, "I wasn't sure the Tyson Company would make it." Dr. Barton went on to become an influencer in the poultry business in his work at the University of Arkansas.

Leland then turned to another Mulerider, James Whitmore, who also grew up on a "two-mule" farm in Nashville, Arkansas. "Whit," as he was known in the company, was endowed with a powerful goal-seeking mechanism. Dr. Whitmore went on to play a key role in the scientific areas of nutrition, food animal safety, food safety and animal pathology. At the time of his death in 1997 at age sixty-two, he was one of the most highly respected scientists in the industry. Most of the young people he mentored have stayed with the company and are in key management positions today.

Life on the campus at the University of Arkansas was characterized by Dr. Stephenson as "no one had cars or money." There were a number of WWII veterans studying under the GI Bill. Other students paid tuition and room costs with part-time jobs and full-time summer work. He remembers Leland, Leland's brother Eugene, Lionel Barton, and another boy renting a four-room house that they furnished with $100 of used furniture.

When they had disposable cash they would hitch a ride to Tontitown, an Italian settlement founded by Father Pietro Bandini, the New York-based Catholic priest, who rescued forty Italian immigrant families from an epidemic of malaria on a cotton plantation near Lake Chico in Southeast Arkansas. They would splurge $1.35 on the sirloin steak at the Venetian Inn.

Dr. Stephenson wondered if campus life was influenced, to some degree, by university President John Tyler Caldwell, who came from North Carolina State University where he was chancellor. Arriving on campus in 1952, one of his first pronouncements was, "There will be no more drinking on campus!" Another significant person and event on campus in 1952 was George Howard, Jr., a third-year law student, and his campaign for president of Lloyd Halls. The university newspaper, *The Arkansas Traveler*, reported, "Howard campaigned on a platform of providing better lounge facilities with more washing machines. He asked fellow members of his residence halls to 'forget my physical stature and forget that I'm a black boy,' and then he asked them to vote for him based on his qualifications for the office." [25] They did, and he won. In the fifties, the races followed separate cultural lives on campus. George Howard, Jr., leader-to-be, was making a difference. In 1980 he was nominated to the federal bench by President Jimmy Carter and the U.S. Senate gave its consent. Today he is the federal district court judge in Little Rock.

From 1952 to 1959 annual sales grew from $1 million to $11 million. The year 1959 was the first of processing chickens in the new Springdale plant with a capacity of 192,000 chickens per week. It was one of very few plants the company built as Don learned that a better use of capital was to acquire and grow by acquisition. Second buyers usually get a better deal.

The components required to achieve the benefits of vertical integration were falling into place: chicken genetics, environmentally controlled hatcheries, control of feed milling, poultry nutrition and live production practices, processing functions controlled by customer demand, and the controlling of all other functions related to meeting the quality and service needs of customers. In the late 1940s a significant volume of chickens were sold "New York dressed." That meant that only feathers and blood were removed. When the consumer got the chicken home, it was necessary to finish the job by removing the feet, head and internals. To the young reader, that is the way it was in the prehistoric time of the late 1930s and early 1940s. Moving from live and/or New York dressed gave rise to the descriptor, ready-to-cook. The phrase, "ring your neck," describes how consumers killed chickens in the era of live chickens.

Before the era of marketing chickens for meat, people grew chickens for eggs. Farmers and others who had little cash, raised hens for eggs to take to take to town and trade eggs for the food they couldn't grow. Sugar, salt, spices, flour, and, in the case of a general store, clothing, kerosene, and shoes.

Mr. John could see changes coming in how consumers wanted their chicken and responded by putting his company into a position to exploit those changes. As a competitive strategy he chose to invest his resources in pursuit of a changing marketplace, while myopic competitors focused on the status quo.

TYSON' MISSION STATEMENT

The words of a Tyson mission statement weren't written until the mid-1980s, when, at a meeting of senior managers at Tyson's Management Development Center, the words were put on paper by identifying what the *people of Tyson had been doing for forty-five years.*

WE ARE DEDICATED TO PRODUCING AND MARKETING QUALITY FOOD

PRODUCTS THAT FIT TODAY'S <u>CHANGING LIFESTYLES.</u>

    Mission statements created by the people who do the work are based on the pragmatic reality of the work required to achieve company goals. Adherence to pragmatic mission statements prevents an organization from wasting resources and straying too far from tasks at hand. All too often mission statements posted in elevators, halls, offices, on stationary, and in advertising promise results the organization doesn't deliver. Words, words, words, and more words, without any basis in reality!

DON TYSON, THE SKILLED POKER-PLAYING COLLEGE STUDENT

    Dr. Burton Elliott, who went on to become the state director of education under Governor Bill Clinton, remembers the hard times of student life at the U of A. Hard though they were, they seemed normal. Burton told me he couldn't afford a dorm room and lived for a time, 1950–1951, at Mom Peterson's Rooming House on West Dixon Street, adjacent to the railroad tracks. Don Tyson also lived there at the time. Social life at Mom's revolved around penny-ante poker. Don's poker skills were already known from his high school days. The first words the writer heard Don Tyson speak, when he announced to the management team of the company he had just acquired, were "Welcome to the world of Tyson Foods. You are another chip in my poker game. Let's have fun making money."

It may be too much to suggest that the skill of poker playing is a marker pointing to a package of leadership skills but we do know for certain that risk taking and risk management are critical skills for entrepreneurial leaders. In the June 1974 interview for *Broiler Industry* magazine, Don was asked, "Can you give us an example of the difference between ROI and ROA?" His response: "It is like sitting down at a poker game. Do you sit down and count all the money you have in the game, or do you count what you sat down with and then borrowed some from Bill and leased some from Joe?"

Poker players, according to Ted Berry [26] of Roseville, Minnesota, are well equipped with the competencies required for entrepreneurial work. He identified them as: being able to read people, being able to read situations, never playing with people who don't like you; knowing that playing with strangers and people you know requires different tactics; understanding and respecting the stakes of the game and the consequences of losing; and being able to think long term—beyond the situation at hand. And it helps when you are in the right game playing with the right people and trust your well-developed intuition. Intuition, hunch, a "blink," instinct, second sight, subconscious perception—whatever it is, Don had it. Tollett said Don could see around corners. Malcolm Gladwell, a staff writer for *The New Yorker*, has published two books [27] that shed some light on Don's ability "to see around corners."

Blink is a book about how we think without thinking, about choices that seem to be made in an instant—in the blink of an eye—that actually aren't as simple as they seem. Why are some people brilliant decision makers, while others are consistently inept? Why do some people follow their instincts and win, while others end up stumbling into error? How do our brains really work—in the office, in the classroom, in the kitchen, and in the bedroom? And why are the best decisions often those that are impossible to explain to others?

Don's intuitive strength served the strategic thinking and planning activities of the young company very well. The writer defines strategic thinking as the process by which Tyson envisioned its future and developed plans, structure, and systems required to achieve that future. Tyson never fell into the strategic planning trap that was popular in the 1950s. It was a trap in that some companies created big departments to produce long-term strategic plans, five to ten years out, and those plans were adhered to as "the gospel," which in effect paralyzed the company's ability to respond to the changing marketplace.

An example of this trap in the meat business was major meat packers who entered the poultry business and tried to manage their poultry assets as subsidiaries. Subsidiaries are like assistants— shadows created by reflected light! The strategic plans produced at their corporate offices lacked the intuitive strengths of the entrepreneurs like Don Tyson. One of their planning errors was to assume that processing and marketing chickens and turkeys was just like processing and marketing cattle and hogs. The first assumption of strategic planning is the plan won't work. It didn't, and those companies planned themselves to death. They didn't notice that chickens and turkeys had feathers!

In his *Strategic Planning in Emerging Companies,* [28] Steven Brandt of the Stanford Graduate School of Business describes a "Hierarchy of Planning Techniques," beginning with *intuition*:

      —intuition
      —sales volume
      —profitability
      —contribution margin
      —return on investment
      —product life cycle
      —experience curve/market share

These were Tyson's strategic thinking processes early on. An analysis of Tyson's annual reports, 1963–1997, identifies them all in detail. Other sources, like the October 1968 *Broiler Industry* interview of Don, provide some insight into his strategic thinking.

Question: Don, just about every time you make one announcement, you're surprising the industry with another move. You seem to be a young man in hurry.

Answer We keep <u>changing</u> our business around—redeploying our capital to where it can earn the biggest return. We have a seven-year average of 14% net return on invested capital. Anytime it becomes possible to forecast that a segment of our business will give us below 7% earnings for a period longer than one year, we begin to phase it out. We think we have a lot more flexibility in that respect than many larger national firms.

Question: It must take a lot of courage to strike off in new directions after a lifetime's experience in commodities.

Answer: Any company, from General Motors to the man just starting his own business, has only a certain amount of capital to work with. It's management's decision to determine how to budget that capital for maximum returns. We set priorities in our capital and operating budgets, and rank on an ROI basis. Question: What's the best single piece of advice you might offer anybody in the industry today?

Answer: Stay well financed. Keep your current ratio strong—for example, two dollars of current assets for every dollar of current liabilities, or more. Don't let your long-term debt position exceed 50% of your equity position. Don't incur payments on long-term debt that exceed half of your depreciation schedule. You can stand a pretty good test of capital with rules of thumb.

HOW EQ, EMOTIONAL INTELLIGENCE, [29] ENHANCED THE IQ OF THE TRIUMVIRATE

One of the critical success factors at work was what we call today the strategic management of *intellectual* or human capital. You can now buy books and hire consultants who have parsed the process as well as any politician running for election. The term *human capital* [30] was first used by Nobel Laureate Theodore Schultz in 1961. The process of matching human talent to the work to be done was one of the triumvirate's strengths. It is a viable test of leadership skill. Leaders know they aren't equipped with all the strengths and skills required to achieve their goals. The process can be highly sophisticated using psychometrics or whatever is for sale at the time, or it can be as simple as knowing the candidate for the job. In either case, it is the beginning of a process that brings together two kinds of human intelligence: 1. IQ—a number/metric noting the relative intelligence of individuals. 2. EQ—the competencies required to manage feelings that are expressed in appropriate and effective ways that enable people to get their work done efficiently and effectively.

Continuing with Daniel Goleman, who for twelve years covered the behavioral and brain sciences for *The New York Times*, has written well and wisely on the "The great divide in competencies lies between the mind and heart, or more technically, between cognition and emotion...Emotional competence is a learned capability based on emotional intelligence that results in outstanding performance at work... Our emotional intelligence determines our potential for learning the practical skills that are based on its five elements: self-awareness, motivation, self-regulation, empathy and adeptness in relationship." These "intelligences" were a part of the glue that held the triumvirate together. Jim Blair, Tyson's general council, is an excellent example of different kinds of intelligence. He earned his bachelor's degree in two years. Two years later, he earned his law degree! As a member of Mensa he was and is in the top 2 percent on the IQ scale. In the January 2005 issue of the magazine *Celebrate Northwest Arkansas,* he said, "When I was eighteen and intellectually arrogant, I joined MENSA. I believe now that there are other kinds of intelligence besides the ones that are measured in traditional IQ. I've always had talent for taking tests, but I think there are other talented people out there that do well in life that may not have that talent for taking tests." Another key to Tyson growing talent was having knowledge of all the variables related to placing the right people in the right jobs at the right time in the right places. Dr. Paul Hersey calls it "readiness" and has developed a practical method to reduce the risk of failure.[31] The triumvirate got the work done without much emphasis on job titles, org charts, and job descriptions. The work was driven by Mr. John's sometimes autocratic style and Don's mantra of being responsible and accountable for doing the work, all the work, whatever the work was, to satisfy customers.

Don said the only time Leland and Buddy let him down was in a meeting with Mr. John whose wrath had been triggered by something. He took immediate and corrective action with vigor that became so vigorous that Leland and Buddy left the room, leaving Don to absorb it all!

Mr. John didn't do annual performance reviews. Any time performance didn't conform to his standards, it was review time. It is interesting to note how contemporary leaders have discovered Mr. John's wisdom. Why save up performance failures for an annual review? Isn't the enterprise best served when performance, positive or negative, is acknowledged and dealt with immediately? Managers who save up worker performance over time are in fact creating a hidden agenda that is irresponsible and flies in the face of accountability! Getting the work done, doing the work right, improving the work, and changing how the work was done was foundational to the formation of the work culture at Tyson Foods, and everyone in the company understood the concept. Don called it "responsibility management."

RESPONSIBILITY MANAGEMENT

An example of how responsibility management influenced Tyson's work culture occurred during a labor dispute in the early 1970s at a newly acquired plant in Shelbyville, Tennessee. Leland Tollett took his management team to Shelbyville during a very hot July to catch chickens to keep the plant running! It was Best Practices 101, for Tyson execs! Some of those executive chicken catchers were Leland, Howard Baird, Aubrey Cuzick, and James Irwin. Can you see these guys catching chickens wearing Armani suits and Vigotti shoes?

On a fishing trip on the White River in North Arkansas at Gaston's Resort, Colonel John J. Torres, [32]commander of the Fifteenth Airlift Wing, Hickam Air Force Base, Honolulu Hawaii/Bellows Air Force Station/Wake Island Airfield, introduced the writer to the leadership training of our Air Force personnel. The training is directed by the Air War College and Air University. Between catching and eating rainbow trout, Colonel Torres and I compared his leadership learning notes with my research notes for writing this book. We both discovered that leadership, the work of influencing, differs little from the work of our Air Force and the work of leadership in business. For example, General Curtis E. LeMay, when asked to provide a one-word definition of leadership, replied, "Responsibility." Writing for *AU–24 Concepts for Air Force Leadership*, Dr. Dewey E. Johnson [33] describes leadership as "a proactive process of influencing people, individually and in groups, to accomplish meaningful organizational missions. This means an influence process up, down, sideways, and diagonally throughout the organization." Responsibility management is an effective antidote to the behavior of blaming others or their job descriptions when the work doesn't get done. As valuable as job descriptions can be, in highly structured organizations job descriptions can be used by irresponsible folks who try to justify work not done or work not done correctly by saying, "It wasn't in my job description!" The folks in the plant did see and knew the new owners of their company weren't ivory-tower-bound execs. They knew about real work, the kind of work they did! They observed responsibility management at work! Another military leader, General of the Army George C. Marshall, was quoted in the *AU-24* story as saying, "A decent regard for the rights and feelings of others is essential to leadership." **HAVING FUN AT WORK.**

Leland and Buddy were known at times to have fun at work—usually away from the office. On one occasion the two of them had scheduled a meeting in a small Arkansas town where Tyson had a plant. They invited Gerald Johnston, the finance/accounting guy, to join them the next morning. They told Gerald they would reserve a hotel room for him. He would join them for breakfast the next morning at their motel's restaurant. They were staying at a fine AAA-rated motel. The hotel room they reserved for Gerald was not AAA, perhaps unrated and cheap, especially cheap for their senior finance guy. Gerald left the office in Springdale late in the day. Arriving at the hotel he walked in and wondered if he was in the right hotel. He tapped on the bell and waited some time for a response. When the desk clerk did show, Gerald inquired about his reservation. The clerk said "Yes, I have a room for you. You are to meet Mr. Tollett and Mr. Wray for breakfast at their motel restaurant at 6:00 a.m." He found his room but felt troubled.

He went downstairs to a public phone to call Tollett or Wray. They weren't available. Gerald went to bed sleeping on top of the covers in his clothes, fearful of entering a bed of bed bugs and other uninvited bed partners! Next morning, arriving at the designated motel restaurant for a 6:00 a.m. breakfast, Tollett and Wray couldn't contain their amusement as they were overcome by laughter!

LEADERS UNDERSTAND THE NATURE OF WORK AND THE NATURE OF WORKERS

This snapshot portrayal of the formative years of three men, Don Tyson, Leland Tollett, and Buddy Wray, is useful in understanding the power of trusting relationships in the pursuit of common goals. It is also useful in understanding the context of the times. Don Tyson did not attempt to clone himself in the selection of these men. Each is unique and different from the other. Each brought different strengths to the management team. Each was encouraged to challenge the others and argue for what he believed. Don gave them veto power! When the arguments were over, they pursued agreed-upon goals with passionate vengeance. Don, the visionary, expressive one; Leland, the analytical analyst; and Buddy, the driver who forcefully kept the energy and company resources focused on company goals—worked together for most of forty years. That is somewhat unusual in U.S. corporate history. They led this company safely through the mine fields of economic crises, political messes, media ineptness, weird attacks from government prosecutors, and others whose behaviors were those of spoiled children who tried to make themselves larger by making their playmates smaller! Kaleel Jamison, God rest her soul, described this behavior in her book, *The Nibble Theory*. [34] This is a must read for folks suffering from ego addiction.

In his *Encyclical Letter on Work and Man,* Pope John Paul II writes, "And work means any activity by man, whether manual or intellectual, whatever its nature or circumstances; it means any human activity that can and must be recognized as work, in the midst of all the many activities of which man is capable and to which he is predisposed by his very nature, by virtue of humanity itself. Man is made to be in the visible universe an image and likeness of God." [35]

THE POWER OF FRIENDSHIPS

David McCullough in his book, *1776,*[36] describes how the friendship of Nathanael Greene and Henry Knox brought together two young men who would be selected by General George Washington to lead the Continental Army to defeat King George III and the British. These three leaders were young—George Washington was forty-three; Nathanael

Greene was thirty-three; Henry Knox was twenty-five. The friendship between Greene and Knox began in Greene's London Bookstore on Cornhill Street in Boston. Both men shared a love for books with an interest in "the military art." Both were self-educated. Near the end of McCullough's story, he writes,

> Of all the general officers who had taken part in the Siege of Boston, only two were still serving at the time of the British surrender at Yorktown, Washington and Greene. Henry Knox, who had become a brigadier general after the Battle of Trenton, and who fought in every battle in which Washington took part, was also present at Yorktown. Greene and Knox, the two young untried New EnglandersWashington had singled out at the beginning, as the best of the "raw material" he had to work with, had both shown true greatness and stayed in the fight to the finish. [37]

LEADERSHIP INSIGHTS

- Leaders wisely acknowledge they are not equippedwith all the knowledge, skills, and abilities to build a great organization. Applying this knowledge, they find the talent required to achieve the goals of the organization.

- Leaders manage their hubris and large egos to Nurture a work environment that encourages fullparticipation by followers at all levels.

CHAPTER 3
"CUSTOMERING"—THE SWEET MUSIC OF PROFITABILITY

But customer loyalty is too important to delegate. It has a crucial effect on every constituency and aspect of a business system; it drives business success and therefore CEO careers. The responsibility for customer retention or defection belongs squarely on the CEO's desk, where it can get the same kind of attention that is lavished on stock price and cash flow. Consistent retention can create tremendous competitive advantage, boost employee morale, produce unexpected bonuses in productivity and growth, and reduce the cost of capital. [38]   Frederick F. Reichheld

Don Tyson's eleventh commandment was "Thou shalt have a profit." His skill in orchestrating each function of the business to satisfy customers created beautiful music for customers, workers, growers, and shareholders. I think it was Warren Bennis who said, "Leaders must encourage their organizations to dance to forms of music yet to be heard." Don had composed music that included melody, harmony, rhythm, and timbre that each team player danced to as they did the work of satisfying customers! All sections of the orchestra—strings, wind, and percussion instruments—worked from the Don Tyson score of customer satisfaction.

Profit was the result of leader functions I have tried to describe with a model. As with most models the Tyson Leadership Model is imperfect—it is a visual representation of events I observed. This model is based on what Kenneth Craik called *mental models*. Craik suggested in 1943 that mental models were "small-scale models" of reality used to anticipate events. Tyson leaders didn't use or need a visual representation describing how to do the work of satisfying customers. They had demonstrated behaviorally and instilled in the minds of Tyson folks mental models that described the what, why, and how of the work of customer satisfaction. Tyson never relied on words fashioned into slick statements or slogans to motivate people. Tyson relied on behaviors, knowing that behaviors were more efficacious than words. This is not to diminish the power of language, but rather to note the cognitive dissonance created when behaviors aren't congruent with words. For an example, consider Enron, now in prison for deceiving their employees and shareholders.

EXPLANATION OF THE MODEL

The center of the model is the *customer*, surrounded by *workers* and *contract growers* who grow Tyson chickens. *Shareholders* occupy the outside ring as owners of Tyson stock who expect and receive very good returns on their investment from 1963 when the company went public through 1997. This is the primary time frame I have written about.

Don's VISION for his company set in motion the actions/behaviors of *alignment, attunement, empowerment, structure and systems,* and *intuition balanced with reason. Visioning* was the process of "seeing a future that was better and different than the present." The process of *visioning* included the rare ability to communicate the vision that causes folks to internalize and adopt the vision as their own.

ALIGNMENT was the work of keeping resources—human, technical, and financial—aligned with business goals. One of the benefits of *alignment* was the ability to achieve right costs by reducing waste caused by folks not understanding the what, why, and how of their work.

The action of ATTUNEMENT was understanding workers and the intrinsic human need for respect, dignity, and personhood; the basic human need for a work environment that was physically and emotionally safe; and opportunities to grow and learn. *Attunement* included equitable pay and benefits to protect families and an opportunity to share in the rewards of the company's success and create personal wealth.

EMPOWERMENT was the work of managing relationships in the workplace in such a way that workers, in the executive suite or on a production line, empowered themselves to do productive work. Risk taking and decision making were encouraged. Micromanagement was not the norm. Managers who had not learned how to lead situationally resorted to micromanaging, thus limiting their effectiveness.

STRUCTURE AND SYSTEMS were created and changed to meet the changing needs of customers, workers, suppliers, contract growers, and regulators.

INTUITION BALANCED WITH REASON was balancing Don's highly developed intuitive skills with the rational thinking of Leland Tollett and Buddy Wray.

DON TYSON—FOOD FUTURIST

"Customering" was an active verb in Tyson's business as evidenced by a satisfied customer base including fast-food restaurants, elegant dining establishments, hospitals, prisons, cruise ships, K–twelve schools, colleges and universities, wholesale clubs, wholesale distributors, the military (including military commissaries), home kitchens, delicatessens, airlines, country clubs, and export customers around the world. Tyson had created a distribution system that satisfied customers' needs for fast and accurate delivery. It gave Tyson a significant competitive advantage.

Tyson was the beneficiary of consumers being told by physicians and food editors that chicken was a healthier source of protein than red meat. He capitalized on the good news. At a meeting of bankers and shareholders, he once jokingly remarked that beef packers should be required to include a warning label on their product as dangerous to health.

His worldview was that of a food futurist. He traveled extensively, searching for more efficient methods of providing meat protein to world consumers. He studied shrimp, catfish, trout farming, and other seafood options. The demand in seafood was high in a few countries, but the world per-capita consumption didn't represent a major growth market.

The issue was always threefold: what does the customer want, what can the customer afford, and can we produce it? In developing countries, low-cost food was grain-based proteins, rather than meat proteins. They couldn't afford the cost of converting grain protein to meat protein. As those countries had more disposable income, Tyson was there to satisfy the newfound demand for chicken protein.

EXAMPLES OF THE ACTIONS OF THE TYSON'S LEADERSHIP MODEL

Rolling the dice for Kentucky Fried Chicken.

I will fast-track a new plant dedicated to producing Lite 'n Crispy chicken!   Don Tyson

The setting was Tyson's Management Development Center located on Lake Dardanelle at Russellville, Arkansas, a hundred miles from the Head Shed in Springdale.

I was hosting a luncheon in the private dining room at The Management Center for Don Tyson, Buddy Wray, CEO Roger Enrico from PepsiCo (owner of KFC), John Cranor, CEO at KFC, and others. The purpose of the meeting was to sell PepsiCo/KFC on building a plant to produce a new product that was being produced in small quantities for testing at KFC. The product, Lite 'n Crispy, was skinless, bone-in chicken designed for consumers who wanted fried chicken with fewer calories.

After some prodding by the PepsiCo/KFC folks for a firm price, Don did what he had done so many times before; he made a decision and a commitment. He said, "I don't know what the price will be because the small quantities we are making for you don't give us enough production data to determine a price. But I will build a dedicated plant in Pine Bluff, Arkansas, to produce Lite 'n Crispy chicken. I'll fast-track construction, 24-7."

The deal was made. Tyson's commitment to customer satisfaction was once again validated. Dessert was served, and the meeting concluded.

PINE BLUFF, ARKANSAS, September 12, 1990

Don Tyson stepped off the airplane at Grider Field, September 12, 1990, and said, "We're going to start clearing Monday morning." By September 20, 1990, the fourth day of construction, men were working around the clock. Thanks to many contractors and our own Tyson Engineering Department based in Springdale, seven months later, April 1, 1991, we started production. Ronnie Hightower, Pine Bluff Complex Manager [39]

Don played his hand. The deal was done. Don liked the word—the process of the "deal." The deal was a $30 million dollar facility. "This is the biggest single plant expansion we've ever done—in dollar amount and size." [40] Three-hundred-forty thousand square feet dedicated to a single customer for a product that was not proven in the marketplace! The plant was to be built in Pine Bluff, Arkansas, where the company operated a hatchery, had good live production capacity with local growers, had a feed mill, and had a good water treatment plant. This facility met all the requirements for a fully integrated production system designed to produce high quality with low cost to the customer. It was also helpful that the city of Pine Bluff wanted Tyson to expand in their town. They competed with several cities and won the competition. Announcements of the new facility were archived by Marilyn Seymour who worked at the Pine Bluff plant and graciously provided a wealth of information about this event.

OPENING CEREMONIES AT THE PLANT DEDICATED TO KFC PRODUCTION—PINE BLUFF, ARKANSAS

Governor Bill Clinton spoke and said, "This is a wonderful day for Pine Bluff and the end of a great year. Tyson now has more than 18,000 employees in Arkansas. That makes Tyson Foods by far our largest corporate citizen. They have more employees (in Arkansas) than—dare I say it—than Wal-Mart does. We are profoundly grateful." [41]

Bill Clinton was governor of Arkansas for eleven years. Arkansas is a very small state with fewer than three million folks. Like governors preceding him, his office door was always open to Arkansas employers, and he worked diligently with employers to improve the Arkansas economy. Don's father John had lobbied Governor Faubus in the 1950s to eliminate a farm tax that was hurting the poultry industry. Tyson Foods protected its interests and the interests of the poultry industry working with Governors Francis Cherry, Winthrop Rockefeller, Frank White, Jim Guy Tucker, Mike Huckabee, Dale Bumpers, and David Pryor.

The Arkansas Industrial Development Project made a commitment of up to $900,000, which was the largest commitment made for economic development. On May

29, 1991, with the band playing, the plant was opened with one thousand folks listening to speeches by Governor Clinton, Don Tyson, John Cranor (CEO at KFC), Pine Bluff Mayor Carolyn Robinson, and David Harrington (Arkansas Industrial Development director). The plant stopped production for three hours while Don met plant workers individually, thanking them for their good work and urging them to continue to grow their careers at Tyson.

Inside the plant there were life-sized cutouts of the colonel in the hallways. Workers wore patches on their khaki shirts with Tyson's Rambo Chicken holding the KFC logo in one hand, the Tyson logo in the other. Every worker in the plant was paying attention at this event. Management of attention is one of Warren Bennis's competencies for leaders. [42] One of those paying attention was Marilyn Seymore, at the Pine Bluff complex, which archived this information and shared it with readers. Thanks, Marilyn!

ROLL OUT LITE 'N CRISPY CHICKEN

This new low-calorie, low-fat, skinless, bone-in chicken was rolled out in February 1991 in seven hundred KFC stores in the Northeast and was expected to be in all five thousand U.S. stores by summer. The company called it the 'biggest breakthrough since Colonel Sanders developed his secret blend of 11 herbs and spices.

According to a report in *Nation's Restaurant News*, February 4, 1991, Kyle Craig, president of KFC USA, said, "I think Lite 'n Crispy is going to give us tremendous sales boost...Incremental sales increases at Lansing, Michigan, test units, ranged from five percent to twenty percent. In the same report, franchisee Bob Peck, president of R.P. Peck Enterprises in Oklahoma City, said, "It's a very good product and will help us with sales...But the biggest problem is that it's a frozen product...many franchisees may have to buy additional freezers to store the product because the containers (freezers) are already filled with such products as Hot Wings, chicken nuggets, french fries and corn."

Five months after introducing Lite 'n Crispy chicken, KFC renamed the product Skinfree Crispy and did a better job of communicating to the consumer that the produce was skinless. The term lite was eliminated. The company said the product accounted for one-third of sales in markets where it was available.

OOPS!

Nations' Restaurant News, November 18, 1991, Louisville, Kentucky:

> Even though KFC has one of the most sophisticated research-and- development facilities in foodservice, the company is clearly stumbling in its

efforts to develop new products. The chain recently suspended testing of its Monterey Broil non-fried entrée, a product seen as a crucial component of the chain's turnaround effort. "I don't think KFC will turn around until it has a healthful non-fried product," concludes Joe Doyle, an analyst with Smith Barney... KFC has spent approximately five years trying to refine a non-fried entrée. Suspension of the effort closely follows the chain's decision to halt the rollout of Skinfree Crispy, a reduced-fat fried-chicken item that similarly was expected to draw health-conscious patrons. The No. 1 chicken chain has also curtailed development of a full line of sandwiches. Instead, it is focusing on the testing and refinement of just two varieties: a barbecued sandwich and a Monterey Broil sandwich made from a grilled boil-in-the-bag chicken breast. Meanwhile, KFC continues to lose market share to hamburger chains touting their new chicken sandwiches, upstart specialty chicken chains that offer non-fried products, and regional poultry specialists.

THE ROLLOUT FAILS

Lite 'n Crispy (Skinfree Crispy) didn't fail for any single reason—it failed for several reasons. One of the more interesting reasons was described by Anthony Ramirez writing in *The New York Times* on March 1, 1991. "For years, fast-food restaurants have promoted foods as being lower in calories or fat than their regular offerings, with decidedly mixed results.

To the frustration of many a market researcher, the consumer is a health-conscious, Dr. Jekyll when answering surveys, but a junk-food-loving Mr. Hyde when fork comes to mouth."

Competition was another factor. Restaurants like El Pollo Loco and Boston Markets were having success selling non-breaded roasted items. Burger King's BK Broiler, a grilled chicken sandwich, was one of its most successful products, selling a million sandwiches a day. Wendy's International invested about $10 million over a year advertising a reduced-calorie menu. A spokesperson said, "No one would bite."

Another problem was resistance from a number of large KFC franchisees to invest in in-store equipment and space required to prepare the product.

When Lite 'n Crispy failed, critics of Don Tyson's risk management style—akin to playing poker, they said—had finally found Don's Achilles' heel. He wasn't infallible. No surprise to Don and his leadership team. They all knew the Pine Bluff plant would be needed to satisfy growing customer demand. When sales were doubling every five years, new or acquired plants would be needed. Lite 'n Crispy was just a bump in the road that slowed progress for a few minutes in the fifty-six-year history of the company. As Leland Tollett described Don's intuitive skills, "He could see around corners."

If you were to do a risk/benefit analysis on this project, it would show significant short-term losses. The long-term analysis would be synergistic, 1 + 1 + 1 = a sum greater than 3. This product failure could have been catastrophic for Tyson had they allowed the relationship to become adversarial. When KFC needed new products or more production, Tyson was there competing for the business. When PepsiCo bought Taco Bell, Tyson was the supplier of choice for a long string of new products.

THE ROLE OF TYSON'S VISION IN THE KFC STORY

Visioning is a process, not a mystical, dreamy or ethereal experience; it is a pragmatic process of how leaders "see" their future and develop strategic plans and create structures and systems required to achieve their future. Value creation is the result of what a vision does. The KFC story is evidence of Tyson's vision of creating value, a process of customer satisfaction. It was sufficiently powerful to pull all the managers involved through the difficult times of disappointments and financial losses—and the customer followed.

The KFC story illustrates the difference between value creation and profit. Frederick Reichheld writes:

> The current approach might be called the profit theory. All business skills and competencies stand or fall on their capacity to contribute to profits.

The new theory sees the fundamental as a vital consequence of value creation—a means rather than an end, a result as opposed to a purpose...Profits alone are an unreliable measure because it is possible to raise reported short-term earnings by liquidating human capital. Pay cuts and price increases can boost earnings, but they have negative effects on employee and customer loyalty and so shorten the duration and worth of those assets. [43]

On another occasion involving a national chain, Bob Womack describes how Tyson's commitment to customering saved a big chunk of business that was being threatened by supply problems.

The first thing I did was get Leland on the plane to go down there and make sure that these people understood that we were going to service their needs. The second thing we did was bring their people in and we all got together. They felt immediately comfortable that we could answer the call in a very short time. They had a president down there at that particular time that was not a good one and didn't last very long. He and the previous seven before him did not last very long. But, at the same time, we molded our company to this individual's needs. He was a hip shooter. He wanted to get the product on the menu in a very short time, and we were able to respond. It took a lot of reading the customer and getting our people involved in the thing very quickly so that we could respond. It's not always good to do things that way. Sometimes it hurts on the front end of the thing, but over time, it develops into a good deal because we did answer the call and they knew very well we answered the call. And they all told me that they will continue to go to the well for us when discussing our own future assignments.

KROGER SUPERMARKETS, CHARLES WYCHE, DON TYSON AND THE OZARK FRY

In 1980, Tyson introduced to the retail market the first frozen chicken sandwich product. Tyson dominated the Rock Cornish hen category in retailers' frozen cases and had a good share of fresh chickens in the meat departments. They wanted to expand space in the frozen convenience section. They looked to researcher Charles Wyche, who had joined Tyson in 1972 after completing his postgraduate work in food technology. He was responsible for product research and development. One morning Don walked into Charles's R & D kitchen and said he wanted a fully cooked chicken breast patty, similar to the one they were selling in foodservice. He described the product and packaging he thought would work and asked Charles if he could make it. Charles said, "Yes, no problem." He assumed the start-up would allow sufficient time to learn how to produce and package the product. Charles asked Don how many cases they should plan for as that forecast would determine packaging and equipment needs. Don was vague—saying something like a few thousand cases a month. Dick Stockland took the product to the Ohio State Fair to test with retail consumers who liked it and said they would buy it in retail stores.

Charles and his team designed the product, packaging, and production methods for a few thousand cases a month. A few weeks later, Don came bouncing into the lab with an order for ten thousand cases from Kroger Food Stores.

Charles Wyche, at this writing, is still there, devoting most of his time to designing Tyson's new, innovative, customer-driven Discovery Center. The press release of April 1, 2004, describes the facility as an "184,000-square-foot research and development and training facility, to be built on the campus of Tyson's corporate headquarters in Springdale. Preparation on the sixteen-acre site has already begun, and construction is expected to begin soon, with an estimated budget of $40 million. The project is expected to be completed in late 2005...The Discovery Center will include:

— Twenty product development kitchens, including a retail presentation kitchen, a foodservice presentation kitchen, and a kitchen of the future.
— Flexible facilities for leadership, management and job-functional training for team members.
— A USDA-inspected pilot plant, which will provide a

manufacturing environment for new concepts to improve "speed to market."
— A consumer focus group area.
— Facilities for packaging design and development testing.
— Capability for shelf life studies.
— Approximately 220 total team members, representing approximately $5 million payroll. [44]

Charles Wyche was wearing golden handcuffs that Tyson used to retain creative and productive talent. It is rumored he still owns the first share of Tyson stock he bought in 1972.

NOTHING HAPPENS UNTIL SOMEBODY SELLS SOMETHING

In the Kroger/Charles Wyche story, Don Tyson was the sales guy who sold Ozark FRYS, the first chicken sandwich product for retail, to Kroger. Dick Stockland sold the product to a state fair to prove consumers would buy the product. In 1988, Dick formed the International Division. Dick came to Tyson by way of acquisition. He was the finance/accounting/sales guy at Prospect Farms in Little Rock. He was something of a renaissance thinker in the chicken business, endowed with an expansive mind that enabled him to see the big business picture.

The 1969 acquisition of Prospect Farms was strategically vital as it gave Tyson access to the growing foodservice market. Bobby Walker, Prospect's sales manager, was recognized by many as the best salesperson in the business. At the time Prospect Farms was a competitor to J.D. Jewell of Gainesville, Georgia. Jesse Jewell was the perennial entrepreneur who pioneered a number of innovative ideas and products. According to Reynolds Skinner, Jewell's customer service manager, Mr. Jewell had an idea a minute and launched several products before their time. He was marketing individually quick frozen chicken long before Tastybird Foods made it their signature item. J.D. Jewell went into bankruptcy in 1972. It appears he made a common error of entrepreneurial thinkers by not balancing his entrepreneurial strengths with rational and analytical thinkers like Leland Tollett and Buddy Wray.

Dick Stockland went on to build a very successful sales and marketing organization selling in retail, club stores, theme parks like Disney, and international markets. He was comfortable and competent in the purchasing office of food retailers Kroger and Wal-Mart and international buyers in Hong Kong, Beijing, and Moscow. Using his organizational skills he put together a unique method of selling surplus leg meat into Japan via a Mequilla D'Oro in Mexico. Leg meat produced in Tyson's U.S. plants was shipped to Mexico and fashioned into a very popular product called yakitori sold in Japanese yakitori bars.

This writer is grateful to Dick Stockland for welcoming him into the Tyson family by taking him to Herman's Restaurant for a special get-acquainted moment. Herman's is a landmark eatery, not far from Tyson's world headquarters. The place has character, absent the plastic motif of the new eateries in town. Most guests enter the restaurant through the kitchen, walking past the grills and work stations, behind the bar into the dining room. Dining there is a kind of ritualistic experience celebrating the successes of whoever dines and drinks there. The Arkansas Razorbacks and their mythic leader, Frank Broyles, are omnipresent on the walls at Herman's and in the memories of the guests. The parking lot is unpaved. The building could use a good paint job.

Proprietor Herman Tuck and Don Tyson were cadets together at Kemper Military Academy in Kansas City. Herman was one of the early investors in Tyson stock, which has made him a millionaire who now enjoys retirement on Beaver Lake. Herman is a perpetual guest at Don's birthday parties and a great storyteller in the Ozark Mountain tradition.

NEIL CAREY TUNES INTO THE CHINESE FOOD CULTURE AND MAKES PROFITABLE MUSIC FOR TYSON FOODS

When Neil Carey left Campbell Soup Company in 1983 to work for Tyson, he never dreamed he would become a key player in his new company's globalization. His boss, Dick Stockland, had formed the international division in 1988. Neil told me he didn't know much about chicken but had discovered in the five years he had been selling for Tyson that when customers wanted a product, they usually got it. His story demonstrates the wisdom of a flat organizational structure that doesn't create barriers of communication between salespeople and the executive group. In some highly structured organizations, it takes so long for a product idea to be implemented that enlightened competitors win the race in new product introduction.

Early one morning, walking through Hong Kong's "wet market," Neil Carey experienced a sales epiphany. When he saw the price of chicken paws (feet) and wing tips at 59¢ per pound it was *voila!* In the United States, those items were worth about 5¢ a pound or less.

Neil is a big, strong, winsome redhead who exudes excitement about his work. On returning to the United States, he went to see Buddy Wray, who headed sales and marketing, and shared his epiphany. He sought Buddy's approval to spend the money required to produce chicken paws in Asia. As they talked specifications, Neil told Buddy that chicken paws in Asia had to be white as snow, free from cuticle and bruises, and needed to come from very large chickens.

Paws had been eaten for centuries as a delectable appetizer preceding a luxurious meal. Legend has it that this Chinese culinary morsel goes back to the time of a government minister named Yi Yin, during the Shang Dynasty, fifteenth to eleventh century BCE. They were fried, served in a zesty sauce and eaten by sucking on the sweet meat that is nearest the bones.

Neil's chicken paws idea was interesting to Buddy. However, his analytical mind and sometimes intimidating style didn't resonate positively to product ideas generated by moments of sales epiphanies. He instructed Neil to go back to Hong Kong and bring back answers to his list of "why/how" questions.

Neil returned to Hong Kong, found answers to Buddy's questions, and returned to Buddy's office. Buddy was still not convinced. This story is an example of why and how Don balanced his entrepreneurial strengths with Buddy and Leland's rational/analytical thinking. It set up a tension that proved over time a pragmatic technique to make profitable decisions in all areas of the business. The relationship was possible because of the ability of each member of the triumvirate to keep their egos from interfering with good decision making.

Back in Hong Kong to satisfy Buddy's need for more information, a predictable behavior of analyticals, Neil was dining with his Chinese agent to discuss how to solve their problem. They knew the profit potential for paws was very good and searched for a way to sell Buddy. They decided to enlist Don Tyson's help. The plan was for Neil's agent to call Don just to inform him of the project and get his advice on the next step. They called Don who listened carefully and asked only one question, "Are you sure?." They assured Don they were sure. The details of the discussion between Don and Buddy are a bit fuzzy, but the details about the huge success of the new product are quite clear. Once again, "Customering at Tyson Foods is an active verb, practiced by everyone wearing the khakis."

To produce the quality the Chinese customers wanted required significant changes in the live production of chickens and in the processing of paws. Growers would have to change how they managed the floor materials in the chicken houses that housed twenty thousand to thirty thousand large chickens. To process these delicacies, new machines had to be modified or invented, line personnel had to be trained, and poultry operations need a "paradigm shift" in their thinking about chicken feet.

David Purtle, VP of Operations, attended the committee meeting that was planning Tyson's 1994 corporate meeting and asked if chicken paws could be placed on the menu. The meeting was at the ski resort at Keystone Colorado. Neil provided an authentic sauce recipe for chicken paws, which was given to the chef at Keystone who agreed to prepare this delicacy for the Tyson meeting. At the luncheon, production managers learned how to eat chicken paws. It was a profound adult learning experience! The message was successfully sent, utilizing all the sensory mechanisms of the diners—sight, smell, taste, feel, and hearing the sucking sound for the sweet meat closest to the bone.

This story is an example of the Triumvirate's commitment to customer satisfaction and open communications without hierarchical restrictions. Profit was the result of a process that was inclusive of the entire workforce from the executive suite to the growers' farms.

CHICKEN PAWS AND VALUE CREATION

When Neil Carey had his "chicken paw epiphany" in the fresh market in Hong Kong and presented the concept to Buddy Wray, he set in motion a typical Tyson value-creation event. According to Tyson's 1996 annual report, Leland Tollett said China had purchased 175 million pounds of paws! Two paws per person in China! For this product to be successful, virtually every function in the company played a role—from the farmer growing chickens to Tyson production folks who learned about the product to seafaring workers transporting the product on the high seas in container ships.

BOB WOMACK PROMOTED TO GROUP VP, FOODSERVICE SALES

Bob joined Tyson Foods in 1970 to become credit manager. He came from International Harvester in Tulsa, Oklahoma. He arrived on the scene a year after Dick Stockland. Both men were promoted in 1983—Dick to group VP, Retail Sales, and Bob to group VP, Foodservice Sales. [45] Together they built the sales organization that managed and grew sales of $603 million in 1983 to $5.5 billion in 1995. They successfully integrated the sales of twenty acquisitions during the same period. Using today's management language, we would characterize these men as "intellectual capital." It is interesting to note that both men had accounting and finance backgrounds. They reported to Buddy Wray, who was named executive VP, Sales & Marketing, in 1981.

Going to work for Tyson Foods was like an eight-year-old learning to ride a bicycle. There are no training wheels. You wobble around a bit on your own until someone or something gives you a shove in the back, propelling you to a speed that causes you to pedal faster and faster—you can't stop as you begin to enjoy the thrill of speed and success and the attendant rewards.

THE TRIANGLE OF TENSION

One of the challenges of leadership in a customer-centered company is the internal tension and conflict that naturally occur in the daily processes of doing the work of satisfying customers. I use the word "natural" as it best describes the tension created when normal behavior of self-interest conflicts with the interest of other departments and the customer. The three functional corners of the triangle of tension are:

1. the pressure to produce quality products,
2. the pressure to deliver quality service, and
3. the pressure to be the low-cost producer.

The center of the triangle of tension is customer satisfaction. When the triangle spins into action it encounters a myriad of forces that can interfere with customer satisfaction. Some of those forces that need to be monitored and managed are quite natural. Occasionally they are not natural nor in the best interests of company goals and they require the interventions of skilled leaders.

At Tyson Foods the traditional tension between production and sales was minimized by how the company was structured. When Buddy Wray managed sales and production, communications distances were very short. Trust levels were high. When a service or product problem occurred, Buddy knew about it quickly and resolved it immediately.

The habit, if you please, of doing the work of customer satisfaction began with Mr. John. When Don came into the business in 1952, he provided the driving force required to counterbalance all the forces that were at work in the triangle of tension.

Here are a couple of examples of how the triangle tension worked. A major distributor of foodservice products that maintained a quality control lab at their distribution hub called to complain that an individually quick-frozen product didn't meet the specified internal temperature of zero degrees. A full truckload was refused. With product codes that identified where the product was produced, the hour it was produced, and in fact, if necessary, the farm where the chickens were grown, the origin of the temperature problem was determined. Someone in operations in pursuit of lower electricity costs to freeze the product to zero degrees short-circuited the system, missing the temperature specification by five degrees—the triangle of tension at work. The cause for unquality was identified, fixed quickly, and balance in the triangle of tension was restored.

In another example, the senior buyer at a national fast-food chain called to advise he was being bombarded with calls from restaurant managers complaining of tough chicken strips. Before additional product was shipped the triangle of tension worked and customer satisfaction was restored fully.

OOPS! HOW A FLAWED INCENTIVE SYSTEM CONTRIBUTED TO UNQUALITY AND CUSTOMER DISSATISFACTION

In large organizations, especially organizations that have grown by acquisition, it is not uncommon for the self-interests of folks who have production-based incentive systems to conflict with other departments and interfere with customer satisfaction. An example of that problem occurred with a sudden increase in legal fees to defend the company from plaintiffs who said they were injured when they ate boneless chicken that wasn't boneless at a fast-food chain.

The cause of bones in boneless chicken was what Buddy Wray described as "wearing out chicken" by moving it all over the country, from plant to plant. Various plants processing and deboning chicken breasts were transferring their product to other plants that completed the process. In the plants that did first processing, feathers were removed by a machine using spinning rubber fingers. The machine had an adjustment that increased or decreased the pressure required to remove feathers. When the pressure was increased the rubber fingers could break the rib bones in the rib cage, leaving tiny rib bone pieces in the product. There was a rule in the plants that did both first and second processing that prohibited workers in first processing from walking into the second processing areas. It was a good rule that eliminated the possibility of cross contamination. Prior to the rule, the person in second processing who finished the product and inspected it for bones could walk down to the defeathering operator and advise of the problem. That communication was stopped by the imposition of the new rule. Simple solution— Communications 101!

It wasn't so easy in first processing plants that sent their product to finishing plants. An incentive system based on yield was in place in both facilities. It was to the advantage of the sending plant to focus on yield, which they did at the expense of the receiving plant. They assumed the receiving plant would inspect out their bones. The tension between quality and low cost was at work. The tension of self-interests was at work.

This was a problem created in the ivory tower when a well-intentioned policy created the silo syndrome or stovepipe effect that always interferes with customer satisfaction by allowing self-interests to trump customer satisfaction.

Any time the "I, me, my, mine, holy, holy is me, I am filled with my glory" behaviors are allowed to exist, customers, shareholders, and profits suffer. It also is a source of childish behaviors that interfere with adult-adult behaviors. [46] Leland had little patience for execs who didn't manage their relationships as highly paid adults. He valued people who believed and expressed their opinions, but when a relationship interfered with productivity and collegiality, Leland acted quickly and decisively. On one such occasion, he was heard saying, "If you can't manage your relationship, I will." And they did, no further intervention required.

In this example the proper interventions were made to correct the lapse in judgment that cost the company dollars to fix. Adherence to quality standards is low cost! When messes are made by messing with quality, the cost of cleaning up messes can be huge. My good friend, mentor, and quality guru Ron Cristofono, gave us the following example. "Have you a sign in a coffee break room, 'CLEAN UP YOUR OWN MESS'?" Ron says that the essence of the message is that is OK. It gives permission to make a mess if you clean it up. [47] That is the beginning of unquality!

"Kurt Lewin (1969) borrowed a technique from the physical sciences and offered it as a way to understand problem situations in social science and to effect planned change. A problem situation exists when there is a difference between *the way things are* and *the way someone wants them to be.*

The concept of force-field analysis is that any situation is the way it is in any given moment because sets of counterbalancing forces are keeping it that way." [48]

CUSTOMERS MAY NOT ALWAYS BE RIGHT, BUT THEY ARE ALWAYS CUSTOMERS—THE SOURCE OF REVENUE

Since customers may not always be right, their demands sometimes create heartburn for suppliers. At Tyson Foods when heartburn started to bubble up, a team was organized to bring relief. The first step was to immediately— that means now, not in the morning—communicate with everyone in the company who had anything to do with the customer. Information flowed up, down, across, and sideways, if necessary! Bob Womack recalls one of those heartburn experiences caused by missing the forecast on pricing breast meat used in a product for a national fast-food chain rollout. "We were several million dollars in the hole on that thing, but we stayed with it. You've got to believe in something like that and we did, and we were able to bring that thing back around to where it's a pretty good profit leader."

THE ROLE OF THE CREDIT DEPARTMENT'S NORRIS PHELAN IN CUSTOMERING

The heartburn team on one occasion required the participation of the credit manager, Norris Phelan, one of the truly great spirits at Tyson Foods. Norris tells about a customer who was buying annually more than $14 million dollars of product from a Tyson distributor. The customer wanted to change to a distributor whose credit was suspect. All the data Norris had on the distributor said no, but his customer commitment said yes. Inside Tyson, Norris called Buddy Wray (Sales VP), Sam Culpepper (sales manager), and Gerald Johnston (chief financial officer). Outside Tyson, he called the customer—the buyer at the distributorship the customer wanted. It was nearing 5:00 p.m. when Buddy called Norris and said he had done business with the guy who was the board chairman of the distributorship before he retired. Norris called the retired board chairman and received his personal guarantee, which released the order for shipment. The solution was temporary, but gave all parties time to craft a permanent solution so the customer got what he wanted. It is what leaders do.

Leadership behaviors are the antecedents to long-term profitability. Customer service or the lack of it is a direct reflection of the leader's myopic vision.

Following the lead of a customer-driven leader isn't a piece of cake. It is hard, daily, demanding, self-induced, and pressure-packed work for everyone who touches the product or is involved with the work across all departments of the business. Customer satisfaction is a very high standard. It is not the ideal situation for those who prefer a more placid work environment where one's goal is to retire "in place" until he or she can in fact retire "out of place." In the Tyson work environment, one was continually involved in moving from a brief stint in a comfort zone of the status quo to the uncomfortable zone of change. Over a weekend, a plant would be transformed to produce products to satisfy customers. A department would be reorganized to meet changing demands. And on occasion, the entire management structure would be changed in pursuit of customer satisfaction.

THE TYSON TORTILLA TEAM PLAYS WIN-WIN WITH TACO BELL

Led by Bob Womack, the Tyson team met a crisis created when Taco Bell understated their forecast for the tortillas needed to support a taco promotion, as reported by the Tyson veteran, Paul Vinson:

> As you know, Taco Bell initiated a national media-supported promotion of a 'super taco' on February 15, 1988...The resounding success of this

promotion caught Taco Bell by surprise. Taco Bell marketing forecasted a 15% to 17% increase in sales of this tortilla…we were prepared for a 200% increase…but the actual increase in sales of this item during the first week of promotion was almost 800%! Our average weekly sale is approximately 2,000 cases. During the week ending 02-20-88, we sold 17,000 cases of this item without shorting any orders. This is a particularly remarkable accomplishment when we consider that this product must be shipped fresh (large quantities cannot be produced in advance) and that large orders of this item were being received on the day of shipment. Obviously, this feat required extraordinary dedication and superhuman effort by many members of our Tyson family. [49]

Tortillas produced by a chicken company? Yes. Tyson acquired a local tortilla manufacturer, Mexican Original, in 1983. Why? Tyson had an excellent distribution system, understood the fast-food business, and Mexican Original owners wanted to sell. Tyson's mission statement doesn't limit products to chicken. It states, "We are dedicated to producing and marketing quality food products that fit today's changing lifestyles."

ALIGNMENT

One of the functions identified in Tyson's leadership model is ALIGNMENT. In these examples of customer satisfaction, it was the ability of leaders to keep all resources aligned to customer satisfaction that proved successful. The alignment of resources ensures that all work functions are focused on the work of satisfying customers, shareholders and workers. When the leadership function for alignment is not functioning, organizations can make fatal mistakes that we read about in today's business news. Enron, the federal government after the Katrina hurricane, the U.S. Department of Veterans Affairs, the Catholic Church (the writer is Catholic) and the pedophile scandals—bureaucracies that don't have the will to reform themselves. However they spin their failure or wherever they place the blame, leadership has failed to lead; to satisfy their customers, patrons, members, patients, taxpayers, or whatever they call the people they serve. Consider recent horror stories about U.S. companies pursuing low costs in China to the destructive point of endangering the lives of children playing with cheap toys, pets dying from contaminated pet food, and human lives driving on dangerous automobile tires—these were leaders who weren't behaving responsibly. Trying to justify their behaviors or blaming U.S. consumers demanding cheap stuff or the Chinese lack of experience in quality production just won't resonate with angry customers or shareholders. Leaders are accountable! Low cost is a worthy goal until greedy companies achieve low cost at the expense of customers' health and safety. Right cost is the work of ethical leaders who know and understand that low cost, when carried to extremes, is toxic behavior that will cause long-term pain and suffering, and sometimes it is fatal.

DON'S THIRTEENTH COMMANDMENT, "THOU SHALT HAVE A PROFIT"

Peter Drucker, who gave us the "knowledge economy," the "knowledge worker," [50] and so much more, defined the purpose of business: "There is only one valid definition of business purpose: to create a customer." In all too many organizations, as Peter Drucker has written, "Despite the emphasis on marketing and the marketing approach, marketing is still rhetoric rather than reality. Profit is not only not a dirty word, in a free market system, profit sustains the system." Drucker's conclusion: "Profit and profit alone can supply the capital for tomorrow's jobs, both for more jobs and for better jobs."

Even in not-for-profit organizations, a source of revenue is critical to their work. Some professionals seem to disdain the idea that they are sellers of products and/or services that depend on satisfying someone—whatever they call them. They appeal to some higher motive for their work, which is betrayed when they send their bills or letters requesting payments or contributions—send your money, it is urgent!

Whatever their motive, the processes of satisfying their sources of revenue is critical to their long-term success. Laying stones for a cathedral or being the bishop, both depend on satisfied followers who provide the money to finance both kinds of work. Semantics aside, the reality is clear.

Most organizations make statements affirming their commitment to customers and hang the statements around their office and places of business to convince customers and employees that their customers deserve some attention. How much attention does the customer deserve and from whom—senior execs, hourly workers, accountants, nurses, doctors, receptionists, ushers, truck drivers, truck dispatchers, teachers, principals, superintendents, flight attendants, gate agents, cab drivers, politicians, preachers, bishops, postal workers, IRS agents, clerks, movie producers, insurance underwriters, and agents, ad infinitum.

The folks in sales and marketing, public relations, and ad agencies do pay attention to customers. Sales folks perceive customers as their career lifeblood. Public relations people create and polish organizational image. Ad agencies serve a couple of functions: one is to create customer demand and project the image of quality products and service, the other is to be the first scapegoat execs use when sales performance goes into a death spiral. Fixing blame on the agency may satisfy a few shareholders but won't resolve systemic customer-related problems.

Beginning with Don's dad John, customering was both an active verb—what people did—and an inactive verb—what people did not do. They learned by observing one of Don's not-do-behaviors—blaming and scapegoating interfered with the work of customer satisfaction.

An example of Don's taking responsibility for his actions occurred when he was interviewed by Mike Wallace on CBS's *60 Minutes*, September 1994. Wallace asked Don about one of his failures—the acquisition of Arctic Alaska Fisheries Corporation.

> Wallace asked him how much he paid for Arctic Alaska.
> Don answered, "$225 million."
> Wallace then asked him, "How much did you lose?"
> Don answered, "About $205 million."
> The next question was, "Who made the decision?"
> Don answered, "I bought it, and it's on my shoulders. What is the next question?"

There were no integrity gaps in Don's leadership. His behavior was congruous with what he thought, said, and did. He understood the absurdity of playing the blame game and scapegoating. He knew that the inelastic resource of time would be wasted playing the blame game. He also understood the freeing power of being responsible and accountable.

Freeing in that one doesn't spend hours trying to justify one's behavior in the organizational swamp of "CYA." Truth is a low-cost behavior and the best friend of productivity and trust. Organizations that practice or condone blaming behaviors empower folks to act irresponsibility.

APPLYING DON'S BELIEF IN RESPONSIBILITY AND ACCOUNTABILITY TO CUSTOMER SATISFACTION

There is an exemplary story in the Hebrew Bible account of Adam and Eve. [51] When they failed, the Creator did a performance review with Adam. Some read the story as Adam trying to blame Eve. One of my rabbi friends says that reading the original Hebrew text indicates that Adam tried to blame the Creator. "It was the woman *you* gave me." Adam's technique didn't work. At Tyson Foods, it didn't work most of the time.

Since customers make the final decisions about the products and services for which they pay their money, we might as well face the reality that customers possess the power to cause supplier success or failure.

As consumers, it is all too easy to be angry with customer contact people for poor service when the fault

Paul Whitley

most likely belongs in the executive suite. When a product or service fails to live up to what is promised in print or in a TV ad, the root causes may lie in policies made by senior managers. Gloria Steinem, in her book, *Moving Beyond Words*, [52] describes the power of actions that harmonize with words. Her book is a useful read for unreformed male managers. American auto makers are still reeling from the gap between what they said and what they did as their customers paid their money to the foreign-based competitors. Their market share of about 95 percent in 1955 has plummeted to 59 percent in 2005, and the point is—customers' wants and needs change and when suppliers stop listening, competitors move in. When this occurs in a company, execs rarely accept responsibility.

There is always an enlightened competitor searching for the weak underbelly of an organization whose words aren't congruous with their behaviors.

Very deep in the corporate genome of Tyson Foods, there was a controlling gene called customer satisfaction. Customering is an active verb that cries out for support! Without the mandate and behaviors of a visionary leader, customering, which is a long-term strategic process, may give way to the short-term need for profit, especially in public companies. When profit becomes its own goal rather than the means whereby a more permanent goal can be achieved, the work of the enterprise ceases to be the kind of work that creates or that adds value to the lives of workers, investors, and customers.

DON TYSON ON THE TEAM PROCESS AND CUSTOMERING

In Don's management notes of August 1, 1994, he writes:

1.) Our greatest asset—People of Tyson

2.) Winning team—Made of great people working together to accomplish a goal.

3.) Today, we are over 52,000 people—Responsible for each other.

4.) We—the management group—are in charge of these 52,000 people, their future and the future of their families.

5.) I believe in the area of Responsibility Management—you manage people and capital. If there is any question about responsibility—it is yours!

6.) We build our company by each of us:

    a.) Taking chances—doing new things.

    b.) Not being afraid to fail.

    c.) No CYA symptoms.

    d.) No Big I and Little U.

    e.) Profit—If we are doing it like we did yesterday, it probably can be improved.

Take care of our people, which will take care of our customers, which will take care of our shareholders.

Don Tyson

THE IMPACT OF MESSAGES INSIDE AND OUTSIDE THE COMPANY ON CUSTOMER SATISFACTION

Consider this: a plant person responsible for monitoring a production quality function returns to work after hearing a rumor circulated in the cafeteria that the company was launching cost reduction measures, a message obviously intended for investors and market watchers. The rumor was based on a story in *The Wall Street Journal* describing why the company didn't achieve its net income guidance given earlier in the year.

The communications distance from the executive suite to the willing worker is long and slow. The rumor mill is nanoseconds fast and can impact quality when the willing worker internalizes the message based on positive or negative experiences in the past. Quality is the result when hundreds of tasks are done well by trained and committed workers. When *messages from corporate* are mishandled, quality can suffer. As coarse as the language is, it is true: When a hard-assed manager delivers a hard-assed message with a hammer, the hard-assed worker may respond in-kind and use the hammer in an adverse way. Trainers call it win-lose behaviors or the zero-sum game. It really is lose-lose behavior.

One of the reasons Tyson invested heavily in supervisory training was to enhance product quality by eliminating causes for unquality behaviors at work. The emphasis on behavioral training was not popular in all quarters, as it was considered to be "touchy-feely." Behavioral training is better described as developing the human skills that have a high probability of influencing the behaviors of all in pursuit of customer satisfaction.

THE ROLE OF INFORMATION IN CUSTOMERING

Leaders in customer-driven organizations insist on actionable information available to all players and knowing the high cost of information blind spots.

Buddy Wray and Sam Walton, founder of Wal-Mart, were on the board of trustees at Harding University in Searcy, Arkansas. Shortly before Mr. Sam died, he called Buddy and asked if he would like to ride with him to attend the board meeting in Searcy. Mr. Sam flew his own twin engine airplane, even though Wal-Mart had a fleet of corporate jets—which says something about Mr. Sam's attitude about expenses and his ego. Buddy said that en route, he and Mr. Sam talked about their common interests in using information as a vital decision tool. Information about customering was becoming an absolute in the process of serving customers profitably.

ROLE REVERSAL IN THE SUPPLIER-CUSTOMER RELATIONSHIP

During the course of a day or in one conversation, a supplier may need information that only the customer has. The role reverses when the customer needs information that only the supplier has. This proved to be a trust-building process. Tyson worked at the task of moving the traditional adversarial relationship with customers toward a partnership based on trust and shared information.

There are always a few folks who try to use information as power. It didn't work too well at Tyson because of the open-door policy in the high-carpet area. If you needed information to get your work done and an information "hugger" wouldn't give it up, you could plead your case with the high command.

Warren Bennis, distinguished professor of business administration at the University of Southern California, in an article, "Culture of Candor" in the 2004 Essay of the Conference Board, writes about the flow of information"

> [F]ew organizations are genuinely committed to openness and candor. Instead, when it comes to sharing secrets, most organizations hold onto inside

information with obsessive zeal. And even within the family, as it were, far too many organizations have traditions and structures that keep essential information from reaching decision makers. History tells us that lack of transparency too often has tragic results. The 9/11 Commission Report is only the most recent evidence of how devastating the consequences can be when vital information does not flow freely within and between organizations.

Don's leadership encouraged candor, transparency and openness by his being candid, transparent, and open. There was no need to wear masks or hide behind layers of armor plate to protect one's real identity.

DON'S SKILLFUL USE OF INTERVENING VARIABLES IN CUSTOMERING

Wendy's fast-food chain had just notified Tyson's sales department that they were moving their business to a competitor. Don overheard a small group of managers discussing how they could send a message of displeasure to Wendy's. Losing a major customer is not easy, especially for the folks who have worked their butts off securing and maintaining the business. Someone in the group was thinking and talking lose-lose thoughts. Don entered the conversation, and after listening for the details he posed a question. "How much money does the Tyson Family Foundation give to Dave Thomas, founder of Wendy's, for his foundation for orphans?" No one in the group knew the answer and probably didn't know of Tyson's contribution. Dave Thomas was an orphan and created the foundation to serve others like him. Don picked up the phone and called someone and said to double Tyson's contribution to the foundation. The whining stopped. The sales folks got to work processing the reasons they had lost the business.

The contribution to the foundation would have no impact on Wendy's purchasing decisions, as the business of the foundation was a separate entity. It did have an impact on Tyson's sales folks. Decision makers often face decisions that have short-term profit and loss results and/or long-term profit and loss results. Managing the variables between short term and long term is a learned skill. It is the skill of a visionary leader who sees more and further than most of us.

Jim Blair, Tyson's longtime general counsel who had seen Don in many litigious situations, told me he never saw Don in a vindictive mode—irritated to the point of anger perhaps, but never vindictive. Don had learned early on that if he expected to never have a bad day, it was best to keep the synapses in his brain moving toward positive thoughts and solutions to common problems.

CUSTOMERING IN THE ANIMAL FEED INGREDIENTS BUSINESS

Jim Cate, Doug Baskin, and Mike Hudlow did a nice piece of customering in the pet-food business when they solved a problem that had plagued the poultry industry from the beginning. The problem was disposal of those parts of the chicken that weren't suitable for human use. For years, pet food and other animal feed ingredients companies bought by-products from poultry processors. Skin, feathers, viscera, heads, tails, wing tips, feet, and blood were converted to animal food. Prices were very low, as the animal-feed-ingredients companies had the advantage, as the poultry companies had no options. Eventually, poultry processors built their own rendering plants, which reduced by-products to a somewhat more valuable product.

In 1986, Tyson Foods, led by the feed ingredients team including David Purtle, VP of Poultry Operations, built a state-of-the-art animal feed ingredients plant at Morrison Bluff, Arkansas. They purchased a high-tech cooker from a European manufacturer that had the capability to convert commodity-priced by-products to value-added ingredients that met specific nutritional needs of pet-food and other animal-feed-ingredients companies. This monster-sized, closed cooking machine accepted truckloads of by-product materials and produced high-protein feather meal for large animals with multiple stomachs. Other by-products were converted to dry or wet ingredients with specific nutrition values enabling animal-feed buyers to get precisely the nutritional values they needed. It was a win-win for everyone, including the environment.

The monster machine was so large it was shipped by sea to New Orleans where it was loaded onto river-going barges and sent up the Mississippi to the Morrison Bluff plant located on the Arkansas River.

EXAMPLES OF TYSON'S PHILOSOPHY OF BUILDING MOATS AROUND THEIR PRODUCTS AND SERVICES TO STAY AHEAD OF COMPETITION

Tyson's investment in their animal-feed business is an example of building moats to give them an eight to ten head start advantage over their competition. In transportation, they installed GPS systems in their fleet to stay ahead of competition.

Bill Lovette and his transportation and warehousing team had the task of moving products to ninety-five of the top one hundred restaurant chains, foodservice distributors in all fifty states, retail grocery chains, club stores, animal-feed-ingredients manufacturers, and military commissaries across the country and around the world. Keeping track of several hundred trucks carrying thousands of customer orders was a challenge. In bad weather, it was especially daunting. The customering cycle wasn't complete until an order was delivered complete and on time. The last Tyson person to touch the product was a truck driver. If one of these experienced a delay caused by weather, an accident, illness, or equipment failure, he or she would have to find a phone (for those who don't remember times before cell phones) and call dispatch for instructions.

Bill Lovette and his team designed a GPS in-truck system that tracked the truck's progress. Initially some drivers were a bit nervous about the eye-in-the-sky but it wasn't long until they experienced the benefits of instant communication. If a trucker encountered a blizzard or broke down, it meant instant contact with dispatch. Customers were advised about arrival times, giving them a heads-up to manage their receiving dock functions. If truckers had a home emergency, they would be informed immediately and could make arrangements to hurry home.

Clark Irwin, who grew up with Johnny Tyson, was a major player in Tyson's transportation system. Clark's father James Irwin left his job as an ag teacher to work for Tyson. He joined the company about the same time as Buddy Wray in 1960 and retired in 1981. Combined, father and son have invested forty-seven years to Tyson, and the number is increasing as today Clark is a senior VP in the Mexican Original group.

At the Tyson Tribal Stories meeting in 1988, Clark said, I guess it's been ten years, since about 1978, since my first transportation experience when I was given the responsibility. I was about twenty-five years old and had been with the company sixty days when J.B. Hunt, up the road, hired manager George Smith, our long haul manager. Instead of giving me a year or two of training, it was just, 'There it is; it's yours.' At that time, we had about eighty-eight trucks. I wasn't really ready for the responsibility of the whole fleet, and shortly after that the fuel prices ran out of sight and we were losing about a hundred grand a month. John McGuire, VP, Finance & Accounting, got involved about that time, and he made it pretty clear to me that there had better be some changes made. I think we finally realized that we had to take the bull by the horns, so we took responsibility for cost controls and cutbacks. I feel like we've become quite a business, and that's great. It just kind of confirms that everybody in this company has had the opportunity to grab it and go with it, and we're pretty proud of some of the accomplishments we've had. I feel like we've got a lot of opportunity in that area in the future.

LELAND CHANGES THE STRUCTURE TO MEET THE CHANGING NEEDS OF THE BUSINESS.

In 1986, Leland changed the management structure to meet the changing needs of the business. Buddy Wray, who had been responsible for sales, marketing, and production, would be responsible for sales and marketing. David Purtle, who came with the Valmac/Tastybird acquisition, would be responsible for production in poultry operations. This structural change had the unintended consequence of cutting what had been the umbilical cord of communications between sales and poultry operations. As each group pursued performance goals, costs began to increase, especially inventory costs. Over production to meet plant goals increased inventory costs. Underproduction increased the number of orders shipped short. Inaccurate sales forecasts aggravated the problem and added cost. Structural noise grew louder and louder. The situation could have become an incubator for destructive behaviors; we call it lack of attunement in Tyson's leadership model. But it didn't, because Leland was listening. He heard structural noise and acted.

Organizational structural noise occurs when departments and job functions are thrown out of alignment with business goals. As the front end of an automobile is thrown out of alignment, tire wear and tire costs go up. The driver begins to feel something is wrong, hears dissonance coming from the front end through the steering wheel. The text of Leland's presentation follows. After several hours of work on "what I need from you to do my job" activities, folks were able to "see" and to behave empathetically, and the team process was restored.

When Leland heard the structural noise, he convened a senior executive seminar on major concerns, December 10, 1986. The event was at Tyson's Management Development Center.

"I REFUSE to HAVE a BAD DAY" -Don Tyson

Dec. 10, 1989

WE HAVE ACQUIRED SOME 18 COMPANYS SINCE THE EARLY 1960'S; SOME WERE FROM PEOPLE WHO WERE JUST PLAIN TIRED AND WANTED OUT (FRANZ-CAVANAUGH), SOME WERE FROM PEOPLE OR COMPANIES THAT DECIDED THEY COULD NOT COMPETE, (OCOMA-WILSON) AND SOME FROM INVESTORS, WHO SIMPLY SAID THIS IS PROFIT ENOUGH ON THIS INVEST-MENT (BASS-VALMAC). IN EACH AND EVERY CASE, THE TRANSACTION WAS AN ACQUISITION, NOT A MERGER. I THINK THAT WE WERE FAIRLY SUCCESSFUL IN UTILIZING THE TALENTS AND THE STRENGTHS OF THE ORGANIZATIONS THAT WE HAVE ACQUIRED DOWN THRU THE YEARS; AND I THINK THAT ALL HAVE BASICALLLY ADAPTED TO OUR WAY OF DOING BUSINESS, "TO THE TYSON CULTURE, IF YOU WILL."

JUST WHAT IS CORPORATE CULTURE, AND IN PARTICULAR TYSON CULTURE. I GUESS A BOOK DEFINITION OF CULTURE IS BELIEFS, BEHAVIORS AND ASSUMPTIONS ABOUT ONES SELF THAT ARE ACQUIRED OVER TIME. I ASKED A FEW PEOPLE TO DESCRIBE TYSON CULTURE.

(1) INFORMAL --MBWA

(2) NO WORRY ABOUT TAKEOVER---CONFIDENT ABOUT FUTURE

(3) PRODUCTIVITY WILL BE REWARDED

(4) SINCERE DESIRE ON PART OF MANAGEMENT FOR ALL OF TYSON PEOPLE TO BE PART OF THE TEAM AND LOOK UPON THEMSELVES AS PART OWNERS

(5) NOT A LAYERED MANAGEMENT STYLE

(6) NOT MANY FORMAL MEETINGS

(7) NO COATS AND TIES

(8) NO TITLES -- MR. IS NOT PART OF THE CULTURE

I BELIEVE THAT WE ARE ORGANIZED TO MEET THE CHALLENGES OF THE FUTURE---WE ARE NOT A PRODUCTION COMPANY OR A SALES AND MARKETING COMPANY. WE ARE A TOTAL COMPANY DEDICATED TO SERVING THE MARKETPLACE. WE HAVE SPENT A LOT OF TIME AND MONEY THIS PAST YEAR GETTING PRODUCTION FACILITIES UP TO SPEED, AND I BELIEVE

TOLLET'S SPEECH
Dec 10, 1989

PRODUCT THAT WE MAKE. WE HAVE HAD PEOPLE WHO COULD NOT ACCEPT THIS SYSTEM.
GEORGE DEDWEILER WAS A COMPLEX MANAGER AT WILSON WHEN WE ACQUIRED THAT COMPANY
AND HE SIMPLY WAS NOT INTERESTED IN ADAPTING TO OUR MANAGEMENT SYSTEM. DON
PERKINS AT SPRING VALLEY WAS ABOUT THE SAME STORY. HE SAID HE WAS ACCUSTOMED
TO RUNNING A COMPANY WITH AN ABSENTEE OWNER, A NON-PARTICIPATING OWNER, AND HE
HAD NO INTEREST IN DOING ANYTHING DIFFERENT. BOTH WERE VERY UP FRONT ABOUT IT
AND BOTH LEFT ON EXCELLENT TERMS. BUT THEY LEFT--THEY DECIDED THEY COULD BE
HAPPIER SOMEWHERE ELSE BECAUSE THEY COULD NOT OR WOULD NOT ACCEPT A DIFFERENT
CORPORATE CULTURE, AND DIFFERENT PHILOSOPHY OF DOING THINGS. DON PERKINS TOLD
ME SEVERAL TIMES THAT THIS WAS NOT THE FIRST TIME THAT HE WOULD NOT CHANGE. HE
SAID I CAN'T QUIT SAYING "WE AND THEY" OR "YOU AND US," BECAUSE HE SIMPLY DID
NOT WANT TO. IT TAKES A CONSCIOUS EFFORT, ALMOST A STATE OF MIND. THIS IS OUR
COMPANY--IT'S US AT WHATEVER LEVEL AND AT WHATEVER FUNCTION. (PRODUCTION/SALES
FOODSERVICE/RETAIL--TYSON/TASTYBIRD) WITHOUT AN INDIVIDUAL MENTAL COMMITMENT, NO
SYSTEM WILL WORK. THE ONE THAT WE HAVE IN PLACE IS ONE THAT I AM COMFORTABLE
WITH AND THAT I AM CONVINCED WILL WORK TO OUR BEST ADVANTAGE.

YOU PEOPLE ARE THE BEST IN THE BUSINESS--YOU HAVE SOME OF THE BEST IN THE
BUSINESS WORKING FOR YOU, AND I WOULD HATE TO SEE SOMEONE IN A KEY POSITION NOT
BE A PART OF THE BEST COMPANY IN THE BUSINESS. BUT, IF WE HAVE SOMEONE AT ANY
LEVEL WHO CAN'T OR WON'T ADAPT TO OUR CORPORATE CULTURE, THEN MAYBE THAT PERSON
SHOULD TRY TO BE HAPPIER SOMEWHERE ELSE.

IN OUR DECISION MAKING PROCESS, TOO MANY DECISIONS ARE MADE BY SENIOR
MANAGEMENT, AND MAYBE THAT IS MY FAULT. WHEN WE ALL UNDERSTAND AND ACCEPT THE
PRINCIPLES THAT I HAVE BEEN TALKING ABOUT, THEN I THINK THAT THIS DECISION
MAKING PROCESS WILL WORK ITSELF DOWN TO THE LOWEST LEVEL POSSIBLE. OUR

"I REFUSE to HAVE a BAD DAY" -Don Tyson

THAT OUR PROCESSING AREAS ARE IN THE BEST SHAPE THEY HAVE EVER BEEN IN. WE ARE GOING TO MAJOR ON OUR FIELD OPERATIONS FOR A WHILE. I WANT US TO SHARPEN UP IN A FEW AREAS. I HAVE ALWAYS BELIEVED THAT IT IS AWFULLY HARD TO OUTMARKET A POOR COST; I DO NOT THINK THAT MAKES US A PRODUCTION ORIENTED COMPANY. IF WE HAVE OUR COSTS IN LINE AND PRODUCTION FACILITIES IN PLACE FOR ORDERLY GROWTH, THEN THE RESPONSE TIME TO A DEMAND BY OUR SALES AND MARKETING TEAM IS MINIMAL. OUR MANAGERS AT THE COMPLEX LEVEL CAN DO A BETTER JOB OF PLANNING THEIR ACTIVI-TIES WHILE DOING A MUCH BETTER JOB OF SATISFYING OUR CUSTOMERS' NEEDS.

LET ME SPEND A FEW MINUTES ON OUR ORGANIZATIONAL STRUCTURE--ESPECIALLY AT THE SO CALLED COMPLEX LEVEL.

A COMPLEX MANAGER IN THE TRADITIONAL SENSE (WAYNE--CON AGRA--WILSON) HAS A LOT OF AUTHORITY OVER THE ENTIRE FUNCTION FROM THE ELEMENTAL STAGES OF PRODUC-TION THRU SALES, (GENERALLY ICE PACK OR FAST FOOD CUT) AND THAT MAY BE OK FOR A COMPANY SERVING A REGIONAL MARKET, BUT THAT IS NOT WHAT WE HAVE BEEN AIMING AT FOR THE PAST 15 YEARS, AND THAT IS NOT WHAT WE ARE AIMING AT FOR THE FUTURE. OUR MARKET IS MORE NATIONAL IN SCOPE. OUR PRODUCT LINES ARE TOO INTERMINGLED AND WE THINK MORE IN TUNE WITH A SOLID, MORE PREDICTABLE FUTURE THAN WHAT SOME OF OUR COMPETITORS ARE DOING.

MAYBE I MADE A MISTAKE IN CALLING OUR SYSTEM A MODIFIED COMPLEX MANAGER SYSTEM--THE BOTTOM LINE IS THAT OUR COMPLEX MANAGER IS IN CHARGE OF A COST CENTER--IT MAY BE A SMALLER OR LARGER UNIT, BUT IT IS A COST CENTER. OUR SYSTEM ALLOWS FOR MINOR LINE ACCOUNTING, AND WE DO NOT HAVE PROFIT CENTERS IN THE TRADITIONAL SENSE OF THE WORD. OUR GOAL IS TO MAXIMIZE THE RETURN ON EVERY SINGLE MINOR LINE, ALL THE WAY FROM INEDIBLE PRODUCTS TO THE MOST SOPHISTICATED

MANAGERS ATTITUDE IS "LET US DO WHAT WE DO BEST--RUN OUR AREA ON A DAILY BASIS.
SENIOR MANAGEMENT SHOULD PROVIDE DIRECTION, GOALS, FINANCE AND THE WHEREWITHALL
TO GET THE JOB DONE." SO, IT IS IMPORTANT FOR US NOT TO CONFUSE CULTURE WITH
MANAGEMENT STYLE.

YOU PEOPLE IN THIS ROOM ARE THE PEOPLE WHO MAKE OUR COMPANY RUN. YOU DO
NOT SPEND ENOUGH TIME INTERACTING WITH EACH OTHER--MORE OFFICE SPACE WILL HELP
ALLEVIATE THIS SITUATION. A CONSCIOUS EFFORT ON SOME OF YOUR PARTS TO SPEND
A LOT MORE TIME IN THE OFFICE--AVAILABLE FOR THE "MANAGEMENT BY WALKING AROUND"
CONCEPT WILL MAKE OUR COMPANY MORE OF WHAT WE WANT IT TO BE, AND ABOVE ALL, WILL
INSURE THAT WE ARE STAYING ON THE LEADING EDGE WHILE ALLOWING OUR PEOPLE OUT
IN THE VARIOUS LOCATIONS TO SHARPEN THEIR MANAGEMENT SKILLS AND PREPARE THEM TO
TAKE A MORE RESPONSIBLE PLACE IN OUR MANAGEMENT CHAIN.

TYSON RESPONDS TO CUSTOMER REQUESTS FOR STATISTICAL PROCESS CONTROLS

Two of Tyson's largest fast-food customers wanted Tyson to add to its quality protocols that some called total quality management (TQM). W. Edwards Deming taught the process to the Japanese in the 1950s, and was the most visible quality guru in the field. Deming didn't use the phrase TQM. He called what he did, statistical process control.

In our search for someone to teach us SPC to satisfy our customers, I was introduced to Ron Cristofono, one of Dr. Deming's disciples. Ron is a native of New Hampshire, the "Live Free or Die" state. Davis Lee was one of our senior mangers whose job was to manage the relationship between

Tyson Foods and one of the suppliers to McDonald's. Davis had worked with Cristofono at the McDonald's supplier's facility.

This writer met with Davis Lee and Ron Cristofono at a restaurant in Oxford, Alabama, January 25, 1991. That evening this writer discovered where he was on the old progressive education measurement chart. The steps are:

- Unconscious and incompetent. I don't know I don't know.
- Conscious and incompetent. I know that I don't know.
- Conscious and competent. I know that I know and have to think about it using my conscious mind.
- Unconscious and competent. I know and I do it.

On the subject of statistical process control, I was unconscious and incompetent. I was not alone. Tyson Foods was approaching the critical mass required for paradigm shift as described by Thomas Kuhn in his work, *Structure of Scientific Revolutions.* [53]

Simply stated, statistical process control was a more effective way to eliminate defects from products and services—the systematic elimination of waste. The old method was to inspect the finished product for defects and get rid of the defective product. Absorbing all the costs that had already gone into the product is expensive and ineffective. We learned from Cristofono how to identify causes for defects and eliminate the causes in the process using statistics. It was about learning to communicate statistically vs. subjectively.

At a plant conference room in Alabama, a very young female line worker described how she used SPC to eliminate bones in chicken. When the statistical data she was collecting told her that a bone problem was developing, she shut the line down. Now, to shut a production line down had not been in the job description of a line worker. Keep those lines running to meet production quotas—defects included! But it was now known shutting down was the low-cost way to eliminate bones from a boneless product. Sitting next to me was a senior operations guy from corporate. He gasped, but remained silent; his body stiffened as his body language betrayed his emotions. The new paradigm was working.

This was another example of the triangle of tension. Tyson leaders understood that tension was a source of energy that powers human systems and, when properly managed, is creative and productive. They also recognized that to destroy human energy sources would prove to be deadly. It would violate their belief in their people and paralyze creativity.

Mr. John Tyson, the founder, laid a solid foundation on which Don Tyson and his leadership team would build a great company as they created value for their customers, workers, and shareholders. Reichheld writes:

> Here we strike bedrock, because creating value for customers is the foundation of every successful

business system. Creating value for customers builds loyalty, and loyalty in turn builds growth, profit, and more value. While profit has always occupied center stage in conventional thinking about business systems, profit is not primary. Profit is indispensable, of course, but is nevertheless a consequence of value creation, which, along with loyalty, makes up the real heart of any successful, long-lasting business institution. [54]

PEOPLE NEED AND DESERVE TO KNOW HOW THEIR WORK CONTRIBUTES TO CUSTOMER SATISFACTION

Seeing the pins fall for a skilled bowler is like working at Tyson Foods and knowing how one's work, whatever the work may be, contributes to customer satisfaction. Keeping workers in the dark and feeding them you-know-what is not only absurd—it assumes human beings are little more than machines of production, void of emotion, pride, spirit, and self-respect.

Folks who do the work of visionaries not only need to see the results of their work, they need to share in the rewards and the joys of customer satisfaction.

THE TYSON LEADERSHIP MODEL

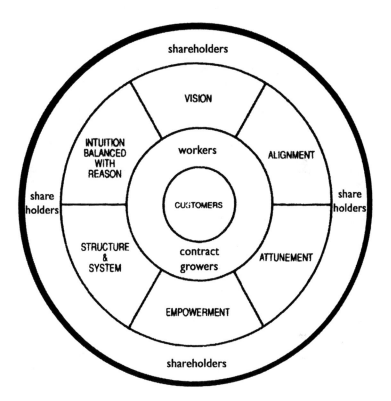

LEADERSHIP INSIGHTS

- There is an economic law at work in virtually all organizations that demands attention— CUSTOMER SATISFACTION! Customers can be called patients, clients, parishioners, patrons, voters, students, constituents, and consumers. Without them, organizations would not have the viable source of income needed to justify a legitimate purpose for existence.

- "There is only one valid definition of business purpose: to create a customer. It is the customer alone whose willingness to pay for goods and services that converts economic resources into wealth, things into goods. What the business thinks it produces is not of first importance— especially to the future of the business and to its success."

  Peter Drucker [55]

CHAPTER 4

THE COHESIVE QUALITY OF ORGANIZATIONAL INTEGRITY

The shift from incoherence to coherence can bring dramatic effects; a 60-watt light bulb whose light waves could be made coherent as a laser would have the power to bore a hole through the sun—from 90 million miles away. **Professor William Tiller, Professor Emeritus, Stanford University.**[56]

Leaders akin to Don Tyson are like bookbinders of old that used glue pots to hold pages together. Thousands of words written by hundreds of people become pages organized into chapters and glued together, bound by the cohesive qualities of a visionary leader, page by page, Chapter by chapter, day after day, event after event.

Events, like the thirty-six acquisitions made by Tyson from 1961 to 1997, are stories of books in progress. Each acquisition was a unique collection of stories about people organized around a visionary leader and held together by the skills and actions of people enrolled in the leader's vision.

In botany, cohesion is the congenital union of parts of the same kind. In physics, cohesion is the process or condition of cohering. In organizational development, cohesion results when centripetal forces keep the energy and resources of the organization proceeding in the direction of the center of the organization, overcoming the centrifugal forces that diffuse and weaken the organization's energies and efforts.

A MULTI-MILLION DOLLAR ACT
OF COHESION

When Tyson Foods acquired Holly Farms in 1989, Holly Farms had a well-managed pension fund that had grown over many years. Holly sources said the fund was worth $117,000,000. Holly's founder and CEO, Fred Lovette, understood the value of organizational integrity. He trusted his people, and they trusted his leadership. The pension fund was a continuing cohesive action of caring for his people. When the acquisition was completed, there was concern on the part of Holly employees that Tyson would raid the pension fund.

During the feeding frenzy of mergers and acquisitions in the 1980s, it was not uncommon for financial sharks to raid pension funds of companies they acquired. It was the same voracious, greedy mind-set that gave us the savings and loan scandals of the early '80s. "There are many notorious examples of how this system was abused by unscrupulous S&L owners reporting high current income on ADC [construction] loans while milking the institution of cash in the form of dividends, high salaries, and other benefits." [57]

In the same report, the FDIC "concluded that the savings and loan crisis reflected a massive public policy failure. The final cost of resolving failed S&Ls is estimated at just over $160 billion, including $132 billion from federal taxpayers—and much of this cost could have been avoided if the government had had the political will to recognize its obligation to depositors in the early 1980s." [58]

Don Tyson did not raid Holly's pension fund. I was not aware of this transaction until, Pete Lovette, finance and accounting executive at Holly, told me the story. Later the story was confirmed by Lois Bottomley-Keller who came to Tyson with the Holly acquisition and became Tyson's VP of Benefits. When I asked Don why he didn't raid Holly's pension fund, he said, "It was their money. It didn't belong to us."

Don's action was an act of cohesion! To the twenty thousand plus workers at Holly Farms, it was an ambiguous time in their work lives. Would their pensions be left intact? Don's integrity as a caring leader was at stake. His decision was one more example of his sense of integrity—his behaviors were congruous with his words.

THE COHESIVE POWER OF ORGANIZATIONAL TRUST

During my research of Tyson's history and over my thirteen years of observations as an employee of Don

Tyson's leadership, I was able to see his leadership through the eyes of those who followed him. He never betrayed their trust. Organizational trust was earned daily by his actions and the policies he created. His actions were concrete, not verbal abstractions such as "people are our most important asset." When he initiated the employee stock purchase plan in 1969 with a generous company match, his people began to experience stock ownership. Every employee with six months' tenure qualified. Each plant posted the stock price so employees could connect their work to the growing value of their stock. He kept the stock price low, encouraging employees to buy a share or two each payday. Nineteen years later, in 1988, *Fortune Magazine* cited Tyson Foods as having the highest total return to shareholders of any of the top 500 U.S. corporations, with an annual growth of 46.4 percent.

The cohesive nature of employee policies was validated when, in 1985, I initiated two companywide surveys at each of the sixteen production complexes. One was to determine the skill levels of our people. The other was a work climate instrument. The work climate instrument indicated Tyson folks were confident about their future and trusted Tyson's leadership. Both surveys were used in developing the training and development curriculum.

THE HIGH COST OF THE CENTRIFUGAL FORCES OF LOW TRUST

On September 3, 1991, the Imperial Foods chicken processing plant in Hamlet, North Carolina, caught fire when a hydraulic line located above a large fryer burst, setting the cooking oil ablaze. Of the ninety workers in the plant, twenty-five died and fifty-six were injured. Employees were trapped inside the plant. They were caged in by locked emergency doors and poor lighting and were suffocated by the superheated smoke. The plant owner had authorized the doors to be padlocked because an employee was suspected of stealing chicken. The owner, his son, and the plant manager were indicted on twenty-five counts each of involuntary manslaughter. On Monday, September 14, 1992, the owner pleaded guilty to the manslaughter and was sentenced on two counts and sent to prison.

The fire example is an extreme example of what happens in organizations when fear replaces trust. In the fire story, the point is that fear of the cost of theft created policies that were horribly destructive. Fear is a natural and productive emotion. It becomes destructive when used to damage persons physically or emotionally. Physical and emotional safety creates productive work environments.

In a cohesive organization, there are more effective and humane ways to solve theft problems. Bill Erwin, VP of Asset and Risk Management at Tyson Foods, knew how to do it right and did so for twenty years. He retired in March 1992. Bill was one of the toughest and gentlest spirits with whom this writer has ever worked.

In the candid culture at Tyson, managers were expected to plead their cases with Leland, Buddy, and Don. At the 1988 Tyson Tribal Stories meeting, [59] Leland Tollett said,

> It's important that you believe in a project. I don't care if I disagree with it or Bob Womack, or Whit, or whoever it happens to be. Go ahead and present your case. Don't just fold up your hands and head for the house. Sometimes we are preoccupied with other thoughts. I know I'm a little bad about that, and Don is terrible about that, especially if it's not a great big deal. Don will not take very much time to analyze a message with a relatively small deal. You would almost get the impression that he doesn't have much interest in it, and that's not the case at all. So, if you have a conviction about something, lean on him. Now, don't get the red ass if he says, "Hey, we believe we want to stay off that deal; it's not enough." That's part of what we're all prone to do; to analyze and make judgments like that. But I can't think of too many times when some of managers, have really believed in something and he's against it.

Barbara Berry, manager of human services, was doing diversity work in newly acquired plants in Mississippi. She was working with the night shifts, moving from plant to plant by car. She noticed a car following her for several nights and became afraid. She needed to communicate quickly, if needed. When she requested a cell phone for her safety, it was denied because policy said so! She went to see Buddy Wray, and pleaded her case and received a cell phone—exhibit A of the benefits of a flat, nonmilitary, nonpapal organizational structure. No one was bent out of shape because she pleaded her case at the Supreme Court—we were encouraged to do that. When you did that, best be well prepared—nibbling on your boss without cause was not permitted!

It was interesting to observe two forces at work in the company as the technologies of cell phones, software and nanosecond-fast hardware, laptop computers, and e-mail arrived on the scene. One force was the commitment to be the low-cost producer. The opposing force was the need to improve communications inside the company and the need to communicate with customers and suppliers in real time. The pro-tech forces pushed and the resisters resisted. Over time, the resisters left their comfort zones when they discovered the value of speed. When Jonathan Livingston Seagull asked his teacher Chang about speed, Chang told his young student that "fast was being there." [60]

DON TYSON'S COMMUNICATION SKILL—A COHESIVE QUALITY

Don's behavioral and communication skills acted like glue holding the pages of the book together. He used his remarkable data reduction skill to pack a lot of punch in the few words he spoke. His short body effervesced with excitement as he spoke, and his smiling eyes kept the listener's attention. He left his audience believing in him, believing in themselves, and believing in their futures as part of the Tyson family.

The writer never heard him make a speech longer than seven minutes. On May 13, 2005, Don, his children, Cheryl, Carla, John, and others were at the University of Arkansas to announce a $7.6 million gift to the University from the Tyson Family Foundation. Don took the platform with Big Red (Tyson's mascot chicken) in his lapel and was quoted by one of the attendees as saying, "My thanks to the folks at the University and to the two guys sitting in the front row who deserve the credit [Leland Tollett and Buddy Wray] for making our company successful. Folks, it is going to rain like hell out here, let's leave before we all get soaked." According to one observer, Don's speech was about ninety seconds. His observation was challenged by another who said, "Couldn't have been more that sixty seconds."

The family's philanthropy to the university exceeds $26 million, as of the winter of 2007.

INFORMATION—A COHESIVE DISCIPLINE

"My people are destroyed for lack of knowledge" (Hosea, c. 750 BCE).

"Indeed, one of the lessons of organizing around information is the importance of concentration to prevent people from becoming fatally confused" (Peter Drucker, *Managing for the Future*).

Used appropriately, information is powerful. When information is abused and used as power, organizational cohesiveness is severely weakened, relationships begin to come apart, and trust is replaced by suspicion and doubt.

When Tyson was doubling sales every five years, full utilization of information became more difficult. As the quantity of data increased, the capability of the system to satisfy internal customers declined. At one point the information team had a cost goal not to exceed one-quarter of 1 percent of sales. The 1984 acquisition of Valmac/Tastybird added so much data, the information system slowed like a plugged-up kitchen drain. The information manager was wedded to a computer technology that couldn't crunch all the data. Internal and external customers began to grumble as the pinch point caused organizational pain. Internal customers of information were forced to invest an inordinate amount of time to find data they needed to do their work.

Field sales people were forced to use stale sales data to review customer purchases. The ability of production planning folks to forecast production/inventory needs was reduced to making educated guesses, resulting in costly inventory buildups. Customer orders weren't being delivered complete and on time. Don placed a higher priority on meeting a goal set years earlier rather than listening to his internal and external customers and pleading their case for an information system in the high-carpet area.

SYSTEM IMPOSED TIME WASTERS

Time is an inelastic resource that, when managed by non-visionary people, causes costs to hemorrhage out of control throughout a company. It is like driving forward using rearview mirrors only. Since you can't change the past, only learn from it, the focus must be on today and tomorrow. Visioning is a process whereby a person envisions a future that is different and better than the present. Information technology does require significant capital investment. Measuring the value of information technology as related to the accuracy of decision making and/or the cost of time wasted is an ongoing process. It is a process that requires input from users of the technology. When users aren't involved in those decisions, the cohesive quality of organizational trust suffers. An ongoing challenge at Tyson Foods was reducing the cost of product inventories. Satisfying customers required either punishingly large inventories or a just-in-time decision-making system.

Other system-imposed time wasters are: bad company policies, conflicting priorities, lack of authority, a culture that encourages people to make messes if they clean them up, waiting for decisions, and, of course, a religious adherence to the status quo.

The causes of the plugged-up system were identified and removed from the system, and usable information began to flow again. A correction was made in management and in policy. In this case, transformational change was caused by pain and suffering. Any time a crack appeared in customer satisfaction, the founder's vision of satisfied customers would appear like an epiphany, preventing fatal mistakes.

Accumulated raw data has value to the degree it is employed in decision making. It is expensive to collect. It is like freezing to death sitting on bed of buried coal. Knowing that twenty-two million pounds of chicken were sold has the quality of rearview management; it is historical and points to the future when it becomes knowledge to be used by managers. At Tyson Foods it was knowledge of which farm produced a specific flock of chickens and quantifying the cost of each chicken by each component, i.e., breast, drumstick, thigh, back, neck, liver, gizzard, wing, etc. Managers need to know where each component was sold and the value of each component.

Visualize a world map that identifies chicken paws from a farm in Georgia sold in Hong Kong; gram-sized drumsticks from a farm on the Eastern Shore sold to a supermarket in Tokyo; hot wings produced in several plants sold in Buffalo, New York, or consumed by students competing in a hot wings contest; chicken nuggets sold to a fast-food restaurant in San Diego; boneless chicken breasts sold to a country club in San Francisco; gizzards sold to a supermarket in Tupelo, Mississippi; animal feed ingredients sold to a Science Diet pet food plant in Nebraska; feather meal made from the feathers of thousands of chickens sold to a cattle feeder in Texas. Equipped with this information, managers made decisions that had a high probability of being right. Without usable information or nonshared information, costs will increase, the quality of service will deteriorate, and structural noise will rise to high decibel levels as customers, shareholders, and workers become dissatisfied.

Real danger lurks in an organization when the information group functions as a silo reporting to and serving primarily accounting managers. When a receiving clerk at a North Carolina poultry plant accepts and accounts for the merchandise received and has the responsibility and the technology to approve payment for the merchandise, it proves to be a low-cost and high-quality transaction—a perfect union! With the high cost of all resources, who can afford to do otherwise? Think about the high cost of all the staples and papers stapled together and unstapled and restapled and passed from desk to desk. But, what if the receiving clerk can't be trusted? Fix that problem by learning how to build a work environment based on trust and respect. Is a stack of stapled papers inherently more accurate, trustworthy, and useful than the same data handled only once and input by a trained and competent person? Is a paper trail more accurate or useful?

BUDDY WRAY USING INFORMATION TO BRING PERFORMANCE INTO COMPLIANCE

Buddy Wray walked into a meeting room of quality assurance people with a four-inch thick, computer-generated report. He asked, "Do you know the cost of the 'material tagged' for rework and identified in this report?" Silence. Cold silence! Buddy, the bull rider, could be very dramatic. Before he spoke, he lowered the thick report to his knees and with leverage heaved it toward his listeners! Memories were triggered, remembering moments of postponement and delay. Others were assembling words into phrases to defend their failure. Silence! If the devil was in the details, Buddy's capacity to know details and understand how they influenced outcomes was one of his most productive strengths. When he intervened in a problem situation that appeared to be a muddy mess, no one had to wait for the mud to settle; it clarified quickly, and rarely did the situation occur again. The woman who described this moment said Buddy didn't need to say another word. Message received! For a moment she paused and then said, "I really miss Buddy Wray. When he retired [March 2000] our department lost a trusted friend, and we miss him. He still comes by to visit. When he leaves, we all feel better about our jobs."

STEVE HANKINS INVOLVING USERS OF INFORMATION TO IMPROVE THE QUALITY OF INFORMATION

When a youthful Steve Hankins, CPA, got his arms around the information function, his ability to sell his vision of a more productive and responsive information system brought about a paradigm shift in the company.

To secure input from and to get the support of all the players, Steve introduced what he called the "brown paper method." Each department created a brown paper. The paper was brown, thirty-six inches wide and as many feet long as necessary—a veritable flowchart. Each job function was entered on the brown paper by the person doing the work and sequenced from beginning to end. Some of these brown papers were sixty feet long!

The results were extraordinary as the understanding of individuals, teams, and departments was elevated high enough that they could "see" how their work impacted the work of others. Bitching and complaining about information was replaced by the question, "What do you need from me to get your work done?" Isn't it interesting how competent people become when they understand their work, make decisions about their work, and have fun doing it?

The process of "brown papering" was a costly investment that met the usual resistance from the "resistance-to-change" crowd. Steve's vision pulled all the players forward and created a highly responsive information system that satisfied customers, shareholders and workers. In a Saturday morning meeting, Steve teamed up with Bill Lovette, who was responsible for warehousing and transportation, to present their work on the information system to the senior execs. They listened. Some asked probing questions and received convincing answers. The green light was given. It was a powerful, cohesive, ongoing, and transformational process that is paying big dividends today. Information systems are organically alive—a state of metamorphosis.

Steve Hankins went on to become the CFO and Bill Lovette went on to become to become group VP of Foodservice at Tyson Foods.

LEADERS INVEST IN FACE TIME WITH WORKERS

Don Tyson didn't manage sitting at his desk. Although his office was inspired by visiting President Carter's Oval Office in The White House, he didn't spend a lot of time sitting there. In Carter's unsuccessful 1980 reelection bid, Don headed the National Farmers for the Carter Committee. This in spite of Carter's embargo of agricultural products sold to Russia that cost the poultry industry millions.

His bent was to be on the move using body language and words to communicate with his people. He would get in his old black Lincoln and visit plant sites to talk and listen to his people about their jobs and their futures. He was especially sensitive about the grounds surrounding plants and other facilities. He wanted to see flowers and grass. When he acquired Valmac/Tastybird he showed up at the Russellville office and invited some of the office folks to come with him. He led them outside and noted the well-manicured lawn and said, "That's nice. Could we add a few 'lumps and moguls' to break up the flatness? It would look even nicer." Ray Griffin, transportation and warehousing manager at Valmac/Tastybird, told me the "lumps and moguls" story and said he was expecting Tyson's chairman and new owner to show up wearing a fine suit, smoking a cigar, and behaving as the chairman. He showed up wearing khakis and no cigar. Ray said, "I liked him and his sense of humor."

When money was tight and they couldn't afford to pave parking lots, he wanted parking lots well graded and free from clutter and trash. He insisted plant cafeterias be brightly decorated, conducive to conversation. His people at all levels observed him walking the plant production lines and offices, asking individuals if they had identified their replacements and if they were grooming their replacements so they could be promoted. He encouraged his people, including farmers, to visit with him in his office. He always had time to listen. I never saw his office door closed during the thirteen years I was there. Don understood the correlation between having fun at work and job satisfaction—the intersection of the affective and effective. Each plant visit strengthened the cohesive bond between leader and followers.

It wasn't uncommon to have him pop into your office and ask, "How's your business?" He believed his people should know how they were doing in their jobs, good or not so good. On one occasion Mitch Newton, director of Refrigerated Sales & Production Scheduling, was in his office on Saturday morning clearing his desk of accumulated problems that seemed to be growing hourly. It was a time of rapid expansion of sales to fast-food chains. Three national chains were rolling out new products so fast Tyson's production wasn't keeping up with demand even though plants and people were working

24-7. As production scheduler, Mitch had to go outside the company to buy raw material from competitors. Prices for raw material were soaring, making it impossible to meet profit expectations. The products these chains were rolling out all required breast meat. Since each chicken had two thighs and two drumsticks, what was one to do when customers wanted only breast meat?

Mitch was the only person in the department that morning when Don came in and said, "Hello, Mitch, how's your business? Mitch paused a moment wondering if he should answer Don's question—then Mitch off-loaded his entire work burden on the chairman! Don listened carefully, patiently, and without interruption. When Mitch finished talking Don said, "Mitch, do you know that police woman who catches speeders driving through Mayflower, Arkansas?" Mitch, who is a very serious man, was dumfounded! Don went on, saying, "Mitch, Tyson Foods got caught speeding and we, all of us, are paying the price. I know what you're going through and we will get through it and be better for it. We are building our company, brick by brick. Right now it's really tough." Don was leading his company, not managing it from his Oval Office. He had an uncanny ability to know who was hurting and where the pinch points were.

THE COHESIVE EFFECT OF DON'S NONARROGANT, AFFIRMING BEHAVIORS

Don's sense of equality and classlessness coupled with nonarrogant, affirming behaviors created a comfortable communications climate in the organization. The wearing of khakis, the absence of titles, and his policy that no one was entitled to a private parking space—was a source of stickiness/cohesion. One exception to the parking policy was the time Buddy Wray had heart bypass surgery. He was granted a space close to his office. The other exception was at production plant sites where the USDA inspectors had reserved parking places. Heaven forbid the feds be treated as mere mortals! Newly acquired companies learned early on that those "reserved for the bosses" signs painted on curbstones would be painted over. He said if we wanted to park close in, come in early! Generals and privates lived with the same orders. Visitors had reserved parking, as did customers and suppliers.

This parking space policy was threatened when, on returning to the corporate office following lunch, the writer noticed workers building what looked like a gate at one of the parking areas close to the executive office. Oops! If this observation was correct, some of the cohesion of Don's spirit was going to be damaged! The decision to create a symbol of an upper class of privileged people could be reversed. The gate came down! The glue worked!

"BIOLOGY, CHEMISTRY AND PHYSICS—NEW LIGHT ON THE FUNDAMENTAL ISSUES OF ORGANIZING WORK, PEOPLE AND LIFE." [61] Margaret Wheatley

The study of organizational development is not unlike the study of chemistry and physics. In chemistry cohesion means "the act or state of sticking together tightly; union between similar plants parts of organs." In physics, coherence is defined as;

> Two or more waves having the same frequency and the same phase (timing) or a fixed difference... Whatever we resonate with determines what our experience of the world will be. Any problem we have simply indicates that one or more wave patterns are vibrating at less than optimal frequency, thus weakening the whole system. These less than optimal frequencies form a structure which may manifest as pain, poor health, difficulty in relationship, business problems, unexpressed creative potential, and inability to make a breakthrough in an area likesport or learning or just feeling "flat." To change the structure that underpins our challenge, or "problem" reality, and regain resonance with life enhancing and

energizing ways of being, doing, and having, we need first to identify the areas of negative resonance…It is a common assumption that when things are not working optimally—whether it's in our physical body or our business—that more energy is required to improve the situation. That is we need to put in more effort or increase our commitments around money, time or some other "fuel" or resource…If we increase the amount of energy, it simply leads to "burn out." The solution lies in creating more coherence. When there is more coherence, less energy is actually required to obtain far more powerful results. [62]

Throwing more money at the problem and asking people to work harder rarely works. I remember hearing a manager say to a group that was not meeting its numbers, "You'll get your life back when you hit your numbers." A leader might have asked, "What do you need from me to get your work done?" It would have been the "cohesive" thing to do. Cohesive behaviors result in the full utilization of all available resources. As an emotion, fear serves our physical needs well; as a source of long-term motivation, it works in dictatorships and totalitarian organizations for a while—until folks tire of being afraid. They can and do revolt, resort to sabotage, drop out, or leave.

This writer has found no better, no more comprehensive, no more accurate way to characterize Don's leadership than that he was the stickiness that glued the organization together. His worldview was the frequency that resonated with the people who did the work of satisfying customers, shareholders, and workers. When Don said, "I refuse to have a bad day," he wasn't sticking his head in the sand. He was saying that while he couldn't control all the events in his life, he would control his responses and would not harbor negative thoughts—profound and simple!

> *To my mind there must be, at the bottom of it all, not an equation, but an utterly simple idea. And to me that idea, when we finally discover it, will be so compelling, so inevitable, that we will say to one another, "Oh, how beautiful. How could it have been otherwise?"*
> John Archibald Wheeler, theoretical physicist

One of Don's closest associates and friends, Jim Blair—Tyson's attorney, told me he never saw any vindictiveness in Don Tyson. David Pryor, former Arkansas governor and U.S. senator, now the dean of President Clinton's School for Public Service, said, when I asked him how Don reacted when he wasn't able to meet Don's request for legislation, "He never expressed anger, he was gracious and thanked me for listening." [63] Dale Bumpers, former governor and U.S. senator, told me that Don never asked for much. When he did and was successful, he was grateful. When not successful, he was never vindictive.

Did Don ever get angry? Yes. When good people did stupid things and when he knew about them, he took decisive action using appropriate methods. People who reported to Don always knew how they were doing. Don didn't save up "stuff" for annual reviews.

On one occasion, when Don was in London, he learned about an ill-conceived internal memo written by an unnamed manager. He was angered and called the manager's boss and said, "I want to see every memo that guy writes before he sends it out!!" In the memo, the sender referred to some small angry group of chicken growers who wanted to organize and described them as "pinkos." The memo got into the hands of a national farm organization, and they were hot! The issue was resolved quickly and all parties involved went on to complete their careers at Tyson.

The difference between vindictiveness and healthy anger is that vindictive people strike back, over and over; people who manage their anger get over their anger and delete it from their memory. Anger embedded deep in a person's psyche causes the person to tune to a frequency that plays ugly and destructive music—over and over and over. The world's major religions all agree that unresolved anger is an enemy of a happy and productive life. Unmanaged anger is antithetical to building and sustaining relationships.

Communication, Verbal and Behavioral, A Key Element in Organizational Cohesion

In every organizational survey I have seen or conducted, communication or the lack of it is at the top of the plaintiff's list. One of the causes is that most folks get very little training in listening for understanding. We are educated to write and to speak. Learning to listen has been on educators' and corporate trainers' back burners. You would think two ears and one mouth would tell us something about which instrument we should use!

We tend not to listen because we weren't trained to listen; didn't have good listener role models; are not interested in the speaker; don't have time to listen; have already made up our minds about the subject; are preoccupied with worry, fear, anger; don't want to hear bad news; are bored or just too tired to listen.

THE OPEN DOORS OF DON TYSON, LELAND TOLLETT, BUDDY WRAY

The always-open doors of Don, Leland, and Buddy were more than symbolic. They were evidence of a listening environment in the executive suite. Buddy was an unhurried listener, listening for daily details about what was going on. Leland was a hurried listener. He wanted to hear facts presented in the fewest words possible. If one began to wander in the forest of the peripheral he would say something like, "Get on with it." Don listened for meaning.

THE OMNIPRESENCE OF THE TRIUMVIRATE

One of the three was always present and available—a commitment to communication. The presence of one of them in the cafeteria during breakfast or lunch sent a message that any one of the thousand-plus folks at corporate could walk into one of their offices for a chat, a discussion about a serious matter, get feedback on a project, or talk about a personal or family matter. It also encouraged verbal communication, which at times was more efficient than long, verbose memos that none of them relished.

Our fast-paced living has made more difficult the skill of listening. Who has time to listen? Dr. Art Robertson, whose research on listening was first published in 1991, writes, "The unabridged English dictionary has 450,000 words, but regardless of education, the average person uses only 400 words in 80 percent of his or her spoken vocabulary. You might think that 80 percent of our communication problem would be solved if we understood the primary meaning of those 400 words. The difficulty is that those basic 400 words have 14,500 meanings. To further cloud the issue, language is changing so rapidly that one thousand new meanings are added to familiar vocabulary each year." [64]

Learning to listen and investing time in the process of listening has a huge payoff in the cohesiveness of leading people who do the work. Refusal to listen may, over time, do serious and permanent damage to a leader's organizational integrity.

Another cause for communication failure is ego addiction or hubris—the big I, small you. I, me, my, mine, holy, holy, holy is my glory! Ego-addicted persons just can't hear; they can't accept the idea that anyone else is as competent as they are. Communicating a message from the top of a pyramidal structure to the bottom is especially difficult. Sending messages from the bottom to the top is virtually impossible if those at the top don't listen. Labor organizers thrive on execs who don't listen and respond to what they hear.

For example, a writer of the memo/message wants to describe an orange. The receiver at the bottom reads the memo or hears the message and sees a lemon! When this happens organizational noise begins to develop making it even more difficult to achieve understanding. Why? One reason is that words have little intrinsic meaning; they are symbols that point to meaning. Behaviors always trump words! The sweet phrase, "I care for you" is trumped by, "No, you can't go to your uncle's funeral because the policy says you can't!" When the writer was asked to intervene in this mess, he learned there were at least three ways the preoccupied supervisor could have cared without violating policy. Caring skills, behaviors, and policies, considered by some to be soft/touchy/feely, become concrete as workers have more choices about where and for whom they will work.

When a leader's words are congruous with his or her behaviors, he or she has organizational integrity—the very foundation of Don Tyson's leadership success as he built a cohesive organization!

There are thousands of sources on the subject of communication. Having been the training and development guy at Tyson, I couldn't have spent enough training dollars to remove all the barriers to effective communication. We learned that effective communication was about both the heart and the head. When one has learned the technical skills of communication and has an "I care heart" that drives out fear, communicating for understanding begins. When head, heart, and soul come together, the hard work of communication becomes more productive.

As the company grew from eight plants and eight thousand folks to sixteen plants and sixteen thousand folks, the work of communication became more difficult. Various media were used to communicate with everyone in the company. Complex sites (a processing plant, feed mill, grow-out operations, transportation, hatchery) published their own newsletters with assistance from the Corporate Communications Group. A weekly video describing all the happenings in the company was created at corporate and sent to each complex for viewing by the workforce. A corporate newsletter was mailed to all employees. Tyson's stock price was placed in each facility. It was a daily measure of company performance as perceived by the market. Picnics at the complex level were encouraged. Softball and fishing tournaments within the company brought a lot of folks together to have fun.

The effectiveness of these communication tools was enhanced by managers whose behaviors were congruous with the messages and activities generated at corporate. One of our plants was experiencing very high turnover. The writer's assignment was to find out why. He was surprised that the line supervisor of the debone line, one of the most difficult jobs in the plant, had a very low turnover rate. Why? When asked what he was doing, the supervisor couldn't articulate what he was doing. When his folks, who worked on his line, were interviewed they said things like, "He knows our names and something about our families. He lets us have fun doing our work. We laugh a lot and sometimes we sing. He encourages us to talk about personal problems that might be interfering with our work and he listens (horrors, we all know we must leave our personal problems at home)." He supervised about seventy people. That span of control is much too large to do what he was doing, but like the humming birds flying, he didn't know the span of control was too large. How did he learn those skills? He observed Don Tyson when he walked through his plant and spoke to each individual on his line. He learned from the behaviors of his parents, who were good listeners, and by observing Don's listening when he visited the plant. Don Tyson not only communicated with words and behaviors, he also used his rudimentary art talent to communicate. At the weekly Senior Management Information Luncheon, he shows his art talent:

"I REFUSE to HAVE a BAD DAY" -Don Tyson

Senior Management Information Luncheon   September 30, 1991   Page

DON TYSON

Today starts a New Fiscal Year for our Company. Last year made the tenth year in a row of record earnings. During this period we have had three poultry cycles but because of our expansion into the food side our record is unbroken.

My thoughts on this year:

1. The economy is not rebounding from the recession but is dragging at the bottom of the economic cycle. Our country needs an upturn in activity. Th layoffs in major industries and the defense cutbacks will make this upturn slow or very difficult.

2. For the first six months we will have too much competing meat products and too much poultry. Pork will be lower than last year and the 5% or more projected increase in chicken will be marketed at very competitive prices.

3. We need to be very careful at this stage of our growth to not expand into another business or other countries, just for the sake of expansion. If we make this mistake, we take capital and management time away from our primar money earning businesses.

   KEEP OUR FOCUS ON THE GOOSE (This means look after our primary activities.)

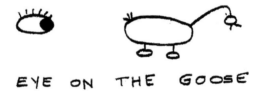

EYE ON THE GOOSE

4. I have always found there will be more places to spend our money than we have money available. This is good because it lets us select the best return on our money so we can continue our earnings record.

5. Earnings need to increase $50 000,000 pre tax this year to maintain our record.

172

<u>Don Tyson</u> - Continued

6. How do we do this:

    a) <u>Buy better</u> - with our volumes we need to rethink how we purchase everything. (Jim Doss was able to buy natural gas over $800,000 per year better in Northwest Arkansas.)

    b) <u>Organize better</u> - whatever and however we did it last year needs to be re-evaluated - (Bill Lovette was able to save 78 people at the Tyson Distribution Center.)

       We also have some plants that we are not getting full volume and their full earnings potential is not being realized. This needs to be corrected immediately.

    c) <u>Sell better</u> - this does not always mean higher prices. Make and sell the product lines that have the best margins. (The Boston Consulting Group says "Milk your cows and kill your dogs".)

COW   DOG

7. Everyone in management this year has a great opportunity to increase the earnings from their Area of Responsibility. We just need 50 or more people to find million dollar increases or 200 of us at $250,000 increases each. It can be done.

As a communicator in a group setting, Don used props to enhance meaning. One of those events was a major meeting of about four hundred folks. To demonstrate the difference between commodity and value-added products, he showed how the value of commodity flour increased as value was added by making cookies. When we arrived in the auditorium we found a package of PEPPERIDGE FARM

COOKIES at each person's chair. He was standing behind a table draped to cover his props. With flair he removed the drape to expose four sacks of flour: one pound, five pounds, ten pounds and one hundred pounds. Alongside were several bags of PEPPERIDGE FARM COOKIES. He said, "One pound of flour in this one-hundred-pound bag has a value of 19¢. One pound of flour in these cookies has a value of $6.64! We're not in the flour or chicken business. We are in the business of adding value to the products we make and sell." No lengthy, sophisticated dissertation on marketing needed; his entire presentation lasted about four minutes!

A caveat for listeners—when you listen for understanding on the individual or group level, you create an expectation that you will respond and act on what you heard. Work climate surveys that don't report back to those surveyed are like bowlers who roll their bowling balls toward the pins and just before the pins fall, a drape is dropped in front of the pins depriving the bowlers of the results of their effort! They hear the noise of pins falling but it is only noise. How stupid and disrespectful is that?

THE COHESIVE POWER OF ENCOURAGING PEOPLE TO DO THE WORK THEY WERE HIRED TO DO.

In the spring of 1967 the Arkansas Gazette published a story saying that Don Tyson and "Bo" Pilgrim, CEO of Pilgrims Pride, had reached an agreement for Tyson to acquire Pilgrims Pride for $162 million. Within the week, the deal was off. When Don asked Leland Tollett to review the "devils in the details" of the deal, Leland voted no. Leland was doing the work for which Don had hired him!

Don learned early on that to achieve his vision of building a great company, he needed competent people he trusted, people who trusted him, and he needed to empower them do the work. To some, this fits the category of a "blinding flash of the obvious." But is it? The leadership journey of many is short lived as they learn too late that they must give some of their personal and position power to people they hire and pay to do the work.

Whatever the reasons, because of their need for absolute control; inability to trust; ego addiction; personal satisfaction of micromanagement; lack of understanding the principles of motivation; the risk of empowering people to fail; their inability to think holistically about the organization— their dearest dreams go unrealized.

Management gurus have provided many rich insights on the causes and effects of empowerment—people like Paul Hersey, Ken Blanchard, Peter Block, Thomas Kuhn, and Warren Bennis.

Bennis writes: "Empowerment is the collective effect of leadership. Empowerment is most evident in four themes: 1) People feel significant—they know they make a difference. 2) Learning and competence matter; leaders value learning; there is no failure, only mistakes that give us feedback and tell us what to do next. 3) People are part of a community—a team. 4) Work is exciting. A "pull" style of influence attracts and energizes people to enroll in an exciting vision of the future. It motivates through identification, rather than through rewards and punishments. Leaders articulate and embody the ideals toward which the organization strives." [65]

THE COHESIVE NATURE OF A LEARNING ORGANIZATION

Don and his people were a learning organization before the idea was popularized. It was based on the principle that when people were empowered to lead they would make mistakes—all of them, including Don. When blunders were made, leaders had the ego strength to take responsibility, learn from the process, and avoid making the same mistake twice. Don was exhibit A.

Leaders know they are not omniscient. When they know they don't know, they engage people who do know to teach them. When Don knew he would be on the CBS program *60 Minutes*, he engaged Robert Keyser III and the Keyser Group [66] to prepare him for the interview. The interview went well as Don, armed with truth, fended off the parries of Mike Wallace. Later, some critics suggested Mike Wallace was easy on Don. He wasn't easy. Don had been to school.

THE COHESIVE RESULTS OF HOWARD BAIRD'S PLAN FOR PROGRESS WITH SECURITY

When Don hired Howard Baird in 1967 as VP, Industrial Relations, his assignment was to create the principles of Tyson's employment relations upon which personnel policies would be based. Howard created Tyson's Plan for Progress with Security, which satisfied Don's commitment to his people.

Howard is a big man, an ex-submariner, gruff and direct in style, and can be as intimidating with his peers as any man with whom I have worked. When I called recently, he said, "Wait a minute while I turn down the volume of my radio. I'm listening to Rush Limbaugh." A conservative of conservatives; a leader in the Episcopal Church; a loving father; married to Naomi who worked in his department and, in my judgment, the woman who keeps him healthy and balanced. And, he meets the requirement that followers demand of their leaders; he is a man of absolute integrity!

Howard's Plan for Progress with Security was a masterwork of communication.

To implement and encourage communications, both down and up:

— a grievance procedure, in the Plan for Progress.
— an employee-elected Quality Review Team responding to customer complaints, posting letters and the team's replies on a U.S. map board showing the "reach" of our quality performance needs.
— A Stock Purchase Plan sharing results of our efforts, with current stock prices shown.
— A retirement Income Saving Plan posting employee savings, Tyson's share, and totals.
— The Round Table bulletin board to "improve management/employee communications"
— A Grand Ideas suggestion plan
— Employee/Management luncheons, with (cafeteria) table tent explanations of the purpose.

HOWARD BAIRD'S PRINCIPLES OF EMPLOYMENT RELATIONS

The Management of Tyson Foods has the responsibility to provide a fair return on investment to Stockholders and Employees through a profitable business.

For the Stockholders, who invest their savings for our use, it is a fair return of interest on that money that provides our jobs.

For the Employees, who invest their time, skills, and energies, it is fair treatment in wages and benefits… and, in their daily association with us.

To meet these responsibilities and effectively work toward our goal of PROGRESS WITH SECURITY, it is important that everyone understand these PRINCIPLES OF OUR EMPLOYMENT RELATIONS:

1. Wages and Benefits
2. Seniority and Ability
3. Promotions and Job Opportunities
4. Grievance and Problems
5. Orderliness and Discipline
6. Communications and Information
7. Unions

Our commitment to these principles with the interest and cooperation of our Employees should provide the maximum of PROGRESS WITH SECURITY where everyone works toward the PROFIT objectives that provide our jobs.

Howard and his people called this Plan a "contract." When labor organizers would surface at a location, the "contract" idea was just right as a vehicle for communicating with employees and labor organizers. "Which contract is best for you?" Employees consistently voted for the Tyson "contract."

The genius of Howard and Don was their pro-people labor policies and behaviors. Once again behavior trumps words. There were no minimum-wage jobs at Tyson Foods. As Bill Ray, retired VP, Plant Operations, told me, "I can give you a list of hourly workers who never earned more than $8.50 per hour who retired wealthy, some of them millionaires."

Creating organizational coherence is a process that must include everyone in the organization from the newest new hire to the folks in the high-carpet area.

Lest my optimism and belief in the leadership principles about which I write suggest perfection, Tyson was not a perfect organization led by perfect human beings. The best behaviors they practiced created a work environment in which highly motivated workers could create personal wealth over time, escaping the degradation of poverty, a workplace where workers could build their own wings and soar as whole persons. The worst behaviors of a few didn't succeed in spreading their toxins very far. In most cases they didn't hang around too long. All organizations are messy. Some are messier than others. When the glue of organizational cohesion is really sticky, messiness is manageable.

TREATING PEOPLE AS PERSONS, NOT AS INTELLECTUAL CAPITAL

"Have you identified and trained your replacement?" This question, which Don asked thousands of Tyson folks, one-on-one, was the beginning of a process to grow intellectual capital inside the company. When Tyson began acquiring companies, acquisitions became a logical and natural source of highly motivated persons. Using today's latest jargon, *intellectual capital*, tends to lump persons in the same category as paper clips and machines. Howard Baird, Tyson's VP, Industrial Relations, refused to allow his department to be called "human resources," for he believed productivity was best served by treating people as persons not machines. Howard understood how the subtle use of words could influence human behavior. Thinking about people in the way managers think about machines is the first step of the law of self-fulfilling prophecy.

Except for the top tier of execs in an acquired company, career opportunities increased geometrically. Once the "dust" created by being acquired had settled, the acquired talent discovered they could compete for job opportunities. Tyson believed proven performance was the guiding criterion for promoting people. The risk of this method was the Peter Principle. To avoid that pitfall folks were moved to different jobs to measure their interest in growing and to measure their growth potential. This pragmatic idea was significantly more effective than the glitzy and excessive costs of psychometrics. Observing and measuring effectiveness of people at work combined with training and development served Tyson very well for many years.

An interesting problem occurred when long-term Tyson folks discovered they too had to compete. When an acquired talent won the competition, which was performance based, a few Tyson veterans would raise the question, "Who bought who?" Job performance became a kind of "Darwinian" process that served the company well—hybrid vigor improving the genes in the work pool. During the acquisition process, talent was identified and assessed. Although the process was informal, it worked well as each manager assumed responsibility for identifying talent and growing it. Growing talent was a mandate. People were encouraged to move to different jobs and to different locations to learn all the skills necessary to run the business.

THE COHESIVE BENEFITS OF GROWING YOUR OWN: WILBURN RIDDELL AND GERALD JOHNSTON

Both men (Wilburn Riddell and Gerald Johnston) grew up poor in rural Arkansas. In their youth, both picked cotton in the cotton fields of Arkansas and the "boot heel" in Missouri to supplement their family's income. Their education experiences were at opposite ends of the education continuum. One completed college, the other the fourth grade. Both men earned the right to become successful and worked their way to the top; one in poultry processing, the other in corporate finance and accounting. Both retired with all the accoutrements of a successful career.

Gerald Johnston was interviewed and hired by Don Tyson in 1970 for a job as cost accountant. The interview was at the Tulsa airport bar. Gerald is one of those nondrinking Baptists. Don asked Gerald if he wanted a drink. Gerald responded, "Mr. Tyson, I don't drink." Don brought him a Coke. The interview was quick with only one possible problem. Gerald asked if he would have to wear khakis. Don said, "No, but you won't appear in many corporate photographs." Gerald didn't appear in company photographs until in the nineties, when he was photographed wearing a suit at an annual shareholder meeting. When Gerald retired in 1996, he was he was executive VP, Finance and CFO.

Gerald was raised on a dirt-poor farm near the small town of Adkins, Arkansas, in the Arkansas River Valley. He was an only child with a very competitive spirit. As a young schoolboy, he would practice hitting rocks over the tin-roofed barn on the farm. He described the scene: bottom of the ninth, two outs, and Gerald was at bat. He hit the first pitch, which hit the tin roof of the barn—a game-winning home run! That scene was repeated many times in Gerald's life, a champion of champions. Rocks were plentiful, money wasn't, do with what you have, didn't need a pricey ball when you had cheap, available rocks. In the summer of 2004 he was on a championship ball team in the senior league.

When he was old enough he would travel with his parents, aunts, uncles, and cousins to the boot heel of southwest Missouri to follow the cotton harvest into central Arkansas. He was as competitive in the cotton fields as he was on the baseball diamond or tennis court. He out-picked everyone by picking four hundred pounds a day! Only cotton pickers can appreciate his performance as a cotton picker. He was educated in the schools of Adkins and graduated from Arkansas Tech University in Russellville with a degree in finance and accounting. He was elected to the ATU Hall of Fame.

As a member of the senior management team, he couldn't be described as being a workaholic. He would be described as having the ability to find and arrange financing for any and all the acquisitions Don could buy. He not only did not wear khakis, he was known to play tennis before arriving at work after the other execs had been on the job a while. And a tennis match in the afternoon was possible. He never measured his contribution to the business by hours invested but by the work successfully completed. He trusted everyone in the world until someone betrayed that trust.

It was customary in those days for Don to invite bankers and investors to a very classy dinner prior to the annual meetings. At one of those meetings, one of Tyson's lead banks in Chicago was represented by an uninitiated banker. Don told the audience he would double sales over the next five years. Veteran bankers and investors in attendance didn't question Don's prediction because of his track record. On returning to the office in Chicago, the uninitiated banker called Gerald asking for more concrete data on how Don would double sales in five years. Gerald said, "Well, let me think about it for a moment." After the pause, he said, "Tell your superiors, Don said it!" Gerald was a card-carrying amiable and mastered the skill of building and maintaining long-term relationships with bankers, investors, and the people who worked for him. He chose talent well, nurtured the talent, and mastered the skill of situational leadership.

He knew his people, built on their strengths, and had more fun at work than some folks could imagine.

Wilburn Riddell walked into Buddy Wray's office in Springdale in August of 1969. He told Buddy he really needed a job. He was working for Arkansas Valley Industries, a chicken processor at Dardanelle, Arkansas, and wanted an opportunity for a new beginning, having just gone through a divorce. Buddy asked Wilburn, "What makes you think you can work for Tyson? Who trained you?" Wilburn identified his trainer as Bill Elam at AVI, a man Buddy knew and respected. Buddy said, "OK, where do you want to work?" Wilburn said he would like to work in Missouri—a place to begin anew. Buddy had a job open at Tyson's plant in Monett, Missouri, just north of the Arkansas-Missouri state line. Wilburn's first job was on the loading dock earning $129 a week. He went on to become the plant manager at Monett, retiring in 1995 to a storybook farm in an idyllic setting east of Monett.

Wilburn, like Gerald Johnson, grew up dirt poor and went to work as a youth in the log woods to supplement the family's income. The family moved from north Arkansas to the Richland Creek area of central Arkansas, not far from where Gerald grew up. Scratching out a living in the log woods of Arkansas didn't provide many opportunities for a strong young man who had learned how to work. When the rains came, shutting down logging, Wilburn met Paul Hogan, the personnel manager at AVI and applied for a job—any job. After several visits, Paul Hogan said he would hire Wilburn if he would start as a chicken hanger. Wilburn's successful career began with hanging live chickens in a darkened room. After a few days of hanging chickens, with blistered hands, Wilburn got advice from George Coffee who showed him how to grab hold of a chicken's leg without damaging his hands. Wilburn had found his way out of poverty, working at every job in the plant, learning at every job he did.

When the writer interviewed him on his retirement farm in southern Missouri, he gave a tour of the place. In one garage, he was storing and restoring old pickup trucks. In a larger metal building, he showed his executive-type motor home and his wife's Lexus. In the house, he explained his adult toys with a stock certificate of significant value. As we walked toward my car he gave me several pictures of his plant folks, many with Don Tyson present. He described Don as a man who loved to make money and have fun doing it. At a company meeting of plant managers in Nashville, Don made one of his short speeches. "Boys, when you go home, I want you to walk around your plant on Sunday when the plant is closed, and ask yourself this question, 'Could I run my plant alone?'"

Before I got in my truck to leave, I told Wilburn I needed to settle a major dispute that had arisen between him and Gerald Johnston. "Dispute, about what? I haven't seen

Gerald in a long time." I said the dispute was about which one of them could pick the most cotton. We called Gerald and resolved the dispute by agreeing that the winner would be the one who picked more than four hundred pounds a day!

This story is one of many, describing the process of growing intellectual capital before we knew what to call the process. The process was neither complex nor sophisticated by today's standards. It was low cost, effective, and met the needs of the company for four decades.

In the early 1990s, some of us attempted to sell a formal career planning system, replete with the consultants, psychometric predictors, and a staff to manage it all. We were not successful, as the informal system was "just fine," so said a wiser man. In our formal training activities we told our folks that they were responsible for their careers. When you come to work in the morning think of yourself as being unemployed and ask yourself the question, "What can I contribute to the business today?" When you leave at the end of the day ask yourself, "What value did I add to my work today?"

Leaders develop their own unique methods of communicating their expectations to their peers and to their people. Leaders see their people not as working machines but rather as whole persons—bodies, minds, and spirits. And they get it right, when they discover that productivity has a direct correlation to worker satisfaction! When they get it wrong productivity goes down and dissatisfied workers exercise one or more of the following options:

— resign in place,
— sabotage the leader and/or the processes of the work,
— slow down and encourage the same among their peers,
— seek justice via a third party such as a labor union or other advocacy group, or retire in place.

Leaders possess what Daniel Goleman calls "Emotional Intelligence." He defines EQ, writing, "Having great intellectual abilities (IQ) may make you a superb fiscal analyst or legal scholar, but a highly developed emotional intelligence will make you a candidate for CEO or a brilliant trial lawyer." [67]

Persons with high EQ don't resort to the use of fear tactics. One of W. Edwards Deming's fourteen management principles is, "Drive Out Fear." [68] Productive people need to feel they are secure players on the team; they are encouraged and free to identify and to communicate problem areas and recommend changes, free to celebrate victories, free to feel the pain and joy of their work, free to be whole persons. Fear tactics cause people to play defense and abandon the productive work of playing offense. The practice of fear tactics creates ceilings on careers and makes work and workers miserable and unproductive. Fear is the basic tool of terrorists. Fear may appear to have good short-term results, but like adrenalin, it doesn't last and it weakens the cohesive qualities in the organization.

Ruby K. Payne and Don Krabill, in their superb and well-researched book, *The Hidden Rules of Class at Work,* describe what they call, "The Krabill/Payne Resource Quotient." The resources identified in their research: integrity, financial, emotional, mental, spiritual, physical, support system, relationships, hidden rules, and desire. They write, "The book is simply intended to look at how issues of class determine one's ability to survive in the workplace—and to offer the tools necessary to move to a different level of the organization if one so desires." [69]

Leaders understand the power of the law of self-fulfilling prophecy—the Pygmalion Effect, which says people tend to behave as you expect they will. In George Bernard Shaw's play, *Pygmalion,* which was popularized in the musical, *My Fair Lady,* the character Henry Higgins believes the Cockney flower girl Eliza Doolittle can be made into a lady. Higgins' belief in her makes it happen.

One of Don Tyson's convictions was to keep the organization flat to diminish the debilitating effects of the "hubris of class distinctions at work—I am the generalissimo, you are the peon."

The cohesive effect of growing our own people inspired and motivated folks to stay with the company, do good work, improve their skills and compete for jobs. The most valuable credential in the worker's portfolio was her or his work successes.

To maintain hybrid vigor in the talent pool and to find people with highly technical/scientific skills, which became more obvious as the company responded to customer demand for more fully prepared foods, the human resource folks recruited on college and university campuses across the country, working with career and development directors on campus. It was rare in those days to use headhunters.

EMPLOYEE WEALTH CREATION AS A COHESIVE ELEMENT

In Tyson's 1987 annual report, Don said: Ownership is a great motivator. People work harder when they have a personal stake in the outcome. Employee shareholders don't look at their work as just a job; they see it as part of their future. Owning stock inspires the salesman to make that extra call. It gets a grower out of bed in the middle of the night to close the windows so the chickens don't get cold. You don't build a successful company with average performance; you build it on superior performance. The best way I know to get above-average performance is to share the rewards with our people.

Don Tyson was a very generous man. I observed early on in my career at Tyson Foods large numbers of folks at all levels who felt they worked for the man, Don Tyson. While that was the attitude of employees, it was not Don's attitude. Buddy Wray, who worked with Don for most of forty years, said, "Don would always say, 'We work together.'" Community leaders remember Don introducing plant workers at community events or local restaurants as saying, "This is Bill. We work together." Of all the personality constructs and leader behaviors that scholars have identified in their research, it was Don's "classless" behavior that endeared him to his people. Wearing his khakis, the absence of reserved parking for execs, or the nonuse of titles and nameplates on desks and office doors were not phony symbols; they were evidence that whether you used a Montblanc pen or sharpened your lead pencil with a pocket knife, you were valued for your personhood. Performance trumped social status! Don, Leland, and Buddy were as comfortable in a chicken house visiting with a grower as they were visiting with a major shareholder in the high-carpet area.

The executive office area was referred to either as Oak Row or the high-carpet area and could have become a major barrier to creating the corporate culture Don believed in, but it didn't because of how the flat organization structure worked. Easy access to the occupants was not only acceptable, it was encouraged. If an hourly plant worker came to corporate to visit with a benefits counselor, he or she was welcome to walk into Don's, Leland's, or Buddy's office and visit. Their doors were open, and they encouraged their "walk-ins" to talk about their work.

Ownership and wealth creation was encouraged by a benefits bundle that included numerous plans:

—defined contribution benefit plan

—401(k)

—profit sharing

—a stock purchase plan that encouraged hourly workers to invest in the company by keeping the stock price low and splitting the stock when its market value hit about $30 per share. Splits were always followed by increases in the value per share.

–September 28, 1968-------------2 for 1

–November 15, 1978------------4 for 1

–April 15, 1983--------------------2 for 1

–April 15, 1985--------------------5 for 2

–April 15, 1986------------------2 for 1

–April 15, 1987------------------3 for 2

–April 15, 1991------------------2 for 1

–February 15, 1997--------------3 for 2

Stock splits became an effective way for workers to multiply not just the number of shares owned, but the rapid increase of the value of each share following every stock split.

—retirement savings plan

—health insurance

—life insurance

Consider the wealth created by a worker who invested in one hundred shares of stock from 1963 to 1968, the year of the first stock split. The company went public in 1963 selling one hundred thousand shares of common stock at $10.50. Those one hundred shares multiplied to a staggering thirty-six thousand shares by the time of the split of February 15, 1997!

Don encouraged ownership by keeping the stock price low and making it easy to buy Tyson shares. At the time of the writer's retirement in 1997, for each share purchased, Tyson added one-half share. Gerald Johnston, CFO, tells about Don coming to his office saying he wanted to give five shares to each employee. Gerald discouraged the idea based on his calculation that the cost of processing all those transactions would exceed the value of the stock. Don's response was, "I know, but I want to show my appreciation to our folks," so it was accomplished.

COHESION AND THE THREE
PRINCES OF SERENDIP

SERENDIPITY—the phenomenon of making fortunate accidental discoveries.

Don Tyson, Leland Tollett, and Buddy Wray may not appear superficially to fit Richard Boyle's story, "The Three Princes of Serendip." However, consider the idea of blogger Jon Udell, who describes serendipity as manufactured serendipity. His idea has merit. Udell writes, "You can't automate accidental discoveries, but you can manufacture the conditions in which such events are more likely to occur." [70]

The cohesion that held Tyson Foods together enabling it to become the world's largest protein-based food company was in part the process of manufactured serendipity.

LEADERSHIP INSIGHTS

Organizational Integrity describes a multilevel organization performing diverse tasks from simple to complex with the minimum "leakage" of resources—time, material, capital, talent, opportunities.

- Organizational integrity is the responsibility of leaders! Organizational integrity is a measure of how much confidence and trust followers have in their leaders at all levels! Integrity and accountability are two sides of the same virtue!

- Trust is the conviction that the leader means what she or he says. Trust is a measure of leaders' integrity. Integrity is the relationship one has with oneself and with the organization. Leaders' actions and professed beliefs must be congruous with organizational policies, practices, words, and behaviors.

- Trust is earned by leaders' consistent behaviors demonstrating the many facets of integrity as understood by followers who make final decisions about leadership integrity.

"It's not what we eat but what we digest that makes us strong; not what we gain but what we save that makes us rich; not what we read but what we remember that makes us learned; and not what we profess but what we practice that gives us integrity."

Sir Francis Bacon, Sr., English lawyer and philosopher, 1561-1626.

Paul Whitley

CHAPTER 5
SEGMENT, CONCENTRATE, DOMINATE
Tyson's Growth Strategy—An Odyssey of Acquisitions

Growth or striving for it is, I believe, essential to the good health of an enterprise. Deliberately to stop growing is to suffocate…Growth and progress are related for there is no resting place in a competitive economy. Obstacles, conflict, new problems in various shapes, and new horizons arise to stir the imagination and continue the progress of industry. Success, however, may bring self-satisfaction. In that event, the urge for competitive survival, the strongest of all economic incentives, is dulled. The spirit of venture is lost in the inertia of the mind against change.

Alfred Sloan. [71]

WHAT IS TYSON'S OVERALL BUSINESS GROWTH STRATEGY?

Don answers the question in Tyson's 1987 annual report. "We say it in three words: segmentation, concentration, domination. We find something we think we can do, focus on it, and then aim to be Number One at it." Eight years later, Leland Tollett at a Consumer Analysts of New York (CAGNY) event in 1995 said, "We're a market-driven

199

company and have as our goal to be the dominant supplier of what we call the center-of-the-plate protein portion of all meal occasions. That means we want to supply the expensive part of the meal, whether the meal be eaten at home or away from home."

The triumvirate built into their strategic thinking a kind of gyroscopic mechanism that kept them on a dual heading—organic growth and growth by acquisition. About the time the organization was getting comfortable, leadership turned up the work environment thermostat by making an acquisition, leading folks out of their comfort zones. Tyson's growth strategy is not unlike Darwin's observations of nature: "It is not the strongest of the species that survive, or the most intelligent, but the one most responsive to change." Tyson's growth strategy proved to be an effective antidote to sleepwalking in organizations that resist change. Many of Tyson's competitors lost the competitive edge when they were seduced by yesterday's successes and lulled into a comfortable state of drowsiness.

Rewards and recognition for successful goal achievement were generous and appreciated, but not long lasting. Don's visionary leadership continued to create the future. Creating the future implies a dynamic process that is quite different from long-range strategic planning, which can impair visioning like cataracts impair eyesight.

Don's ability to see the future was demonstrated in his interview in October 1968 for *Broiler Industry* magazine. The context of the conversation was the future of the ice-pack business. "I can see the time when a full-line processor, with cooked items, would become attractive to a retailer. However, he'd probably be a chain who would want to use the institutional field as a means of recapturing volume he loses in his stores, and volume that will carry a higher margin to him. *To summarize, I don't think we'll recognize our industry ten years from now. We're in the middle of a revolution right now. Tyson Foods expects to be in the front lines then, as now.*"

Today a consumer who wants to serve a fried chicken dinner with potatoes and gravy or roast beef with broccoli and cheese sauce can pick up the meal at a fast-food restaurant or at a fine dining restaurant with an Internet menu and take-home order service. Hundreds of prepared or partially prepared foods are now available for the time-pressed consumer to pick up on the way home from work or shopping. Don's prediction from thirty-five years ago was right on! Tollett was right—Don could see around corners!

A Vasco da Gama Moment

In a recent interview of Don, I presented him with a copy of the October 1968 issue of *Broiler Industry* magazine. He smiled broadly, spun around 180 degrees in his office chair, retrieved the original article from his credenza and said, "Here it is!"

Of the many hours I was privileged to be with this man, this moment and the several days to follow were the most insightful intellectually and emotionally. It was as if a retired Vasco da Gama, the fifteenth-century Portuguese sailor/navigator who charted an ocean route to the east and India, had unfolded those heavily soiled, old charts and remembered the many stops in Africa—problems with Muslim traders who didn't want anyone interfering with their profitable trade routes, naysayers who said it would be impossible because the Indian Ocean was not connected to any other seas, and the tragedy of some of his sailors dying at sea from scurvy before the explorer finally reached Calcutta on May 20, 1498.

Don's odyssey of acquisitions and his philosophy of managing capital were reported in a 1974 interview with *Broiler Industry* magazine when he responded to this question, "Do you think the size of company will limit diversification?" His answer: "Size is not really the criteria. *Management of capital is the key*—how you manage it and how you employ it. Your stockholders deserve the return. They have enough liquidity to take their capital to other places if you are not managing it properly. So our guide is *how well we can manage capital* in this industry compared with alternative uses." Don's vision for the company combined with his ability to manage capital are perhaps the two skills that gave Tyson an ongoing competitive advantage, guiding his odyssey of acquisitions.

Hard evidence of his skill in managing capital appears in the 1986 annual report: "The company's total capital employed, as represented by shareholders' equity plus long-term debt, at fiscal year-end 1986 was $415,519,000 compared to $273,285,000 in 1985. Shareholders' equity increased 31.6 percent during 1986 and has grown at a compounded rate of 34.3 percent over the past five years, inclusive of $40.1 million received from the public sale of common stock during 1985. At fiscal year-end, the company had construction projects in progress that will require approximately $70,000,000 to complete. The company *anticipates funding the expenditures through working capital provided from operations and borrowing under existing lines of credit.*"

His success in managing capital in the interest of shareholders created an environment that enabled him to effectively run the company as a sole proprietorship. Satisfied shareholders don't revolt; satisfied workers don't need unions; satisfied customers tend to be loyal to the brand—a mutually beneficial relationship. Plus the fact that the family's Class B stock gave them ten votes to one for holders of Class A stock. As government regulations became more invasive, sole proprietorship thinking began to create problems for the company.

It is important to note how well Don balanced shareholder interests with commitment to customers and workers. Among public companies there is a temptation to satisfy shareholders by making short-term decisions that may impair the ability of the company to satisfy customers and workers. I think of him as an existential futurist.

ACQUISITIONS PRODUCE PHENOMENAL FINANCIAL RESULTS

Investor, banker, employee, and customer confidence in Tyson's leadership performance grew as Tyson's financial behavior produced solid financial results. From Tyson's 1987 annual report: "For the fifth consecutive year, financial results hit record highs. Sales rose 18.8 percent to $1,785,969,000 from $1,503,719,000 in fiscal 1986. Net earnings were $67,764,000, up 34.7 percent from last year's $50,289,000. This solid performance enabled us to reduce short-term debt to zero, and further strengthen the company's financial position. In February the company declared a 3-for-2 stock split, the fourth split in five years. In its April 27 issue, *Fortune* magazine ranked Tyson Foods, Inc., first in the Fortune 500 in terms of total return to investors, with an average of 58.27% a year for the last decade."

When Leland was asked if Tyson's production capacity could keep up with revenue growth, which was at 28.5 percent a year, he said, "In the last three years we have spent over $300 million on capital improvements and $188 million on acquisitions, which *we made to increase our supply of chicken and to enhance our ability to serve the marketplace.*"

Growth was driven by the marketplace and Don's vision of how to dominate a marketplace that was changing like the river Greek philosopher Heraclitus described: "The river where you set your foot just now is gone—those waters giving way to this, now this." As the river changed, the Triumvirate made the necessary midcourse corrections in pursuit of long-term goals.

Max DePree, visionary leader, who led Herman Miller, Inc., the Grand Rapids, Michigan, office furniture company to a position of dominance, writes about a leader's ability to "move constantly back and forth between he present and the future. Our perception of each becomes clear and valid if we understand the past. The future requires our humility in the face of all we cannot control. The present requires attention to all the people to whom we are accountable. The past gives us the opportunity to build on the work of our elders." [72] At Tyson Foods the elder was the founder, Mr. John Tyson.

RATIONALE FOR GROWTH BY ACQUISITION

1. Per capita consumption of chicken rose from 23.6 lbs. in 1960 to 71.9 lbs. in 1997.

2. Per capita consumption of beef in 1960 was 63.3 lbs., rising to a high point of 94.4 lbs. in 1976 and declining to 65.7 lbs. in 1997.

3. Per capita consumption of pork in 1960 was 59.1 lbs. and declined to 47.9 lbs in 1997.

4. Per capita consumption of shellfish and commercial fish was 10.3 lbs. in 1960 and rose to 14.6 lbs. in 1997.

5. In the 1970s and '80s, healthcare providers were touting the health benefits of chicken vs. beef.

6. By 1997 the time required to produce a beef animal was two years or more vs. about 5.5 weeks for a broiler chicken, and that time was being reduced by one day each year.

7. Chickens convert grain to meat more efficiently than beef or pork. The conversion ratio for chicken was below 2 lbs. of grain for 1 lb. of meat; beef was about 5 to 1 and pork 3 to 1.

8. Americans were eating more meals away from home, creating opportunities for Tyson to capitalize on the advantage they had captured in

the development of value-added products for the growing foodservice market.

9. Fast-food restaurants were expanding rapidly and needed fast-food chicken products.

10. Most countries of the world preferred leg or dark meat over white creating an export market for what was becoming a surplus leg meat problem.

11. The chicken industry was entering a period of consolidation for Economic and/or personal reasons of owners who had made their fortunes and wanted to retire. [73]

INDUSTRY TIPPING POINTS

The Great Depression was something of a tipping point in the chicken industry when farmers discovered chickens and eggs as generators of much-needed cash. Farmers needed feed for their chickens, a need that was filled by John Tyson's Feed and Hatchery; Jesse Jewell's feed store in Gainesville, Georgia; and Harold Snyder with Arkansas River Valley Feed Mill in Russellville, Arkansas. These three companies went on to become vertical integrators.

Another tipping point occurred when Harold Snyder went to the public market in 1961 to raise capital for his fully integrated Arkansas Valley Industries. A year later, Fred

Lovette in Wilkesboro, North Carolina, founder of Holly Farms, traded Holly stock for ownership of sixteen hatcheries, feed mills, and related assets. Tyson Foods and Jesse Jewell went to the public market to raise capital in 1963.

In the late 1960s and early 1970s, the chicken industry was dominated by feed millers like Ralston Purina, Allied Mills, Cargill, ConAgra, Pillsbury, and Central Soya. Major meat packers, such as Swift, Armour, and Wilson, who had enjoyed some success processing and selling chickens, began to lose interest in chicken, as they never learned how to consistently make money at it. Making money or the lack of it was related to the inability of the industry to match production to consumption—the universal problem in most commodities. Don Tyson told the Food Service Marketing Workshop in 1988, "When the industry gets into over capacity, 75 percent of the industry has to take medicine. The question is, does it take medicine slowly over a long period of time, or does it gulp it down and get rid of the problem really quick?" [74]

A WATERSHED TIPPING POINT

In 1972, the feed companies, led by Ralston Purina and their corporate planners, concluded they couldn't manage the great price swings caused by over capacity and sought ways to limit their exposure. Case in point, "Red"

Hudson, manager of Ralston's feed business in northwest Arkansas, with the help from George's Feed & Supply, was able to buy Ralston's northwest Arkansas operations.

Another tipping point occurred following World War II as more and more women entered the workforce creating new demand for chicken products that were easy to use. In 1965 Holly Farms was getting rave reviews for their Chill-Pak system that increased shelf life of cut-up chicken by controlling the product temperature throughout the channels of distribution—from their plant in Glen Allen, Virginia, to the supermarket refrigerated meat counter. A few months later, Don Tyson and Fred Lovette answered a request that Safeway Stores made to Lovette. Safeway needed a second supplier, especially for Safeway's West Coast stores. Tyson introduced its Country Fresh Chicken or T-28 (temperature 28 degrees). The deal was a big boost in the retail market. From that day till the day Fred Lovette died in 1988, they continued to be fierce competitors on the street, but good personal friends. It was a kind of Jack Nicholas-Arnold Palmer golf relationship as each competitor pursued the green jacket at the Masters in the 1960–1966 period.

Another tipping point was the work of *Broiler Industry* magazine, which became the forum for industry leaders who had common problems, especially issues related to the U.S. Department of Agriculture and the Food & Drug Administration. In 1954, the National Broiler Council was established at a meeting in Washington, DC. Those poultry and egg pioneers were: Charles Vantress, Clyde Hendrix, Ray Firestone, J.D. Jewell, Otis Esham, Roy Titter, B.C. Rogers, Jerry Hinshaw, Marshall Durbin, Ray Purnell, Henry Saglio, E.S. Kendrick, Clyde Fore, H.C. Kennett, W.R. Shaffer, Henry Tilford, Jr., and Frank Frazier. The organization evolved to become today's National Chicken Council based in Washington. In addition to this group, the U.S. Poultry and Egg Association of Tucker, Georgia, provided education services to the industry and sponsored the annual International Poultry Exposition in Atlanta, which brings the industry together from around the world. In 1977, Garden State Publishing merged with Watt Publishing to increase the number of publications that focused on industry issues.

The growth and development of poultry science and related degrees in the curricula of several colleges and universities added to industry tipping points. By 1950, there were poultry science programs at forty colleges and universities. [75]

DON TYSON, THE ROMANTIC ADVENTURER

To fully understand Don Tyson's Odyssey of Acquisitions, it is helpful to get inside the heart of this man. As a leader, he had good balance of head and heart. Some leaders and observers of leader behaviors are reluctant to talk about the soft/touchy/feely skills of leadership, preferring to focus on the macho-Machiavellian, hard-ass, bottom-line skills of the head. Some leaders are described as not having a single altruistic bone in their body. To reject the anima in male leadership behavior or the animus in female leadership behavior is to create a one-dimensional, incomplete human being. The Don Tyson I observed over thirteen years was one of the most transparent, authentic persons for whom I have ever worked. He wore no masks as he had nothing to hide. Because he possessed balance of head and heart, he could be tough, gentle, angry, direct, indirect, quiet or loud—sensing both the needs of the situation and the needs of the person or persons involved. In our research for curricula development, we discovered the principal of versatility. Reid and Merrill called it the third dimension of behavior "versatility." [76] Versatility is the degree to which a person is sensitive to the stress of the other person in a situation. Don Tyson demonstrated high versatility behaviors.

Leaving Don's office on October 6, 2005, the writer was able to scratch the itch that prompted the writing of this book. Don's answers to two questions gave the writer a little peek into his heart of hearts. The first question: "What is it that lures you to the sea?" He described the first vacation he and his wife Jean had taken after his working seven days a week from 1952, his first year in the company, to 1963, the year he took the company public. He came home from work one evening and Jean told him they were taking a vacation. They were going to Granada. He described the event as a love affair with blue sky, blue water, the white sands of the beach, and catching big-bill fish (marlin, sailfish, spearfish, and swordfish). This man is more than a hard-working, intuitive visionary; he is a romantic in touch with the natural world. The itch was scratched. This book would be written. As I walked to my car I could see something in this man that I hadn't seen before and realized that we rarely have enough information about leaders to know the measure of the leader. The insight I gained from this interview was that Don Tyson was a Hemingway man.

SUPER BOWL I, JANUARY 15, 1967— THE TRAGIC DEATHS OF DON'S PARENTS

The second question, "What was the most difficult year for you?" He said it was 1967. "I lost my dad and my stepmom. It was the Super Bowl I weekend, Sunday, January, 15." The Packers beat the Chiefs 35 to 10 in the Los Angeles Memorial Coliseum. Tickets were $12. He went to say, "During that three-month period I lost $300,000. My chickens were dying with chronic respiratory disease. That was just about all the money we had."

Don's answer to the second question said a lot about this man. He was more than an economic man. His business success was not the sole measure of this man. This "I refuse to have a bad day" man lived his life experiencing the full range of human emotions. There were several bad events in the business. 1974 was one of the worst years in the chicken industry. Bob Justice, Tyson's public relations man, described a day in 1974 when the execs at Tyson watched in disbelief as Tyson's stock price fell hourly. It was the only year they had experienced an annual loss, $2.7 million on sales of $168 million! This "tycoon, entrepreneur, chicken king" or other descriptors used by the business press, missed the full measure of the man. Some macho men of hubris would not have revealed their inner feelings.

THIRTY-SIX ACQUISITIONS FROM 1962 TO 1997

In an interview with Leland and Buddy, February 22, 2005, they described the reasons for each acquisition and noted a few that were unique in the impact they had on the business. The reasons ranged from, "The owner wanted to sell or got into financial difficulty" to "We needed capacity to support our growth" to "Some event or someone opened the door, we were ready, we walked in."

Most acquisitions were friendly as opposed to hostile. The degree of friendliness was determined by the acquiring company's business needs and how one's skills met those needs. Being caught up in mergers and acquisitions is kind of like rowing your boat from a small, shallow river that you know well into a faster-moving river whose currents, rapids, and depth you don't know. If you read the currents and rapids well, it may be friendly. There is one, predictable absolute: when you are acquired, things will change—in both the acquired company and the acquiring company. It was in the very process of change that Tyson improved its competitive advantage—hybrid vigor bringing new genes into the management gene pool as described by geneticist, Dr. John Hardiman.

Track and field enthusiasts will remember the Fosbury Flop. It became the wonder of the track world when Dick Fosbury set a new American and Olympic high jump record of 7 feet, 4¼ inches. The technique he developed enabled him to clear the bar with his body, as his own center of gravity went beneath the bar—a paradigm shift! Fosbury introduced new genes into the high jump competition.

Today, at the Tyson Track Center on the campus of the University of Arkansas in Fayetteville, high jumpers, using the Flop, compete from around the country. The story of how the Track Center came to be begins with a chance meeting at Uncle Gaylord's Restaurant in Fayetteville. Don

Tyson was having breakfast at Uncle Gaylord's, reading the paper. Head Track Coach John McDonnell, one of the most successful college track coaches, came in for breakfast. As he waited for his meal and as he watched Don he was prompted to do something his boss Frank Broyles, the athletic director, told him never to do. That something was to solicit funds to build a new track center. Frank Broyles was and is a football guy. Coach McDonnell had been winning track titles on top of track titles without spending capital dollars for a new facility. He decided to take the risk. He left his table, walked to Don's table and said, "Mr. Tyson, I am…" Don interrupted the coach and said, "I know who you are, please sit down." After a few minutes of conversation, Don asked, "What can I do for you?" Coach McDonnell began describing his vision for a new indoor track center. Don found a piece of paper and asked the coach to lay it out on paper, which he did. They talked generally about costs, ended the meeting, and went on about finishing their breakfasts. On February 12, 2000, the Randal Tyson Indoor Track was dedicated! [77] Coach McDonnell pushed himself outside his comfort zone when he approached Don and shared his vision.

What do Dick Fosbury, Coach McDonnell, and Don Tyson have in common, and why do they appear in this book on the subject of growth by acquisition? They share the common belief that change is requisite to growth and improvement. In a changing environment, doing the same old things the same old way produces the same old results. They also have in common a willingness to take risks in pursuit of a goal. They also have in common a worldview of abundance rather that scarcity—a worldview that refuses to behave in miserly and curmudgeonly ways.

HOW MUCH IS AN ACQUISTION WORTH?

Included in the process of due diligence, Tyson used a simple rule of thumb to determine the value of an acquisition. How much more was one chicken worth in Tyson's hands than in the hands of a targeted acquisition? Fundamentally, the goal was not to grow more chickens but to do more with the chickens grown. When you do more with the chickens you grow, the profit earned enables you to acquire more chickens to earn more profit—the Tyson cycle of growth. Profit was one measure of how well Tyson satisfied customers, workers, and shareholders. Profit was both effect and cause and getting the order is important! Profit was an intermediate goal in pursuit of a larger goal—becoming number one in the industry. Tyson avoided the common trap of making profit the ultimate goal, knowing that when that ultimate goal was reached, the numbing forces of satisfaction and comfort would smother the "fire-in-the-belly" of the greater vision.

One of Don's "thou shalts" was, "Thou shalt have a profit." What this writer observed during his tenure at Tyson was that Don understood that without satisfied customers buying value-added products, he would be back in a low-profit commodity business that was based only on cost. Leland Tollett said over and over that a company could not out-market high cost, and he kept the hammer down on cost containment. Buddy Wray and the production folks had numerous discussions about the question, "Are we building too much quality into the product?" The ability of these folks to find "right cost" is a testament to Don, Leland, and Buddy avoiding the obsessive trap of cutting costs to the point that customers lost confidence in the company. Peter Drucker wrote in *Management, Tasks, Responsibilities, and Practices:*

> A business is not defined by the company's name, statutes, or articles of incorporation. It is defined by the want the customer satisfies when he buys a product or a service. To satisfy the customer is the mission and purpose of every business. The question 'What is our business?' can, therefore, be answered only by looking at the business from the outside, from the point of view of customer and market. What the customer sees, thinks, believes and wants, at any given time, must be accepted by management as an objective fact and must be taken as seriously as the reports of the salesman, the tests of the engineer, or the figures of the accountant. And management must make a conscious effort to

get answers from the customer himself rather than attempt to read his mind.

Another aspect of Don's acquisition mind-set was the idea that being the second buyer was historically a better deal than being the first buyer or first investor. It was especially true in buying assets of commodity producers whose futures were in fact controlled by the realities of commodity pricing rather than by adding value of fixed-priced products.

ACQUISITIONS BY DECADE, 1962–1997
THE SIXTIES

1962—Oklahoma City Poultry & Egg

1963—Garrett Poultry

1966—Washington Creamery

1967—Franz Foods

1968—Chicken Hut Subsidiary

1969—Cavanaugh, Monett, Mo.

1969—Prospect Farms

1969 SALES—$61.9 million
STOCK SPLIT IN THE SIXTIES
1968—2-for-1

THE SEVENTIES

1972—Krispy Kitchens

1972—Ocoma Food

1973—Cassady Poultry

1974—Vantress Pedigree, Inc.

1975—Bologna/Wiener Plant

1977—Tyson Carolina Mountaire Poultry Subsidiary

1978—Wilson Foods Poultry Div.

1979 SALES—$382.2 million

STOCK SPLIT IN THE SEVENTIES

1978—4-for-1

THE EIGHTIES

1983—Honey Bear

1983—Mexican Original

1984—Valmac/Tastybird Foods

1986—Heritage Valley

1986—Lane Processing

1988—Trasgo of Mexico Joint Venture

1988—Agrimont of Montreal

1989—Holly Farms- The Federal Company

1989 SALES—$2.5 billion

STOCK SPLITS IN THE EIGHTIES

1983—4-for1
1984—5-for-2
1986—2-for-1
1987—3-for-2

THE NINETIES

1992—Arctic Alaska Fisheries Corporation

1992—Brandywine Foods

1992—Louis Kemp Seafoods

1993—A Poultry Plant, Sedalia, Missouri

1994—Culinary Foods1994—Gorges Foodservice

1994—100 percent Cobb-Vantress

1994—Majority Interest in Trasgo

1995—Star of Kodiak Seafood

1995—Int. Multifoods Seafood Processing Plant

1995—JAC Creative Foods

1995—Cargill Poultry

1995—McCarty Farms

1997—Mallard Foods

1999 SALES—$7.6 billion
STOCK SPLITS IN THE NINETIES
1991—2-for-1
1997—3-for-2

ACQUISITIONS OF NOTE

Every acquisition is an acquisition of note to most of the folks directly involved, either as the acquirer or the acquired. The writer has "been acquired" three times and was present during eighteen acquisitions made by Tyson. Except for the top tier of execs in the acquired company, history tells us that for most folks, once the mud had settled, Tyson ownership was an opportunity for highly motivated individuals to advance their careers. Since a company didn't need two CEOs or two CFOs, those folks took the wealth they had created and went on to other things. Consider the wealth created for Holly Farms shareholders when Tyson paid $70 per share for their stock that was selling at $39 on October 11, 1988, the day before Tyson announced intentions to acquire Holly Farms.

1963—Garrett Poultry of Rogers

Charles L. Garrett founded his company, Farmers Produce Co., in 1920. He purchased and sold fruits, vegetables, poultry, and eggs. When the drought of 1927 severely damaged the Big Red Apple crop, he restructured his company to focus on poultry and called it Garrett Poultry. He built a hatchery, feed mill, a processing plant, and several chicken houses to grow chickens. He also operated the Warehouse Super Market and owned a bank in Rogers.

He was enjoying his successes until disease invaded his chicken houses. At the time, little was known about disease prevention. Don Tyson approached him, asking if he was interested in selling. He was, and they negotiated a deal that included a significant earnest money figure. At the time Tyson Foods was working with underwriters to take the company public. Delays by the underwriters kept pushing the closing date for the public offering back. As the due date for payment of the earnest money to Mr. Garrett drew closer and closer, the anxiety level began to soar—especially the anxiety level for Mr. John Tyson who made no deals without cash in the bank! On the day before Mr. Garrett's earnest money was due, the public offering finally closed, saving Don's earnest money and the acquisition—the agreement stipulated that Don would not only lose his earnest money, the acquisition would be null and void. Once again the poker player held the right cards.

1966—WASHINGTON CREAMERY— A MARKETING COMPANY

This acquisition is an example of Don's use of acquisitions to acquire talent. In this case, it was marketing talent he needed to enhance his competitive advantage. A case in point comes from geometry and Buckminster Fuller's work, *Synergetics, Explorations in the Geometry of*

Thinking. [78] Fuller uses two wire triangles to demonstrate his principle of synergetics. "By conventional arithmetic, one triangle plus one triangle equals two triangles. But in association as left helix and right helix, they form a six-edged tetrahedron of four triangular faces." The writer asked engineering to make two wire triangles to demonstrate Fuller's principle; engineering sent him two wire triangles with twelve-inch sides. We used the triangles to demonstrate the power of synergetics by manipulating the two triangles to produce the four triangles of a tetrahedron, the base and three sides. Fuller describes the why and how of the triangles: "Therefore, the triangle is a spiral—a very flat spiral, but open at the recycling point." Consider Tyson as one triangle with $38 million in sales in 1966. Tyson acquired the Washington Creamery for $1.5 million. The synergistic effect of the acquisition exceeded the arithmetic effect. Washington Creamery, according to Leland, introduced Tyson to professional marketing and dominance in the Rock Cornish game hen market.

The 1966 annual report identifies three execs from Washington Creamery who occupied key jobs at Tyson: Joseph Woglom, executive VP, Marketing; Isadore Rosen, executive VP; and Ken Potterton, VP, Marketing. At the time Leland was VP, Broiler Production, and Buddy was VP, Processing. Buddy described the cultural differences between these "New York Yankees and the natives of Arkansas as challenging."

Joe Woglom was a hard-drinking Polish guy, Isadore Rosen was a hard-talking New York Jewish businessman, and Ken Potterton a hard-drinking Scot who loved Scotch whiskey. Washington Creamery had been marketing Tyson's Rock Cornish game hens in the Northeast. They were marketing game hens at a fixed retail price of 50¢ each rather than on a cents-per-pound basis, removing them from the vagaries of the commodity market. For the next seven or eight years this diverse leadership team built on each other's strengths and experienced the pure joy of the multiplication of shared resources. While most of Tyson's competitors couldn't escape the insanity of doing things the same old way, Don Tyson, the visionary, entrepreneurial romantic, led his company to a future that was different and better than the past.

THE MARKETING EXPERTISE OF WASHINGTON CREAMERY

The following is a Joseph Woglom quote from the October 1968 issue of *Broiler Industry* magazine.

> We're taking a strong look at the institutional field [foodservice], as reflected in our recent negotiations to acquire Prospect Farms. By cooking chickens, we upgrade them and put them on a segment of the market where prices don't fluctuate as often as they do in ice-packed and frozen retail packs.

Our Cornish picture is strong and prices have not changed in a year. We're plugging Cornish hard on TV and radio and magazines (*Family Circle, Sunset, Better Homes and Gardens*) in west of the Mississippi markets. We consider that area to be our natural marketplace in relation to our plant locations.

The oven-baked turkey breast is our newest— Lord knows what is next, except we know it's going to start out on the farm as a chicken! We're recognizing the strength of Prospect Farm's precooked chicken in the institutional area and hope to marry our own institutional products to Prospect's success story. As to retail, we never stop banging away. In five years we've become the world's largest producer and marketer of Rock Cornish hens and we're not satisfied.

We've introduced our Tyson 28 program— meaning controlled temperature chicken shipped from plant to store in dry-pack form, already pre-priced and packaged to retail specifications. For this we have a full-time staff of merchandisers to help chain personnel get the deep-chill program off the ground.

"You might say," concludes Joe Woglom, in a sonorous voice, looking deadpan at an incoming tele-type message from the peripatetic Don Tyson in Arkansas, "that we can never be sure what's coming next...except that it'll mean a helluva lot more work...and fun!"

1969—Prospect Farms

This acquisition gave Tyson immediate access to the growing fast-food market with fully cooked fried chicken products. Prospect Farms had a well-trained broker (commission agents) sales force. The synergy of the combined companies was pivotal in Tyson's goal to move away from commodity products to value-added, fixed-price products.

Dick Stockland, who was to play a key role in Tyson's future, was the finance guy at Prospect and instrumental in the deal. Dick possessed a rare combination of skills: finance, accounting, sales and marketing, and superb human skills.

1972—Acquired Ocoma Foods from Consolidated Foods (now Sara Lee Corporation)

Broiler Industry magazine interviewed Don for their June 1974 issue and asked, "How has the Ocoma acquisition worked out for you?" He answered, "Well, it was a helluva bite. We bought a company as big as ours in sales and one that was losing twice as much money as we were making. We were strong financially, and Consolidated Foods considered its Ocoma Foods division a loser—at least as measured by its income expectations for the future. So we strained our management and our resources to make it break even."

The losing assets included a turkey plant that Tyson disposed of in forty-two days. The management staff at two plants that were losing money had to be replaced. The Berryville, Arkansas, plant was a winner with a winning management team. Bill Ray, considered to be one of the most knowledgeable persons in the technology of cooking chicken, was in the talent pool as was Don Tharp, plant accountant. Within a few weeks of being acquired by Tyson, Bill sold his Consolidated Foods stock, investing the proceeds in Tyson stock. For the next twenty-six years he was a major contributor to the success of Tyson Foods. Bill was a VP when he retired in 1998.

The story of Tyson Foods is a story of rural agriculture and small towns that depended on the success of rural agriculture. It is a story of satisfying consumers with agricultural products using high-tech food technologies, low-cost production methods, and efficient distribution.

Over lunch at Myrtie Mae's restaurant in Eureka Springs, Don Tharp and Bill Ray described how life has changed in this Ozark Mountain Valley that is traversed by U.S. Highway 62 between Eureka Springs, Berryville, and Green Forest. In chamber-of-commerce fashion, they told stories about subsistence farms becoming prosperous growing chickens that produced fertilizer to grow grass for more income from the sale of cattle; young people being able to stay in the valley to fill jobs in the processing plants and related industries; new schools, thriving churches, new healthcare facilities—Tyson dollars growing the infrastructure in one of the most beautiful mountain valleys in the United States.

Annual payroll generated in Tyson facilities in the valley was estimated to be $37,440,000—dollars that bought groceries, clothes, houses, tractors, pickup trucks, campers, insurance, health care, etc. Dollars that turn seven or eight times in the valley, becoming something like $262 million annually.

1974—Acquisition of the Vantress Male Breeding Lines—Vantress Pedigree, Inc., a genetic research and breeding firm

This acquisition initiated a process of genetic improvement that gave Tyson a dramatic competitive advantage in the early 1980s. In 1974, the Upjohn Company acquired Cobb at the same time Tyson acquired the Cobb male breeding lines. In 1986, Cobb-Vantress formed a joint venture with Tyson and Upjohn. With over 120 years of combined breeding experience, Cobb became the international leader in poultry breeding. In 1994, Tyson acquired Upjohn shares making Cobb-Vantress, Inc., a wholly owned subsidiary.

In Tyson's 1976 annual report Don wrote, "With the purchase of Vantress Pedigree, Tyson Foods has accomplished two important goals: (1) assured a continuing supply of the

Vantress breeder cockerel that has proven itself in the Tyson broiler programs and throughout the poultry industry, and (2) acquired the Vantress system of 'applied genetics,' which can be utilized in the continuation and improvement of the breed and in the development of new breeding lines for the future."

The wisdom of this acquisition was demonstrated in 1981 when Leland Tollett had a meeting with Dr. John Hardiman, senior geneticist at Cobb-Vantress, and asked Dr. John if he could increase the quantity of breast meat on a chicken by five percent. John said yes. Leland saw the demand for breast-meat products exploding, and he needed and gained the competitive advantage available via genetics. One again Tyson was listening to customers in the U.S. market who preferred white meat over leg meat. It was critical that Tyson produce more breast meat per chicken, as leg meat was being sold well below the cost of production. Supermarket consumers were buying whole legs, drumsticks and thighs, at prices as low as 25¢ per pound—about half of production cost.

In Tyson's candid and open culture there didn't appear, in this writer's experience, to be many proprietary secrets. The one big exception was chicken and hog genetics. Both biosecurity and genetic security were extremely high.

Dr. Hardiman remembers Leland coming to him at various times inquiring about ways to alter the basic design of a chicken, based on consumer demand. For instance, when wings were of low value, change the design to reduce wing size. When Hot Wings, which were invented at the Anchor Bar in Buffalo, New York, created exploding demand for wings, Leland wanted smaller legs and more wings. The University of California at Davis worked on reducing feather content on a chicken as feather disposition was a problem. While they had some success, it was concluded that naked chickens didn't do well. Today chicken-feather meal is a high-protein ingredient in cattle feed.

Dr. Hardiman was the subject of an article in the April 2005 issue of *National Geographic*. "This has become a world of chickens. It's Planet Pollo. It's an astonishing triumph for the descendants of the humble creature called the red jungle fowl (*Gallus gallus*)...Hardiman reported, 'In the 1980s 10% of a typical chicken's weight was breast meat, but that has risen to 21%.'" Today, Cobb-Vantress dominates broiler genetics around the world.

1975—Mountaire's Springhill Louisiana Wiener and Bologna Plant

This story of a small acquisition is a story of empowerment as told by Buddy Wray at a 1988 meeting of several of Tyson's Warriors who had gathered to tell leadership stories.

This was the purchase of a little old bologna and wiener plant down in Springhill, Louisiana, back in the 1970s. We had been getting some product co-packed for us, and we had heard through the grapevine that these people were thinking about selling the plant. On the third of July, I made a trip to Little Rock to find out if they were going to sell it or not.

They did not want to sell it to Tyson because they were afraid Tyson would come back in and gather some other market shares of products they were doing. This company was Mountaire Poultry Company. They had a plant in De Queen, and several plants in Arkansas, and they were kind of like some of this list that Leland read earlier; Mountaire Poultry Company was one of the larger companies back in the early 1970s in Arkansas, and today they don't even exist in Arkansas and barely exist at all.

Anyway, the negotiations started out. They wanted something like one-half million dollars for the company and we kept talking. When I left Springdale, I had not thought of really going down to buy the company. They had told Don, though, that it was going to be for sale, and I went down to find out what I could do about it. But, in the course of the day, and in talking back and forth, I realized that if we didn't do something quick, we not only wouldn't have the opportunity to buy the company, but we were going to be out of a source of supply. So, before the day was over, we negotiated, and finally, the guy told me, "Tomorrow is the Fourth of July, and I don't plan to be here all night"...I said, "That's fine; let's strike a deal."

We wound up buying the plant for about a third of what they wanted for it, and within about four months, we had made enough off the plant to pay for it."

At the Warrior meeting Buddy was asked, "Who gave you the authority to buy the plant?" He said, "Myself!" [79]

1978—Wilson Foods, Poultry Division

This acquisition is noteworthy for several reasons. First, it demonstrates the reality of Don Tyson's intuitive skill. The market went up a penny-per-pound each week for eleven weeks following the acquisition! Once again, what did Don Tyson know that the giant meat packer didn't know, and how did he know it—intuition, adaptive unconscious, gut instinct, luck, IQ, nanosecond-fast cognition, rational thinking? Research in the neurosciences is helping us to understand and use intuitive skills. In Don Tyson's case, he learned to trust his intuition and balanced it with the rational thinking of Leland and Buddy. He knew his intuitive skills were very good but were not infallible. In the Wilson acquisition, the value of the 01¢ per pound increase, based on the acquired capacity from Wilson during the eleven weeks, was over $5 million! Tyson paid $25 million for Wilson Poultry.

The second noteworthy reason is how the deal reinforced Tyson's strategy of segmentation, concentration and domination as related to Rock Cornish game hens. Some of the production and sales from the four plants was used to increase Tyson's share of the Rock Cornish market to 60 percent. At the time Rock Cornish hens were selling at twice the price of mature broilers.

1983—Mexican Original

This producer of corn and flour tortillas, based in Fayetteville, Arkansas, was riding the growth wave of Mexican fast-food restaurants and doing well, but wanted to sell for family reasons. Tyson and Mexican Original shared a common customer and distributor base that made the deal a win-win for both companies and customers.

Consolidation in the fast-food business (e.g., PepsiCo buying Kentucky Fried Chicken, Pizza Hut, and Taco Bell) worked in Tyson's favor because of its ability to satisfy their volume and product-development needs. Today, a company named YUM! Brands, Inc., based in Louisville, Kentucky, owns nearly thirty-four thousand restaurants in more than one hundred countries—KFC, Pizza Hut, Taco Bell, Long John Silver's, and A&W.

1984—Valmac Industries, Inc.—Tastybird Foods Brand

A convoluted acquisition made to order for Tyson Foods.

It was Saturday morning in Don Tyson's oval office. The triumvirate, Don, Leland, and Buddy, were doing what they had done sixteen times before—planning the next acquisition. It was time to acquire Valmac Industries, Inc., owned by Bass Brothers Investments in Ft. Worth. Don picked up the phone and called Sid Bass, asking if Valmac was for sale. Bass said anything Bass owned was for sale. They agreed to meet on Monday at Bass headquarters in Ft. Worth. They met, negotiated, and the deal was made. It was a checkmate move. The checkmated king was Clift Lane of Grannis, Arkansas.

Valmac, headquartered in Russellville, Arkansas, came out of the company founded in 1947 by Harold Snyder, a vocational education teacher who went into the contract-growing and feed business by organizing Arkansas Valley Feed Mills. In 1958 Snyder created Arkansas Valley Industries (AVI) from fourteen feed dealerships, a feed mill, a processing plant and a hatchery. In 1961, it became the first integrated chicken company to go public, selling thirty thousand shares of common stock and $600,000 in convertible subordinated debentures.

THE COTTON CONNECTION

Circa 1968 George H. McFadden & Brothers, a Memphis cotton merchant, bought control of Valmac. Robert D. McCallum, who spent his career with McFadden and its successor corporations, became the chairman of Valmac Industries.

Cotton money played a role in at least three chicken companies: Gold Kist in Georgia, Valmac in Arkansas, and Holly Farms in North Carolina. In 1968, the Federal Compress & Warehouse Company, Inc., sold its cotton compressing and warehousing business to a New York group for $33 million and bought Holly Farms. Money made in cotton was used to buy Valmac. In 1933, D.W. Brooks, agronomy instructor at the University of Georgia, and thirteen farmers in Carrollton, Georgia, borrowed $2,100 to form Cotton Producers Association. In 1972, the name was changed to Gold Kist, a co-op until they went public in 2004. The business evolved from a supplier of animal feed and other supplies into one of the largest chicken companies in the country.

Clift Lane, the checkmated king, began processing chickens in the railroad station in Grannis, Arkansas, in 1952. Through the 1970s he grew his company, and by 1980 it was one of the largest processors in the country. In 1979, Lane began buying small blocks of stock in Valmac Industries. At about the same time, Willard Sparks also began buying small blocks of Valmac Stock. The two of them had accumulated about 74 percent of Valmac's stock. These two men, both with roots in Oklahoma, were radically different in every other respect. Sparks earned his bachelor's and master's degrees from Oklahoma State University and his doctorate in agricultural economics from Michigan State University.

Sparks was regarded as one of the nation's leading agricultural economists, businessmen, and philanthropists. In 1977, he founded Sparks Commodities, where research analysts and consulting specialists served hundreds of the world's leading agribusinesses. He was part owner of Cattlco, Inc., one of the nation's largest cattle-feeding operations, and Vining-Sparks, a NASD-registered general securities firm in Memphis. He was affiliated with Refco, LLC, one of the world's largest futures commission merchants headquartered in Chicago, and held membership in the major U.S. commodity exchanges. He was a close personal friend and partner in numerous businesses with Shelby Massey, chairman of Valmac Industries.

Clift Lane has been described by some of his work associates as a "country boy who discovered his entrepreneurial skills growing and selling chickens." One of Lane's successful managers, Myer Westmoreland, was moved to Lane headquarters in Grannis, Arkansas, to stop some of the hemorrhaging that was draining Lane's cash reserves. Westmoreland identified two operations that were losing money daily. He told Lane they had to be closed. Lane's response was, "Close them if you have to, but how can we make money if we don't grow chickens?" Westmoreland is an example of not only how to survive being acquired, but how to thrive as a major contributor to the acquiring company. At the time of his retirement in 1997, he was a poultry operations executive at Tyson Foods.

Paul Whitley

The name "Valmac" is a contraction of McFadden and Arkansas Valley Industries. In 1979, Blake Lovette was lured away from his family's company, Holly Farms, by Shelby Massey, Valmac's chairman. When Lovette left Holly Farms, he was executive VP for poultry operations. Under Lovette's leadership and Dick Hill's marketing expertise, Valmac had become a successful marketer of value-added products to several niche markets: individually quick frozen (IQF) products to the U.S. Military Commissary; gram-sized bone-in IQF chicken parts to the foodservice market that needed precisely sized parts at a fixed, long-term price that enabled operators to fix menu prices for long periods of time; IQF chicken for the budding club store market; fresh, cut up, sized chicken parts for the chicken fast-food restaurants with an efficient delivery system to the restaurants; and boneless specialty products designed to the specs of the fast food segment. Valmac had become a low-cost producer under the direction of David Purtle, who became known as the low-cost-driver guy in the industry.

BLAKE LOVETTE'S ACHING BACK TRIGGERS A CORPORATE NAME CHANGE

Tastybird Foods, the business/image name of Valmac, came out of an experience Blake Lovette had watched a

NASCAR race. He introduced himself to the man sitting behind him as the president of Valmac Industries. There was a vacant seat with a back next to the man. The man said he didn't recognize Valmac and asked Blake what Valmac did. When Blake identified the brand Tastybird, the man smiled and said, "I am one of your customers!" Blake proceeded to change the name of Valmac to Tastybird Foods.

Valmac/Tastybird was doing quite well with sales near the $400 million level until in 1980, when Valmac Industries, the parent company located in Memphis, suffered heavy losses in commodity trading, especially coffee. Simultaneously, the checkmated king Clift Lane, who now owned controlling interest of Valmac, encountered the dual problems of a soft market and double-digit interest rates during the Carter presidency. At this time, Lane was the fifth-largest processor in the country. Tyson knew of Lane's problems and proposed an infusion of cash for a piece of the company. Lane rejected the offer and borrowed $9 million from Worthen Bank in Little Rock using his Valmac stock as collateral. In November 1982, Don Tyson bought the note from Worthen Bank through Stephens, Inc., and demanded repayment or foreclosure, which forced Lane to file for bankruptcy. Court records show, "On November 7, 1982, the Lanes, LPI and their affiliates filed petitions in the United States Bankruptcy Court for the Middle District of North Carolina, Greensboro Division, under Chapter 11 of the bankruptcy Code case numbers B-82-02012-C-11 to B-82-02031C-ll."

In April 1983, with a gaggle of attorneys representing creditors, three companies came prepared to make offers for Valmac. Tyson, who had seen Valmac as low-hanging fruit on the acquisition tree, was there. Archer, Daniels, Midland (ADM), the giant agri-company, was there with an offer in hand. Bass Brothers Investments was there, represented by an older, smallish-in-stature, gray-haired man. To most folks in court, including the judge, Bass Brothers was an unknown entity.

When the bids were opened, the judge acknowledged the Bass Brothers offer as the winning bid. Speaking to the attorney representing Bass, he said, "Sir, your bid is superior to the others. I've never heard of Bass Brothers. How does the court know they have the cash?" The attorney rose and identified a national brokerage company with local offices who had a cashiers check from Bass. Their bid was $35 million. The Bass acquisition of Valmac delayed Tyson's goal of owning those assets only briefly. In the late summer of 1984, Tyson acquired Valmac from Bass for about $70 million. In 1986, Tyson acquired the balance of Bass poultry holdings, buying Lane Processing for $108 million, making Tyson the nation's largest poultry processor.

Shelby Massey, Blake Lovette, and their team, combined with market economics, created a tailor-made acquisition target for Tyson. Don Tyson described the Valmac acquisition as one of the best he ever made in terms of return on his investment, niche market share dominance, and talent. Tollett said he thought they got their money back in less than two years.

The 1984 Valmac acquisition achieved Don Tyson's goal of doubling sales in 1985. It was a goal he had announced to securities analysts. Tyson sales FY1983 were $603,536,000. Sales FY1985 were $1,135,712,000. Once again, Don's goal-seeking mechanism worked perfectly.

GERALD JOHNSTON—DON'S GO-TO GUY TO FINANCE DON'S ACQUISITIONS

The work of arranging financing Tyson acquisitions was the work of Gerald Johnston, CFO. As described in Chapter 4, Gerald grew up poor near Atkins, Arkansas. He developed his work ethic and competitive spirit as a youth picking cotton to earn school money for the family. Gerald earned a finance and accounting degree at Arkansas Tech University in Russellville, Arkansas, where he was elected to the Arkansas Tech Hall of Fame. His finance and accounting skills served him well when he was assigned the task of arranging financing for Don's acquisitions.

Along the way Gerald had been working on his negotiating skills and building productive relationships with several banks around the country. Don called Gerald after he made the deal to buy Valmac and said he needed $71 million in two weeks. He had already signed a contract. Don had not provided Gerald with all the documents needed to satisfy bankers to secure $71 million. No problem—his competitive spirit of winning took over.

He contacted the bankers he had been grooming for just such a moment and invited them to a meeting in Dallas. He took one of his associates with him and at dinner the night before, he said that since he didn't have documentation the bankers would want, it was necessary to get their attention quickly by appealing to their ego needs to be successful. At 9:00 the next morning, several bankers came to the meeting room. Gerald thanked them for coming and said, "My boss has signed a contract to buy Valmac/Tastybird from Bass Brothers. I need a commitment for $71 million for this deal. Because of the short time frame, I don't have all the documents I know you will need. If any of you is nervous about this deal, please leave, as I need a commitment today!" No one left the room! Gerald Johnston, empowered by Don Tyson and confident in the relationships he had been building with bankers, produced the desired results.

GERALD JOHNSTON AND THE PROCESS OF EMPOWERMENT

Empowerment is another of those overused buzzwords that, when understood as a process, begins deep within the psyche of individuals. It is not something one person does for another.

The universal question is, how do we empower others? How do we get other people to take responsibility for their actions and our business? The answer is, you don't empower other people. You don't give other people their freedom. You don't legislate self-esteem. You begin with yourself. You cannot give to others what you have not claimed for yourself. Claim your autonomy, your vision; declare the organization you wish to create. Live that out at every moment. Then, and only then, make it easy for others to do the same. If top management wants to create a vision or a set of values for the organization, let them create it and live it out for themselves first—for two years or more. Then let them worry about how to engage others in the vision. Stop enrolling, start embodying. Enrollment is soft-core colonialism.

Peter Block [80]

1988—Trasgo, S.A. de C.V. (Trasgo) Mexico

Yakitori! Maquidora! Yakitori! Maquidora! Yakitori!

Yakitori is boneless chicken meat skewered on a bamboo stick, sauced with soy, marin, or sake, and sugar and honey, grilled over high quality charcoal, served in yakitori bars in Japan identified by red lanterns on the building and mouth-watering aromas wafting to the sidewalk.

Maquidora is a partnership arrangement designed by the Mexican government to create jobs along the Mexican border. Tyson acquired an 18 percent stake in a Mexican chicken processor based in Gomez-Palacio in northern Mexico. This enabled Tyson to capitalize on the maquidora idea by creating an international partnership with Japan and Mexico. Leg meat produced in the U.S. was shipped to the maquidora in Mexico, which was converted into yakitori and sold in Japan. In 1994, Tyson acquired 50.1 percent of Trasgo.

This acquisition "had pups," a phrase Leland used to describe product development, as Tyson applied its segment, concentrate, dominate strategy to Latin America.

A June 7, 2005, news release:

> Greg Huett, president of Tyson's International Operations, announced that in Mexico, Tyson has entered into an agreement that allows Tyson to purchase the interests of the Villegas family in Tyson de Mexico, S.A. de C.V. ...Additionally, Tyson de Mexico, S.A. de C.V., has purchased the poultry assets of Nochistongo S.P.R., a fully integrated broiler production with a capacity of approximately 500,000 birds per week, also located in Gomez Palacio...Tyson has also signed a joint venture agreement with Chinese partner Zhucheng Da Long

Enterprises Co., Ltd., to own and operate a further processing plant in China. This plant, located in the Shandong Province, is expected to be operational in September of this year. Par-fried, breaded, boneless leg meat products from the plant will be marketed into Japan, other countries in the Pacific Rim and certain countries in the Middle East...Tyson Foods joint venture operation in Panama City, Panama, with Aliment Procesados Melo, S.A., announced in April of 2000, has begun processing in a new facility. According to Huett, "These efforts move us quickly forward along our strategy of producing quality products for our worldwide customers from cost-effective global locations.

Greg Huett is another example of Tyson successfully acquiring and growing talent. Greg's first job was as a service tech working with growers producing chickens for the Tastybird Plant in Dardanelle, Arkansas. He attended the first Hispanic immersion training at Tyson's Management Development Center, led by Barbara Berry. When Tyson needed a manager for their Mexican acquisitions, Greg was ready. Following a successful career in sales he moved his young family to Torreon, Mexico, close to Gomez-Palacio, Mexico, where he was responsible for managing Tyson's operations in Mexico.

Don Tyson's interest in global marketing was noted in a *Broiler Industry* interview in June 1974. He had just returned from London where he was a project leader for the Harvard Business School and was describing the change process in his life:

> We all change. Goodness knows I've changed in the twenty-two years I've been in this business. For example, could you have imagined my need to get an international perspective on my food business at a business seminar in London, say, ten years ago?" Earlier, in the October 1968 interview in the same magazine, he said, "We're selling some products overseas now; it's less than 5% of our sales. What has happened to us in the past is that as soon as good international markets open up, trade barriers are erected and we lose these markets. The only way we feel our company can work outside the domestic United States is with production units overseas. As long as we have investment opportunities in the United States that will measure up to our ROI criterion of a 14% rate of return, we'd probably be reluctant to go overseas."

LEADERSHIP INSIGHTS

- Leaders think strategically. Strategic thinking is the process by which leaders envision the future and develop plans, structures, and systems necessary to achieve that future.
- In the twenty first century's competitive and rapidly changing market, twentieth-century bureaucratic methods of long-range strategic planning are becoming the buggy-whip symbol of the nineteenth century.

CHAPTER 6
1989 HOLLY ACQUISITION
The Mount Everest of Acquisitions
"Great things are done when men
and mountains meet."
William Blake

I treat this acquisition in more detail because it is a very human story about two men who were friends, competitors, and industry leaders; men who played together, shared ideas, made tongue-in-cheek calls to each other suggesting it was time for one to buy the other or the reverse. They were men who had demonstrated their capacity to be visionary and to put motive power behind their visions. Both of them had demonstrated by their behaviors that they cared deeply for the people in their company. They had big, healthy egos that were not allowed to get in the way of objective business decisions. Fred Lovette was a man of the Appalachian Mountains; Don a man of the Ozark Mountains. They had similar learning and working styles. Each man's sense of organizational integrity created productive work environments based on trust and knowledge of the human side of leadership.

On February 24, 1924, C.O. "Charlie" Lovette hauled three coops of live chickens and a few cases of eggs from Millers Creek, North Carolina, to Charlotte and sold his chickens and eggs to cafes, boarding houses, and hotels.

As he sold his produce, he took orders for the next week. This event marked the beginning of one of America's great poultry-based food companies, Holly Farms.

When Don Tyson announced on October 12, 1988, his intentions to acquire Holly Farms Corp., the parent company of Holly Farms, he set in motion the ultimate odyssey in pursuit of his goal to stand alone on the podium, winning the gold as a competitor in the poultry-based foods industry. Like Sir Edmund Hillary, a New Zealand bee keeper, nearing the top of Everest said, "I will know I am at the top when there is no more mountain to climb."

The three giants in the chicken business were Tyson, ConAgra, and Holly Farms. Two of the giants, Holly and Tyson, were family companies. ConAgra, a food conglomerate, had origins in Nebraska; in 1919 Alva Kinney brought together four grain mills as Nebraska Consolidated Mills. They funded the establishment of Duncan Hines in 1951, which was successful. In 1956, they sold Duncan Hines to Procter & Gamble and chose to expand in raw foods like poultry and livestock feeding. In 1971, they shortened the name to ConAgra.

The 1970s brought the company to the brink of ruin as it lost money expanding into fertilizer, catfish, and pet products. In 1974, Charles M. Harper (Mike), an experienced food industry executive, took over the firm and brought it back from the brink of bankruptcy…[T]he company set off on a decade-long buying spree, purchasing over 100 prepared food brands starting with its 1980 purchase of Banquet Foods. It moved heavily into the frozen-foods business and the packaged meat industry, and then picked up a selection of other brands from firms like RJR Nabisco and Beatrice Foods among others as the leveraged buyouts of the 1980s gutted and sold off many major American consumer product firms. [81]

Great adventure odysseys have their dramatic moments. Buddy Wray describes a dramatic acquisition moment in the nine-month battle to acquire Holly Farms. It was mid-April 1989; Don was in New York City working to close the deal. Buddy and Leland were in the offices of Stephens, Inc., the investment banking house in Little Rock. Don called to tell them he had raised the price from $63.50 to $70.00 per share!

The outcome of this odyssey of poultry giants would propel Tyson Foods to the top of the mountain as the poultry industry leader in the U.S. and the largest poultry-based food company in the global marketplace. The triumvirate had agreed early on that Holly Farms would be a good acquisition. The price to be paid for Holly stock had been discussed but not yet agreed upon. Before Leland and Buddy could move the conversation to a discussion of price, realizing the captain had made a price decision and was going to reel in the biggest catch in pursuit of his goal, Leland said, "OK, Don, anything you can buy, Buddy and I can manage!" And, so they did, thirty-six times between 1961 and 1997.

On several occasions, when Don was asked if there would be more acquisitions, his consistent answer was, "We'd buy this afternoon if the right opportunity came along. Acquisitions are like fishing—you never know when you're going to snag one. Our hooks are in the water all the time." [82]

THE LOVETTE FAMILY OF HOLLY FARMS

C.O. and Ruth Lovette-Bumgarner had seven sons (one died hours after birth) and one daughter, Bonnie Ruth. Fred was the eldest of the living sons—Fred, Rex, John Maurice (Pete), William Wade, Blake Duane, and Gene Allen. Fred was the visionary leader of Holly Farms, the nation's third-largest poultry company in 1988. This Scotch-Irish family of Millers Creek, North Carolina, lived and worked in that part of the Appalachian Mountain chain called the Blue Ridge. The Lovette family grew the business under Fred's visionary leadership. Pete (John Maurice) Lovette described his elder brother as a visionary man who loved the people in his company.

The Blue Ridge Mountain village of Millers Creek in Wilkes County was a generator of entrepreneurial leaders who found ways to create wealth. Lowe's home improvement centers began in Millers Creek with Lowe's Hardware store when Carl Buchan, part owner of the North Wilkesboro Hardware Company, bought out his brother-in-law, James Lowe, in Millers Creek. Lowe's Hardware sold overalls, horse collars, wash tubs, work boots, and an assortment of hardware items. Buchan could see the post World War II building boom coming. He bypassed wholesalers to keep prices low and focused on hard-to-find building materials and added home appliances.

THE NASCAR CONNECTION

North Wilkesboro, North Carolina, was the site of NASCAR's HOLLY FARMS 400 race. Both Holly Farms and Lowes were involved in auto racing. Holly Farms sponsored or worked with a number of drivers including Junior Johnson, who grew up in Ingle Hollow, not far from Millers Creek. Some of those early drivers were Cale Yarborough, Darrell Waltrip, Bobby Allison, Lee Roy Yarborough, Charlie Glotzback, Geoff Bodine, Bill Elliott, Jimmy Spencer, Neil Bonnett, and Terry Labonte.

Junior Johnson was working behind a mule pulling a plow when he was approached by his brother L.P. to drive one of the cars in a fill-in race at the North Wilkesboro Speedway. Using lessons he learned eluding the law hauling moonshine whiskey, he became an icon and a leader in NASCAR racing. Junior Johnson envisioned a personal future behind the steering wheel of a race car that was better and different than walking behind a mule and plow. He became a student of the behaviors of the lawmen whose goals were incongruous with his. Eventually the lawmen won, but not before the intrinsic seed of leadership had taken root deep in his soul.

JUNIOR JOHNSON, NASCAR AND HOLLY FARMS

Consider this: when tobacco advertising was banned from television, Junior approached R.J. Reynolds about sponsorship of his racing team. He met with Ralph Seagraves of RJR. He learned that RJR had budgeted millions for advertising and had no place to spend the money. Junior connected Seagraves with Bill France at NASCAR and a new partnership was created. This move inspired Budweiser, Tide, Maxwell House and others to spend their advertising dollars on the sport.

Junior Johnson's dad, Robert, operated one of the largest copper stills in the area making moonshine, which Junior succeeded in delivering to customers by outmaneuvering the federal agents, who in fact never caught him in a car. He was arrested at his daddy's still and spent eleven months in a federal reformatory. In 1986, President

Ronald Reagan granted Junior a presidential pardon and his record was wiped clean.

In 1960, Junior approached Holly Farms to sell them on sponsoring his race team. They made the deal. Junior was the primary driver until an accident in 1966 forced him to retire from driving. "Things race fans take for granted today were once unheard of. For example, NASCAR fans and teams alike can thank Junior Johnson when they use their scanners and radios. The first time a race team used radio communications between driver and crew was at Martinsville when Junior ran the race wearing a helmet equipped with speakers and a microphone. His sponsor, Holly Farms Chicken, used two-way radios to dispatch their trucks. Johnson says crew chief Rex Lovette and crewman Fred Johnson, "hit on the idea of using a couple of these radios to talk to me in the race car while they watched from pit road." [83] This was also the first time a driver turned the radio off on his crew chief. Junior's team warned him to take it easy after he had a commanding four-lap lead. It was not in his nature to slow down, and he did not back off. Junior wrote, "Rex kept cussing' and raisin' the dickens on the radio. He was on there so much that he was distractin' me, so I cut the darn thing off." [84]

"In 1960, Junior was driving a Chevy and struggled to be competitive against the dominant Fords and Pontiacs. As a privateer Johnson received no support from Detroit.

His Chevrolet was giving up 5–10 mph to the factory-backed machines. Trying to get a feel for race conditions in practice at Daytona, Junior tucked the nose of his car near the bumper of Fireball Robert's Pontiac and the Chevy took off. The concept of drafting in a stock car had just been applied for the first time. An aerodynamic phenomenon, drafting allows two cars running nose to tail to go faster than either could run alone…In the 1960 Daytona 500, Johnson drafted his way through the field, past the Pontiacs and to victory lane. A legend was born. By defeating factory-equipped teams Junior Johnson became a hero. Thousands of hardworking, blue-collar fans loved Junior (no last name was needed) and were proud that one of their own had 'made good.' Author Tom Wolfe wrote in his 1965 Esquire profile, 'God! Junior Johnson was like Robin Hood or Jesse James or David.' The sport of stock car racing would never be the same; quite by chance Junior had drafted NASCAR into a new era."

William Blake's line about what happens when "men and mountains meet" was right on as related to many of the pioneer leaders in the chicken business. The 2,015-mile long Appalachian Trail ends on Springer Mountain in the Chattahoochee National Forest, forty miles as the crow flies from Gainesville, Georgia, the home of Jesse Jewell, who started raising chickens in a wooden shed in 1936. He was working in his mother's feed, seed, and fertilizer business.

When he couldn't sell the feed to the poor farmers in the area he borrowed $6,000 from a local bank to lead his company to prominence as an innovator. Jesse Jewell was the first president of the National Broiler Council, 1954–1957. In 1963, he took his company public, the same year Don Tyson took his Ozark Mountain Company public.

The Appalachian Trail goes through the heart of chicken country. Maine, Vermont, Massachusetts, and New Hampshire were the source states of chicken genetics with the New Hampshire Reds leading the way. The states of Maryland, Pennsylvania, West Virginia, Virginia, North Carolina, South Carolina, Tennessee, and Georgia played a major role in the growth and development of the chicken industry. The Appalachian Mountains and the Ozarks made good sense to farmers as they sought cash crops that could be produced on small farms in mountainous and rocky terrain. On very few acres, farmers growing chickens could produce eight or ten "chicken crops," generating enough cash to sustain their farms. Cattle required hundreds of acres of grazing land and up to two years to produce one crop, and hogs required about a year to generate cash. These mountain people loved their way of life, and the economics of chicken farming enabled them to stay on the land.

The Appalachians, from Mt. Katahdin in Maine to Springer Mountain in North Georgia, produced a large number of the entrepreneurial pioneers in the chicken industry. As William Blake said, "Great things are done when men and mountains meet."

SIGNIFICANT EVENTS IN THE HISTORY OF HOLLY FARMS

Fred Lovette, Holly Farms founder, died March 16, 1988. Tyson announced their intention to acquire Holly Farms on October 12, 1988. Observers who knew both Fred Lovette and Don Tyson have speculated that Tyson would not have pursued Holly Farms as long as Lovette was alive.

The winter of 1988 saw the three largest poultry companies in a high-stakes legal battle. A precursor of the ensuing battle occurred when Charles Harper at ConAgra explored the possibility of a stock swap in the spring of 1988 with Lee Taylor II, chairman of Holly Farms Corp. The deal was sealed on June 24, 1989, after Tyson raised its bid to $70 per share.

A clarifying word about the ownership of Holly Farms: in 1968, Federal Compress & Warehouse Company, Inc., headquartered on Front Street in Memphis, Tennessee, sold their cotton compressing and cotton warehousing business to a group in New York for $33 million. Federal Compress & Warehouse Company, Inc., was founded in 1888 by Lee "Red" Taylor. He was followed by his son Bill Taylor, who was followed by Bill's son, Lee Taylor II. When the Federal

Company acquired Holly Farms Poultry Industries in 1968, Federal changed their name to Holly Farms Corp. Samuel Hollis, majority shareholder, said Red and Bill Taylor had accumulated a lot of cash over the years, much of it literally cash in the vault. Mr. Hollis is past president and founding member of the Memphis Society of Entrepreneurs and now lives in the Atlanta area. In 1968, Bill Taylor sold the Federal Company to a New York group for $33 million and used those assets to buy Holly Farms Industries in Wilkesboro, North Carolina.

INTERVIEW WITH FRED LOVETTE

(Based on an interview of Fred Lovette, January 17, 1984, by Dr. Ken May for the American Poultry Historical Society. The author acquired the audio interview from Michigan State University's Vincent Voice Library. The audio is identified by DB 153.)

1925—C. Fred Lovette was born January 1 to C.O. and Ruth Bumgarner-Lovette. Six more children followed: Bonnie Ruth, Rex Lane, John Maurice (Pete), William Wade, Blake Duane and Gene Allen.

1928—C.O. Lovette built the first "hot-house" in Wilkes County, growing three hundred chickens per house and selling live chickens delivered to grocery stores in coops and sold live to housewives.

1942—On completion of high school Fred borrowed $3,100 from his father to go into business for himself on Tenth Street in North Wilkesboro, North Carolina. His goal was to earn $75 per week buying and selling country produce in High Point and Greensboro, North Carolina, Washington, DC, Miami, New York City, and Chicago. He had learned the business riding with his daddy, C.O. Lovette, buying country produce from farmers and selling to grocery stores. C.O. bought eggs, chickens, cow hides, pork hams, pork shoulder, rabbits, and anything else that could be sold for a profit. Live chickens were delivered in wire coops and placed on the sidewalk in front of the stores. Housewives bought live chickens, took them home and processed them in the backyard. Fred said he remembers riding with Dad from his fifth birthday forward. Some family members said the mentoring of Fred began as early as age three.

1946—To level out the supply of live chickens Fred and E.S. "Izzy" Kendrick created New Way Feed Supply. They contracted with growers on a no-loss basis, which protected growers against loss and guaranteed a steady supply of live chickens. By 1948, they were selling fifty thousand live chickens per week.

When the war was over in 1946, the chicken market plunged as a result of overproduction. Fred had oral contracts with growers at 40¢ per bird. The market went to 30¢ per bird. Fred had accumulated considerable money and was able to keep every contractual commitment at 40¢.

1947—Harry Hettiger and local investors built a processing plant in Wilkesboro.

1953—On the first day of February, Fred bought half interest in the Wilkesboro plant that at the time had an operating deficit of $100,000. The plant was processing eighteen birds per minute. As the president, Fred plunged into the task of learning every function of plant operations from hanging live chickens to loading trucks with ice-pack chickens, while Izzy Kendrick managed the live grow out side of the business. By 1955, the plant had wiped out the deficit and had a net worth of $100,000. Fred bought Harry Hettiger's half interest and over time bought the outstanding shares owned by local investors. He then sold stock to Izzy. At the time they owned a hatchery and realized they needed to buy a feed mill. Izzy invested in a feed mill at Mocksville, North Carolina.

1957—They were operating three ice-pack processing plants. The Wilkesboro plant was producing seventy birds per minute; the Winston-Salem and Hiddenite plants, thirty birds per minute. They were selling five hundred thousand ice-pack chickens per week along the East Coast from New York City to Miami.

1961—There were sixteen chicken or related companies in the area including the Mocksville feed mill. Fred bought these companies using Holly stock and cash. There were sixteen people involved. Four of them took cash and went home. The other twelve took stock and made up the board of directors. By 1968, they had acquired thirty-eight more companies. Added to the sixteen, this made a total of fifty-four companies.

1963—In November, Gordon Johnson, an equipment manufacturer, presented a system of processing and packaging cut-up, case-ready, fresh chicken with extended shelf life for supermarkets. Johnson invited twenty-nine processors to a two-day seminar in Kansas City to demonstrate the process. The meeting began on Thursday morning. By about 4:00 p.m. his audience had dwindled to Fred Lovette and Francis Garvin. Lovette and Garvin said they were interested and would like to meet Friday morning and work out details. In the Friday morning meeting Johnson offered to reduce the franchise fee by fifty percent for the first year. A specialist who was working with Johnson, Bob Montgomery, was invited to fly to Richmond, Virginia, with the Holly men and drive to a plant in Glen Allen that was for rent. On Saturday morning, they looked at the plant and asked Montgomery to determine what it would cost to convert the plant to produce what they were to call "chill pak" (28 to 32 degrees) cut-up and packaged chicken. The cost was estimated to be $50,000, and the deal was consummated. The next task was to call on Safeway, Grand Union, and Giant supermarkets to measure their interest. They all responded affirmatively.

Lovette said, "You could never imagine their interest. They really wanted to get cutting and packaging chicken out of the stores." On February 1, 1964, they ran their first "chill pak" chickens and began to supply fifty-five supermarkets. After about six months of operating experience and major modifications to the process and incurring a loss of $100,000, Lovette had to go to the board and sell them on investing about $500,000 into the program. After a long and hard day of selling, the board voted to approve the deal. Lovette said the board meeting lasted until about 9:00 p.m. as the board wasn't convinced the concept would work. He encountered all the arguments of the resistance-to-change crowd. He said that if he had taken a vote at 10:00 a.m., the vote would have been fifteen against and one vote for spending the half million dollars. During the twelve-hour meeting at a late lunch, the board was served forty-two-day-old chill-pak chicken that had been held in ideal conditions. That was thirty-five days longer than the seven-day guarantee. There was no need for a forty-two-day shelf life; it was a test to prove a point. Lovette didn't tell the board until after they had eaten it. It was a convincing argument, and at about 9:00 p.m. the board approved the expenditure. They changed the name to "Holly Pak."

During the first full year of Holly Pak, the Safeway Store converted all 230 stores to Holly Pak. By 1976, all plants had been converted to Holly Pak. The Holly Pak process propelled Holly Farms to the top of the mountain of chicken suppliers to the retail food business.

Dr. Ken May concluded his interview of Fred Lovette by asking him about the key innovations that made Holly successful. He described the innovations in genetics, nutrition, and disease control that reduced the time required to produce a 4.5-pound chicken from eighteen weeks to seven weeks. He said the two major innovations were moving from New York dressed chickens to Holly Pak and Holly's success in branding their product by partnering with supermarkets to provide the consumer with the "perfect meat."

A FUNDAMENTAL DIFFERENCE IN STRATEGIC THINKING

In 1964 and 1965, Holly Pak became the standard by which supermarkets measured the value of fresh, cut-up, prepackaged-at-the-plant, pre-priced chicken versus doing that labor intensive work in the meat department. Holly was the brand preferred by consumers and retailers. The product commanded a premium price that became Holly Farms' unique selling proposition (USP). Both companies started by selling live chickens to grocery stores before the supermarket era that began when Clarence Saunders created the concept of self-service grocery stores with U.S. patent # 1242872. Sanders opened the Piggly Wiggly supermarket in 1916 in Memphis, Tennessee. The store had four aisles and was the first to have checkout stands. ^{cg} Before Saunders, grocers put their merchandise on shelves behind the counter, keeping the customer away from their merchandise preventing shoplifting (You can't trust the customer, you know!). According to the Smithsonian, the first true supermarket in the United States was opened by ex-Kroger employee Michael J. Cullen, on August 4, 1930, in a six-thousand-square-foot building in Jamaica, Queens, New York.

Tyson's strategy took the company in the direction of the food-away-from-home market—foodservice. With the 1966 acquisition of the Washington Creamery, Tyson was dominant in one category in the supermarket frozen case, Rock Cornish game hens. With the Prospect Farms/Dick Stockland acquisition of 1968, Tyson gained quick access to the foodservice market with fully cooked chicken products and a competent foodservice marketing organization. Although Tyson continued to sell ice-pack fresh chickens, frozen cut-up, and specialty items, it applied most of its resources toward the goal to segment, concentrate, and dominate profitable niches in foodservice.

The strategic decisions these two companies made in the 1960s caused very different outcomes. As Holly was enjoying success with Holly Pak in supermarkets, it continued to invest resources to expand its domination of the supermarket category. Tyson's heading on its investment compass was prepared products to foodservice. The acquisition history of the two companies bears that out. With the Krispy Kitchen acquisition of 1972, Tyson had success in the supermarket frozen-food case with their Ozark fried chicken sandwich product and with other specialty entries. Holly had success with their 970 chicken patties which they sold into both market segments.

Another differentiating factor was Tyson's *inability* to get comfortable with successes. If there were ever a question about the pragmatic power of one man's visioning, Don Tyson's leadership behaviors provide ample evidence of that power. For about a ten-year period, during the 1960s and into the 1970s, Holly Farms had not expanded their poultry operations all that much.

GROWTH HISTORY OF HOLLY FARMS

1961 sales—$31 million. From 1961 to 1968, sales grew 15 percent a year. At that time there were 326 shareholders, which was close to the number of 350 that required filing with the SEC.

1968 sales—$97 million.

1984—sales exceeded $700 million. Holly employed ten thousand folks and sold seven million chickens per week.

1988—At the time Tyson acquired Holly Farms, sales of the poultry division were in the $900 million range. Total sales of the parent company Holly Farms Corp. were at $1.5 billion. Poultry products accounted for 50 percent; flour and bakery 19 percent; national by-products 9 percent; food service 22 percent.

Beginning in 1963 and continuing to 1967, Lovette began talking to folks about going public. A couple of chicken companies, J.D. Jewell and Tyson Foods, had gone public, and they looked pretty good. Because of extreme fluctuations in the market, they were unable to convince a broker to take the company public. The brokers suggested Holly merge with a conglomerate, and they brought several conglomerates to them. A few of them were Ogden, Textron, International Foods, Ward Foods, and others. Finally in February 1968 they were introduced to the Federal Company in Memphis. The Federal Company was in the cotton compression and warehousing business and was looking for a way to leave that business as the future didn't look good. They sold their cotton business to a group in New York. In May 1968 they reached agreement and the Federal folks said they had about $40 million they could put into Holly.

WHY DID DON TYSON WANT TO ACQUIRE HOLLY?

Perhaps the most accurate answer to this question is found in observing Don's leadership behaviors over his forty-three years of leading the company from 1952 to his retirement as chairman of the board in 1995. Frederick Reichheld, in his book *The Loyalty Effect,* describes the importance of studying a company's performance over long periods of time.

Take the phenomenal success of *In Search of Excellence,* first published in 1982. In the tradition of American management "science," this book, based on theories of the authors developed by studying high-performance companies, became a bible for a whole generation of managers. It sold five million copies and spawned a whole new genre of business books claiming to reveal the key to business success. *In Search of Excellence* represented the best thinking of the business establishment. Its research included a painstaking analysis of twenty-five years worth of data, and a Who's Who of business leaders contributed to and endorsed the book's ideas. But over the course of the ensuing ten years, who do you suppose would have become richer: an investor who built a stock portfolio out of the companies profiled in *In Search of Excellence,* or someone who merely matched the mediocre performance of the S&P index? Believe it or not, mediocrity trounced excellence! Two-thirds of the publicly traded "excellent" companies have underperformed the S&P 500 over the last decade. Some have stumbled badly, and a few are close to extinction. The authors acknowledge that only one-fifth of their original group remains excellent today, while the remainder fall somewhere on a continuum from merely good to downright bad.

Don believed his shareholders deserved a good return on their investment, and his shareholders were the beneficiaries of his leadership.

When Don built Tyson's first processing plant in 1958 and began acquiring poultry companies in 1962, it was clear he was going to lead his company to the top of the chicken mountain. Charles Hobbs, a time management guru, gave us the principle of "concentration of power": "Concentration of power is the ability to focus on and accomplish your most vital priorities." [86] Don Tyson's focus to achieve his goal never went fuzzy. He never allowed his remarkable successes along the way to divert his attention from *growing* his business. His commitment to growth energized his people. His actions were consistent and congruous with his words that kept the workforce attuned to his vision. *Attunement* was the process whereby Leland and Buddy answered workers' question, "Why are we asked to do what they ask us to do?" Howard Baird in his many years in industrial relations at Tyson insisted that workers had a fundamental right to know the "why, what, and how" of their work. Leland and Buddy kept all Tyson resources *aligned* with Don's vision. Consider the fact that Don never lost control of his company. He managed the balance sheet so they could take advantage of opportunities and avoided any situation that might cause them to relinquish control. The fact of two classes of stock assured family control. They never, as Leland said, "piled up a lot of cash" that made publicly held companies a ripe target for being acquired.

TYSON FOODS AND HOLLY FARMS "BETTER TOGETHER"

When Don announced on October 12, 1988, his intention to acquire Holly Farms, he triggered one of the most fascinating acquisition battles in the food industry. It has been reported that on two or three occasions in the mid-1980s Don approached Fred Lovette about a "merger," followed by Fred approaching Don about a "merger." "Merger" is one of those soft words sometimes used to mask the reality of a takeover. This was not a merger as anyone who has been "merged" knows; it was about ownership, who ultimately had the deed to the mountain. Neither company could accept being in second place. Tyson was dominant in foodservice, and Holly was dominant in the fresh retail sector. Together, Tyson and Holly produced nearly enough chickens each week to equal the next three top poultry produces combined (ConAgra, Gold Kist, and Perdue).

Pete Lovette, one of the execs at Holly, told me that when he read *Barbarians at the Gate,* the story of the fall of RJR Nabisco [87], he could identify with the acquisition process. The story of Kohlberg, Kravis, and Roberts leveraged buyout (LBO) of RJR Nabisco broke in *The Wall Street Journal* in October and November 1988, the same time Tyson announced their intention to acquire Holly. The only common characteristic of the RJR Nabisco/KKR deal and the Tyson/Holly deal was the time the events occurred. LBOs have been variously described as using phony money to buy companies or stealing them. Tyson, after nine months of intense negotiations, used real money. Gerald Johnston, Tyson's CFO who led the financing of the deal, has a wall plaque in his home office from Bank of America with a copy of the check payable to Holly shareholders in the amount of

$1,559,000,000! Gerald also said that finding financing for the Holly deal was much easier than finding $70 million for the Valmac deal in 1974, as Tyson had proven to bankers over the years its ability to make money and succeed as a public company. Success begets success.

For nine months, from October 1988 to June 1989, the struggle for ownership of Holly was treated as a hostile takeover by Holly Farms Corp. (the Federal Company). They used every known legal defensive tactic as Tyson used every known legal tactic to complete the deal. The bidding began at $49 per share and increased several times until the Holly board accepted $70 per share.

One skirmish in the battle was described in *The M & A Journal:* It is the spring of 1989. The fax machine hums to life at the offices of Wachtell, Lipton, Rosen & Kats, then at 299 Park Avenue. It is just minutes before the 5:00 p.m. deadline for offers to be submitted for Holly Farms Corporation. ConAgra (a White Knight) is sending in its bid aimed at clinching its seven-month acrimonious fight against Tyson Foods for control of Holly Farms. Two pages emerge from the fax machine, with 31 pages to follow. Then—nothing. ConAgra's chairman, Charles Harper, has abruptly cut off the transmission. The fax machine comes alive again an hour later, this time disgorging the full text of the offer. The target's team (Holly) has no way of knowing what has happened. Harper and his rival Donald Tyson were in the midst of a telephone slanging match. The two sides had agreed that Tyson would pay ConAgra $50 million to withdraw from the fight, leaving Tyson with the target. The Holly Farms board and their advisors at Wachtell were waiting for final bids in the third auction for the company. ConAgra was not going to make an offer this time and planned on walking away with its $50 million instead. But Harper (ConAgra) decided to throw in another bid when, his side says, Tyson cut the $50 million down to $5.5 million, roughly equivalent to ConAgra's expenses, based on advice from Tyson's lawyers at Skadden. After two pages had gone through, Harper got a phone call from Tyson putting the $50 million back on the table, so Harper ended the fax. He asked to indemnify ConAgra for any liability that might ensue from the two-page transmission. When Tyson refused, the ConAgra chairman sent in his full bid to the Wachtell offices…Much of the frustration felt by Tyson, and much of the credit for the greatly increased price, can go to the lockup and to the fact that the target did not seek a final adjudication of its validity. Says one lawyer on the Holly Farms side: "They were mightily pissed off." [88]

When all the legal tacticians on both sides had exhausted their arguments and neither side could find a final solution in the courts, Tyson raised its tender offer to $70 per share. After Don Tyson and Charles Harper, in a limo trip from the airport in Fayetteville, Arkansas, to Don's office, offered ConAgra $50 million to vacate their interest, the deal was made.

Analysts, some Tyson folks, and others, debated the question as to whether the price for Holly was too high. In the end, price was negotiable; Don's goal of becoming number one wasn't. Leland Tollett at Tyson, Pete Lovette at Holly, and Holly shareholders generally agreed that Lee Taylor II met his obligation to his shareholders. One of the driving forces of the Tyson triumvirate was their responsibility to their shareholders. It was a matter of honor and respect.

Don had reached the top of the chicken mountain. In William MacPhee's book, *The Rare Breed* [89] Don is quoted as saying, "In my life, there has always been a mountain to climb and conquer. When you finish one mountain you are eager to see the next and the next. It's a never-ending quest to achieve; it's excitingly perpetual and a driving force."

Paul Whitley

RAMBO

The business press picked up on a symbol Vice President Kristin Ferguson, Foodservice Marketing VP, and her staff had created in an advertising campaign that targeted beef as the enemy of chicken. In the foodservice market, beef was the dominant protein on menus. The symbol was Rambo from the movie by the same name. The campaign was evidence of the third element in Tyson's strategic thinking—segment, concentrate, and dominate. The campaign employed war terminology and all the attendant war visuals. The campaign was very successful, not only as designed, but because it became something of a symbol of Tyson's battle to acquire Holly Farms. David Matassoni, [90] marketing guru in Tyson's marketing group, was the lead guy in creating Rambo and described the campaign as "having fun," one of Don Tyson's mantras about how to do good work. He outfitted Don, Leland, and Buddy with Rambo shirts, which in a special way relieved some of the stress tension that developed during the nine-month-long war. Sales folks who had extraordinary success in the sales campaign received plaques on which "dead" grenades were mounted. They acquired the grenades from a war surplus store. Some of those plaques were confiscated by the security folks at the Fayetteville, Arkansas, airport.

Rambo posters were placed in all the plants in an effort to enlist production workers in the war effort against beef. Matassoni tells the story of Tyson's VP of Industrial Relations, Howard Baird, calling him when one of the plant personnel managers discovered a Rambo poster on his bulletin board. Howard asked, "Is this Rambo character the end of a gentler and kinder Tyson Foods?"

This Rambo figure was picked up by *The Wall Street Journal* in a story dated October 13, 1988, one day after Tyson's intentions were announced. The *Journal* described a poster Don had unfurled at a stock analysts' meeting showing a muscular chicken standing upright and dressed as Rambo with battle helmet, grenades, and machine gun. Tyson's combat-ready chicken was a symbol of corporate tenacity and strength and the tremendous patience and iron will that Don displayed in his deep-sea fishing expeditions. [91]

KEY ACQUISITION INDICATORS AS TYSON PURSUED ITS GOAL TO BE NUMBER ONE

In the 1970s, the key acquisition indicators were Ocoma Foods in 1972 and Wilson Foods in 1978. These were key indicators because the two acquisitions gave Tyson a production capacity to solidify and expand its customer base in those market segments that were making money—removing the company further and further from commodity products. These acquisitions also made it costly for a competitor not only to play catch-up, but to move ahead of Tyson. These acquisitions were like moats protecting the castle. This was especially true for those competitors who had failed to build their business on value-added products—competitors like Cargill and ConAgra who were conglomerates with multi-interests in food marketing vs. Tyson's single focus on chicken.

In the 1980s, the key acquisition indicators were Valmac in 1984, Lane Processing in 1986, and Holly Farms in 1989. Leland Tollett describes the Valmac and Lane acquisitions as two of the most important. Valmac's product lines were a natural fit with Tyson's value-added products for the foodservice market. Each product was highly profitable in niche markets. The price paid for Valmac was right. The Lane acquisition met a huge need for more production capacity. Tyson really needed more chickens, brick, and mortar. These were key indicators because they increased Tyson's lead in market share, production capacity, and capital resources. Or, perhaps it is more accurate to call it a critical mass as a scale or volume at which processes become self-perpetuating. It was the process of moat-building to ensure Tyson's competitive advantage. The move to acquire Holly Farms was a checkmate move. One major exception was Pilgrim's Pride of Pittsburg, Texas, who, by smart acquisitions, including ConAgra's poultry division in 2003, has become the nation's second-largest processor.

ACQUISITION INFLUENCES ON TYSON'S CORPORATE CULTURE

Scholars of corporate culture have generated a bunch of empirical knowledge on forces that change a corporation's work culture. Some Tyson acquisitions had little change effect, as their way of getting work done was similar to Tyson's. Acquisitions that moved Tyson's work culture a few degrees were the 1966 Washington Creamery acquisition, the 1974 acquisition of Vantress, the 1984 acquisition of Tastybird/Valmac, and the Holly acquisition of 1989.

- 1966: Retention of Washington Creamery senior execs influenced the way marketing would be done by Tyson for years to come. They provided the professional expertise Tyson used to move its products from the vagaries of commodity products to value-added products.

- 1974: Vantress became a key factor in how Tyson used chicken genetics, nutrition, disease control, and breed management, which gave Tyson a significant competitive advantage. This acquisition completed the vertical integration process that gave Tyson virtual control of all the processes at work in satisfying customers, shareholders, and workers.

- 1984: Tastybird/Valmac's product line not only fit Tyson needs perfectly, it also brought a competent low-cost team to Tyson. Tastybird's CEO Blake left the company, after discovering there can't be two kings in the same palace. David Purtle, Tastybird's production VP, had developed a reputation of being one of the industry's best low-cost operators. That was validated when Tyson saw Tastybird's numbers. When David was moved to the Production VP job at Tyson, he brought his experience with him and became what some perceived to be a need—an influence on Tyson to alter its focus from being a sales-driven company to becoming a production-centered company. Leland became the chairman and CEO in 1995 when Don reached his sixty-fifth birthday. He managed these cultural conflicts very well as he kept the players behaving in the adult mode most of time. In the 1995 annual report, he wrote, "First, a little about our organization. We have only one profit center—our sales and marketing organization. It is focused on the customer and the consumer; all other departments are cost centers serving sales and marketing. The cost centers focus on product quality and cost reduction rather than market pressures, thus contributing to a longer-term focus."

- 1989—The Holly acquisition was a case of one giant swallowing another giant, as they were about the same size. Having made more than thirty successful acquisitions, Tyson had learned how to maximize acquired resources by dominating the culture of acquired companies, evaluating and accepting cultural differences as ideas that would supplement and/or improve on Tyson's culture. The Holly acquisition introduced a new variable into the cultural equation. First, it was by any definition "hostile" as evidenced by the nine-month legal battle. Second, it is more difficult to integrate two giants than it is for a giant to integrate a smaller organization. Third, both companies, though publicly held, were historically "family" companies. The heads of acquired family companies encounter for the first time in their history the loss of power and influence acquired over many years—it can't feel good. Many Lovette family members and relatives stayed with Tyson and made significant contributions to Tyson's future successes. There was some concern that if family members and their relatives bailed, Tyson would lose good people and complicate the process of integrating the two companies. Most stayed and did very well.

Don had developed a reputation of dealing fairly with employees of an acquired company. Pete Lovette, who stayed on through the acquisition process assisting with finance and personnel issues, told the writer that Don deserved high marks for protecting the pension plan. In that era, greedy and avaricious "Wall Street acquisition barbarians" targeted companies that had large, vulnerable pension plans. Don, once again, behaved as a man of integrity.

To "sell" Holly folks on Tyson, Don convened a meeting of senior and middle management folks in Atlanta to begin the process of "Tysonizing." Next, he convened a meeting in North Carolina of Holly workers in an auditorium and shared his philosophy. The workers were paid while they were away from their plants. He also walked the production lines of Holly plants, shaking hands and introducing himself. He presented a list of seven hundred names of key Holly supervisory and management folks to the Management Development Center in Russellville with the task of bringing the two cultures together. In those training sessions, Holly folks and Tyson folks identified possible problems that could cause conflict and committed to resolving them. This writer had never experienced such an emotional and pragmatic coming together of persons emerging from a potentially "hostile" situation.

The Holly Farms Corp. acquisition included businesses in flour milling, bakery supplies, a Pennsylvania-based poultry company, a pork processor in Michigan, a beef and pork processor and distributor in Le Mars, Iowa, and two breaded-beef processors in Texas. Tyson immediately sold off the flour and bakery supply business and integrated the beef and pork companies into its product mix. Management had aspirations that beef and pork products would be accepted by their foodservice distribution base as part of Tyson's goal to become the dominant supplier of all center-of-plate proteins. After a couple of years experience, the company learned it just didn't have the muscle in beef and pork to achieve what had been achieved in chicken. Tyson sold those businesses and introduced a marketing campaign called, "We're Chicken."

When the integrating processes were complete and management folks were able to get back to their daily work routines, subtle, almost imperceptible, attitude changes began to surface in hall conversations about the future. It was kind of like an NFL football team winning a Super Bowl and learning there would be no more Super Bowls! "When you have climbed to the top of the tallest mountain…" Don had said he would retire as chairman on his sixty-fifth birthday, which he did on April 21, 1995. Leland was fifty-eight and became the chairman and CEO; Buddy became the president and COO at age fifty-eight. Don's son, John, age forty-two, was president of the beef and pork division. Gerald Johnston, CFO, was fifty-nine. Bob Womack, former senior exec in sales, was the first to leave corporate; he moved to Seattle in 1993 to head up the Tyson seafood group. He left Tyson in 1995.

One by one, senior managers retired early, taking their considerable wealth to do other things. The writer has interviewed all of them. Their reasons for taking early retirement ranged from "It was just time to go" to "I knew I couldn't move any higher in the leadership hierarchy." One of them said, "I got tired of the Buddy notes," which I am sure Buddy would consider a compliment to his communications methods.

1992—ARCTIC ALASKA SEAFOODS CORPORATION—OOPS!

In pursuit of their goal to be the dominant supplier of all center-of-plate proteins, Tyson had flirted with the seafood category for some time. At one point the company researched shrimp farming in Hawaii. The idea was discarded. In 1992, Don went beyond the flirting stage and fell in love with Arctic Alaska Seafood Corporation, based in Seattle with operations at Dutch Harbor, Alaska. When Don presented the idea to Leland and Buddy, they nixed the deal, temporarily. One of Don's axioms was, "Never acquire a business you don't know how to run." We had also heard him say that he didn't want to be in a business that didn't control the sex life of the animal. They had certainly done that with chicken—one rooster with ten hens had worked well. As is often true in love, flirtatious behavior leads to marriage, which is how Tyson got in the seafood business. They didn't just "get in" seafood—it was full throttle ahead as they quickly acquired Louis Kemp Seafood Company from Oscar Mayer, a subsidiary of Kraft-General Foods. Kemp was a processor of *surimi*, a Japanese word that means "minced fish." The end products were faux crab and lobster-flavored delights. In 1995, Tyson added Multifoods Seafood, Inc., acquired from International Multifoods Corporation.

Arctic Alaska was founded by Francis Miller, who took advantage of the Magnuson Act (federal legislation that extended U.S. territorial waters from twelve to two hundred miles offshore). The Act gradually phased out the dominant Russian and Japanese fishing fleets, reserving for U.S. boats some of the richest fishing grounds in the world. Miller acquired fishing vessels to integrate fishing, crabbing, at-sea processing, sales, and distribution through a series of partnerships that were consolidated in 1988. Ron Jensen joined the company, and Merrill Lynch packaged Arctic Alaska to sell. When Tyson completed the acquisition, Miller took his money and invested in the floating-casino boat business. Arctic sales at the time of the acquisition were in the $200 million range. Jensen stayed on. John Tyson ran the division for a time, followed by Bob Womack in 1993. Womack's job was to stop the hemorrhaging as losses continued out of control. He successfully turned the business from a loss to a profit. He retired from Tyson in 1995 when it was clear that Arctic had become a victim of a bunch of what strategic planners called "environmental barriers" to success. There were too many high-tech fishing boat captains chasing too few fish, complicated by federal and state regulations and biomass replenishment. It was an "oops" acquisition. In July 1999, they completed the sale of the assets of the Seafood Group.

In a *60 Minutes* interview, Mike Wallace asked Don about the Arctic Alaska acquisition. Wallace asked Don how much he paid for Arctic and how much he lost. Don answered, "I paid $225 million. I lost about $205 million." Wallace then asked, "Who bought it?" Don answered, "I did. It's on my shoulders." How refreshing to find a man taking responsibility for his decisions—good or bad—a freeing kind of behavior! Don never wasted time blaming others. Mea culpa—next question, please!

Twelve more acquisitions were made up to the time the writer retired in 1997. In the Mike Wallace interview, Don told Wallace that in business there was no second place—you have to win. He led his people and shareholders to the winner's podium for all the gold medals in the chicken business. What was Don Tyson's motive for all those gold medals? Was it the gold content? Was it accumulated power? Was it greed? At the risk of walking into the quicksand of moralistic judgmentalism, considering his leadership behaviors and their impact on the lives of persons of acquired companies, most of those folks have done very well. The exceptions were those at the very top of the acquired companies whose careers were changed. They were compensated fairly; those with large blocks of their company stock added to their personal wealth. The writer, based on personal knowledge, analysis of the record, and research into the lives of workers at all levels, believes Don's controlling motivation was to be number one by being the best in the chicken-based food business.

Don believed he could have a bigger piece of the pie by making the pie bigger and finding more ways to satisfy customers with innovative products and services.

LEADERSHIP INSIGHTS

- Leaders possess and accumulate power, which they can use for the common good, a diminishing idea in a culture of individualism and celebrity, or misuse for uncommon evil. How they use their accumulated power defines their legacy.

- "When my *power* serves my sense of *justice*, I am *loving*.
  When my *love* really guides my use of *power*, I serve *justice*.
  When my *love* and my commitment to *justice* are rightly connected, I get true *power*."

Paul Tillich, theologian and Caryle Marney, philosopher, clergyman, theologian.

CHAPTER 7
INVESTING IN SCIENCE AND TECHNOLOGY TO ACHIEVE A COMPETITIVE ADVANTAGE
"By the way, Lord, thanks for the chicken!"

Tyson invested heavily in technology and science to build a protective moat around the business to achieve a competitive advantage. Their objectives were to get ahead and stay ahead of competition by using science and applied technology in the areas of product development, manufacturing proficiencies, food safety, warehousing/distribution, and information management. The investment paid significant dividends over time.

Tyson's investment in science and technology was well known. Knowing this prompted Reverend Jim Anderson, pastor of Wesley United Methodist Church at Russellville, Arkansas who was giving the dedicatory prayer at Tyson Management Development Center in Russellville. Reverend Anderson is a tall, slender, distinguished southerner with beautiful white hair, whose bass voice has god like qualities. He prayed and lifted up to the Lord all those seated on the platform. Don Tyson, Leland Tollett, Buddy Wray, and other execs were properly honored for their achievements and contributions to the industry and to the community.

He concluded the prayer, "By the way, Lord, thanks for the chicken! Amen." The audience sat quietly. Time passed—was this a sacred or secular moment? When the audience "got it," they broke into a noisy, secular applause. Brother Jim, as he was known to his parishioners, like the prophets of old, gave the event a sense of proper perspective.

Don Tyson on a number of occasions had said, "I was lucky to have a daddy who was in the chicken business." The chicken was the raw material, the commodity stuff that was transformed using science and technology.

Science and technology were among the basic building materials used to build a moat around Tyson products that gave them a significant lead on their competitors, which they never surrendered.

In the late 1940s, the industry paradigm for breeding was to breed only pedigreed birds—no crossbreeding allowed. Mr. John Tyson changed the paradigm of the always risky status quo mentality by flying in New Hampshire Reds from the "Live Free or Die" state to crossbreed with other breeds. The experiment began in 1946. He bought a forty-acre farm to test his theory. When the single airplane landed at Drake Field in Fayetteville, the press was present to record the event. Crossbreeding proved to be the superior method, enabling breeders to pick and choose genetic characteristics they desired.

Pioneer ag-aviator Ray Ellis, who managed South Central Air Transport (SCAT), began flying baby chicks into Drake Field from distant hatcheries. "By the early 1950s, the situation had reversed itself; northwestern Arkansas was producing more baby chicks locally than they could use. Consequently, Ellis began flying baby chicks out." [92]

The work and worth of science was one of the critical success factors in the growth and development of Tyson Foods. Don Tyson studied poultry science at the University of Arkansas. Buddy Wray and Leland Tollett earned degrees at the U of A in animal husbandry and poultry nutrition. Leland hired Dr. James Whitmore to succeed himself as poultry nutritionist. Whitmore did his undergraduate and master's work at the University of Arkansas and his doctoral work at the University of Nebraska.

Visitors arriving at Northwest Arkansas Regional airport (XNA) discover something of the role of poultry science at Tyson Foods when they look at the Points of Interest display in the arrival lounge. The large display gives directions to the University of Arkansas in Fayetteville and the John W. Tyson building at the Center of Excellence for Poultry Science.

The Center is a $26 million facility for training poultry scientists. At the 1993 ground-breaking ceremony, department head Dr. James H. Denton was leaving the tent set up for the event. Don Tyson caught up to him and asked him how many students were enrolled in the department.

Dr. Denton said, "Nineteen."

Tyson asked, "How many would you like to have?"

Denton answered, "Two hundred."

Tyson, always seeking ways to make his company better, said, "I'll help you, and I want a crack at the best of the bunch."

Denton and Tyson—two visionaries who shared individual visions for mutually beneficial objectives that, when achieved, would influence the poultry-based food industry and consumers around the world.

The groundwork for the Center of Excellence for Poultry Science was laid in two preceding events. Dr. T. Lionel Barton, winner of the Pfizer Poultry Science Extension Award for distinguished service and president of the Poultry Science Alumni organization, told me the story about event number one. The University of Arkansas, College of Agriculture was established in 1905. Dr. Barton joined the faculty as Extension poultry man in 1967. He was Mr. Poultry. In 1979, Dr. Barton received a phone call from Dr. Whitmore at Tyson Foods. Whit said, "Get your stuff together. We have a $1.5 million grant from the state Legislature for you to use to expand poultry science at the university." Dr. Barton targeted those dollars to build the essential requirements to eventually become a world-class poultry science department.

The second event occurred circa 1987 when the Good Suit Club, an organization of leading business leaders in the state, proposed and promoted funding a poultry science center at the university. A goal of $20 million was set for construction funds for the Tyson building and a pilot processing plant included $10 million in federal matching funds shepherded through Congress by Senator Dale Bumpers, who sat on the powerful appropriations committee in the Senate. The state issued bonds for $5 million, and $5 million was raised from poultry companies and Arkansas utility companies. During construction, they discovered they were short about a million dollars to complete the project. The board decided to eliminate something from the plans to stay on budget. My university contacts tell me that Don Tyson said he would pick up the difference to make the dream come true.

THE INTERNATIONAL ASPECT OF POULTRY SCIENCE

Long before the threat of the avian influenza virus H5N1, poultry scientists around the world collaborated to expand their knowledge of Reverend Jim Anderson's chicken. Several years ago scientists at the University of California, Davis, produced a featherless chicken that was designed to solve the problem of feather disposal. In Israel, "An Israeli researcher had developed a strain of featherless chickens that were less fatty and better adapted to survive in tropical climates where cooling systems are needed to raise poultry." [93] In Nanjing, China, April 14–17, 2006, Dr. Robert Wideman, associate director and professor of poultry physiology from the Center of Excellence for Poultry Science at the University of Arkansas, was the keynote speaker at the International Conference on Avian Nutritional and Metabolic Disorders.

The success and growth of the food-based poultry industry has been inextricably connected to the "excellence" of the scientific work in poultry science at a dozen or more poultry sciences schools.

ACADEMIC VISIONARIES AT WORK

Dr. James Whitmore, group VP, Research and Quality Assurance at Tyson Foods, directed the scientific work at Tyson for twenty-six years until his untimely death caused by heart disease in 1997 at age sixty-two. Dr. James Denton at the University of Arkansas described one of Whitmore's many strengths as his understanding of the critical societal issues of food safety, environmental stewardship, and waste management.

Whit, as he was known by his associates, met James Denton when Denton was at Texas A&M where he did his postgraduate work. Whit was on the staff at the poultry science school at A&M until he came to the University of Arkansas as director and department head at the Center of Excellence for Poultry Science. These two men collaborated on and developed a food safety program for educating poultry growers, processors, retailers in foodservice and supermarkets, and consumers.

Whit was known to be a direct and candid communicator. He did not waste words in circuitous dialog. As the science czar at Tyson, he seemed to always be in a hurry, except when it came to mentoring his staff. He was the epitome of the law of self-fulfilling prophecy—his people lived up his high expectations.

The writer knew Whit as a dedicated team player who had mastered the art of negotiation. One of the bright, young talents on the training staff at the Management Development Center, Scott Stilwell, was leading the task of teaching the organization how to apply process management principles advocated by W. Edwards Deming. He was doing an effective and affective job. Whit called the writer and asked for a meeting to discuss Scott's future. At the meeting, Whit, using a combination of his well-developed negotiating skills and the cold logic of a scientist, convinced the writer that Scott's talents would be multiplied several times over by transferring him to Whit's department. Whit was right. At this writing, Scott is a senior exec in the department. Scott described one of the guiding principles of his young life this way: it is more effective to idealize the real than to realize the ideal—wisdom beyond his years.

Scott was a fearless instructor as he went about his work of introducing a sometimes misunderstood concept that was difficult for some managers to buy into. On one occasion he was teaching a group of German engineers who lived by the "inspect out the defects" mind-set that was contradicted by Deming's concept of eliminating defects from the process. David Purtle in poultry operations was working with a German manufacturing firm that had little manufacturing experience in the poultry business. Picture this: eighteen middle-aged German engineers listening to this young American teacher with an Arkansas chicken company describe how statistically based process management principles were superior to precision German engineering methods! Scott said, "Japanese automobiles are better than German automobiles using the old 'inspect out the defects' model—achtung!"

What followed was a perfect picture of the power of adult learning methods to change paradigms. After several minutes of Mercedes-Benz versus Toyota talk, sometimes in German, sometimes in English, sometimes both, Scott succeeded, as he proved statistically that managing the process produced a higher quality product at a lower cost than the inefficient method of inspecting out defects.

DR. JAMES WHITMORE, THE MAN

Whit grew up on a "two-mule farm" in South Arkansas, not far from where Leland Tollett grew up. Two mules meant they didn't have tractor. He had an environmentalist's respect for the land and enjoyed living on his farm north of Springdale where he raised cattle. His son, David, who works at Tyson's corporate office, said he saw his dad in the stands at most of his school's sporting events. Whit was a scratch golfer and a bird hunting partner with Tollett and Wray.

His custom-made office desk, a gift from Don Tyson, made trips to his office especially interesting—interesting in that when he was behind that remarkable desk, his visitors were conscious of being with a remarkable human spirit. As a scientist, he knew and understood living things. Like Black Elk, the Oglala Sioux holy man, he knew and understood man's relationship with Mother Earth. Today, Dr. Rick Roop, department head, sits behind Whit's desk and speaks with affection and professional pride of the man who mentored him. Whit's being in a hurry never kept him from being on the school board or participating actively in his church and his community.

His successor at Tyson, Dr. Ellis Brunton, said Whit was one of the most highly respected scientists among his peers and among the federal regulators at the USDA.

Dr. Brunton described Whit's relationship with the regulators as 90 percent partnership and 10 percent adversarial.

During the Clinton gubernatorial and presidential years, contrary to most press accounts, the two Clinton administrations were not particularly friendly with the poultry industry. Clinton writes in his autobiography, [94] describing his losing the governor's mansion to Republican Frank White in the election of 1980: "He [Frank White] had strong support from all the interest groups I'd taken on, including utility, poultry, trucking, and timer companies, and the medical associations." President Clinton, in the White House, transformed the partnership relationship established by the George Herbert Walker Bush administration into an adversarial one. The industry was pushing for science-based inspection and regulation while the administration clung to the more traditional inspection-by-eyeball functions of the USDA and the Food Safety and Inspection Service (FSIS).

Perhaps part of Whit's legacy will be his long and stubborn commitment to improve food safety using science vs. some of the archaic and arcane methods of an unscientific past.

WHITMORE'S INFLUENCE ON THE HIGHER-LEVEL THINKING AT TYSON FOODS

For several years, researchers in neuroscience, education, anthropology, and sociology and curiosity-driven adult trainers have pursued ideas of higher and lower levels of thinking. The *Journal of Agricultural Education* at Texas A&M University, [95] using Bloom's Taxonomy and Newcomb-Trefz models, describes the differences:

Blooms taxonomy---Newcomb-Trefz Model----Two-level skills model

Knowledge--------Remembering-------	Lower-order thinking skills
Comprehension--Processing----------------------	" " " "--------------
Application------------- " ----------------------------	" " " "--------------
Analysis----------- ------" ----------------------------	" " " "--------------

Synthesis----------Creating-------------	Higher order thinking skills
Evaluation--------Evaluating---------------------	" " " "--------------

Consider the genius Nikola Tesla and his fluorescent lightbulb, neon lights, speedometer, automobile ignition system, radar electron microscope, and the microwave oven. Chances are most moderns don't know about him, even though they use products of his inventive mind.

Now consider the alkaline storage battery, carbon-button telephone transmitter, cement work, electric distribution system, electric generator, electric locomotive, electric pen, incandescent lamp, mobbing picture camera, microphone, mimeograph, ore separator, perforator for automatic telegraph, phonograph, printer of stock ticker, printer for telegraph, and the telegraph repeater, This genius, of course, is Thomas Edison.

Both are recognized as geniuses. Both possessed lower-level thinking technical skills. A basic difference in the outcomes of their work was Edison's higher-level thinking, which included conceptual and human skills. Tesla was a loner. He worked alone and was reluctant to trust another human being. Edison was the epitome of trust and collaboration. He understood, as did leaders like Don Tyson, James Whitmore, and James Denton that one person doesn't possess all the skills required to achieve their goals and to maximize their effectiveness as leaders.

Across the careers of these men, they found those persons who had the skills they lacked and partnered with them. They also learned to process and transform failures into profitable learning experiences and profitable products.

BACKWARDS THINKING—A METHOD TO MODERATE THE PERCEPTUAL BLOCKS OF NONVISIONARY PERSONS WHO DO THE WORK OF VISIONARIES

The Triumvirate used a thinking technique to evaluate innovative ideas and systems called *backwards thinking*, or what Stephen Covey in *The 7 Habits of Highly Effective People* [96] called "begin with the end in mind." The purpose of backwards thinking is to moderate the influence of those in the organization who can kill an innovative idea by their total focus on all the things that can go wrong. President Kennedy used backwards thinking when he announced to a joint session of Congress on May 26, 1961: "We will land a man on the moon and return him safely to Earth this decade!" On July 16, 1969, Apollo 11 left planet Earth. Three and a half days later, July 20, astronauts Collins, Aldrin, and Armstrong touched down on the Moon with less than thirty seconds of fuel left in the lunar module Eagle!

There were those naysayers who didn't buy into Kennedy's vision for a variety of reasons. One reason is what J.L. Adams calls *perceptual blocks,* which he describes as "obstacles that prevent the problem-solver from clearly perceiving either the problem itself or the information needed to solve the problem." [97]

One of the vital skills of leaders is their understanding of perceptual blocks and having the intellectual tools to moderate the negative effect of these blocks in problem solving. Don Tyson and James Whitmore used this skill, which on the surface seems so easy yet in practice is difficult for some. The consummate micromanager has difficulty seeing beyond the problems of innovative ideas of entrepreneurial visionaries. Micromanagers need the balance of those whose vision is always forward to moderate their vision, which tends to be yesterday—the overuse of rearview mirrors. Micromanagement may be a useful parenting skill; it is not a productive leadership skill. However, leaders need those with highly developed analytical skills to prevent fatal mistakes of flawed visions.

Backwards thinking is an effectual antidote to a vision defect that blinds persons to seeing distant objects. The skill of visioning is absent from the tool kit of some in the organization. Everyone at Tyson didn't have what Tollett described as Don's "ability to see around corners." From an organizational perspective, that was good. Most of us did our work in the present tense, implementing our leader's vision.

THE PERCEPTUAL BLOCK OF COMPLEXITY

The mind-set of complexity was, in Don Tyson's mind, a deterrent to productivity. Over and over in many situations and in many ways, we were reminded of the value of simplicity. William Occam, a fourteenth-century English logician and Franciscan friar, gave us the expression, "Given two equally predictive theories, choose the simpler, and the simplest answer is usually the correct answer."

Peter Senge writes about dynamic complexity: "Evidence is overwhelming that human beings have cognitive limitations. Cognitive scientists have shown that we can deal only with a very small number of variables simultaneously. Our conscious information processing circuits get easily overloaded by detail complexity, forcing us to invoke simplifying heuristics to figure things out." [98]

THE INNOVATIVE IDEA OF AN ANIMAL FEED INGREDIENTS PLANT: TRANSFORM AN INDUSTRY PROBLEM INTO A TYSON PROFIT

Tyson's practice of challenging industry assumptions gave it a dramatic competitive advantage. For years, the industry lived with the disposal problem of blood, feathers, and guts. They built rendering plants to alter the products to be used in some profitable fashion. Rendering plants weren't particularly welcome in the community, and if the wind were blowing in one's direction, one's olfactory nerves came alive! Rendering plants were used by all, providing little competitive advantage.

In 1986, Tyson invested big dollars to build an ultramodern and technologically superior animal-feed ingredients plant at Morrison's Bluff on the Arkansas River in the River Valley of central Arkansas. It gave them a seven- to ten-year advantage over the competition by a process of converting by-products from commodities to value-added ingredients for animal food manufacturers. It was environmentally friendly and produced feed ingredients to the specifications of animal feed manufacturers.

Five years earlier, Leland Tollett, seeing the demand for white meat exploding, met with Dr. John Hardiman, geneticist at Cobb-Vantress, a Tyson subsidiary, and told Hardiman that Tyson needed a 5 percent competitive advantage by designing a chicken with more breast meat. In a relatively short time Hardiman met Leland's goal!

The lowly barnyard chicken, humblest critter of all the critters in the food chain, proved to be the most valuable, because the chicken, whether by intelligent design or evolution, was the most receptive and responsive to change.

Reinvention of the chicken by scientists was one of the keys that unlocked the door to developing the most efficient and healthful animal protein for human use. The chicken became the ultimate protein-conversion machine!

TYSON INVESTS $52 MILLION IN A DISCOVERY CENTER

Tyson's Discovery Center—the name exudes Don Tyson's belief as a food futurist—to learn, to discover, to create, to apply, to satisfy consumers!

On June 2, 2003, Chairman and CEO John Tyson announced the grand opening of their newly expanded and upgraded Food Safety Laboratory located a few blocks south of Tyson's world headquarters.

> The $5.2 million expansion more than tripled the laboratory's square footage, providing a state-of-the-art facility that has greatly increased Tyson's capabilities in analytical testing and food safety research. This laboratory has devoted a sizeable area solely to food safety research where new food safety products and processes will be tested for effectiveness. Additionally, each year hundreds of Tyson Foods' more than 3,000 Quality Assurance team members attend training and certification classes in the latest laboratory techniques at the Springdale facility...The new lab is set apart from other food laboratories in the United States, in that it is one of the few that

has earned two International Organization of Standardization (ISO) certifications. The lab holds certifications for ISO 9001-2000, which creates guideline standards for quality management and improvement through prevention of nonconformities, and ISO 17025, which is a standard specifically for testing and calibration.

To update ongoing investments in scientific work at Tyson, Greg Lee, CAO and international president, and Hal Carper, senior VP, Research & Development, e-mailed their description of Tyson's Discovery Center (at the time of writing it was under construction). The e-mail, dated October 21, 2005:

> In the areas of food technology and research, Tyson Foods has made dramatic industry-leading commitments to the future. At the time of this writing, the Research and Development professionals include over 50 who hold advanced degrees. Of those, 11 have earned the Ph.D. The company's widely admired heritage of investing in people will be further enhanced by the $52 million investment in the new Discovery Center, due to open in December 2006. The project is over 100,000 square feet with 20,000 square feet devoted specifically to kitchens, a 39,000 s.f. USDA-inspected Pilot Plant, and a 42,000 s.f. office to house the Research and Development team. The Discovery Center will be the focal point for the development of insights, people, processes, and new and innovative products. Bringing together Tyson's protein research and development

into a single location, the workspace is designed to maximize communication and collaboration with learning optimized and applied across all the proteins (chicken, beef, and pork).

The Discovery Center will contain:

- seventeen product development kitchens
- separate focused consumer products and foodservice presentation kitchens for key customer visits and product presentations.
- a consumer focus group area.
- a proprietary sensory testing lab packaging lab for development of new, value-added packaging solutions.
- a dedicated facility for shelf life studies.
- pilot plant with three highly versatile production areas featuring an enclosed viewing area for visitors to see the entire production area without entering the plant.

From establishing consumer insights, to innovative idea inception for new products, to pilot plant trials, through commercialization, the Tyson team will have the best available resources to power their consumers and customers with innovative, value-added products for the future.

In a more recent news release, "The network, which includes eighteen Tyson laboratories across the country, has received the Quality Award presented annually by *Quality Magazine* and DuPont's Qualicon award." Dr. Neal Apple, VP of Network Services for Tyson, leads a team of 235 professionals who conduct research and millions of food safety tests each year, protecting consumer health and consumer satisfaction and safeguarding the North American food supply.

Dr. Apple, leading a tour of his facility, described some of the scientific work being done there including a microbiology research center, which conducts complex studies on microbiological pathogens, and a DNA-based technology that will enable the microbiology department to identify microbial strains according to genetic composition. Emphasis will be placed on: innovative microbiological interventions; shelf life evaluations; expanded nutritional analysis for food products and poultry feed; expanded research on pathogens such as listeria monocytogenes, Salmonella and Campylobacter; pathogen lethality studies; microbiological challenge studies; allergen testing; and expanded pesticide and feed ingredients testing.

On the tour, the writer spoke with several of the folks who work there. One of them called him aside and suggested he read Dennis W. Bakke's book, *Joy at Work*. [99] When asked why she recommended the book, she said, "Bakke has captured Don Tyson's passionate belief that people should have fun at work."

Neal Apple's team has learned to have fun at work. Neal Apple possesses the pragmatic balance of head and heart, which has served Tyson leaders very well. His followers create personal power for him that serves him well, especially working with his superiors' position power. He is one of those leader-followers who models Don Tyson's principles of leadership. His leadership behaviors have created a results-driven team, focused on satisfying their internal and external customers.

COBB-VANTRESS, QUINTESSENTIAL DESIGNER OF CHICKENS

Investing in genetics gave Tyson a competitive advantage by defeating in-breeding depression with the hybrid vigor of genetic design. As early as 1976, Tyson was counting the dividends of their investment in genetics. The 1976 annual report states the following:

YEAR	AGE (days)	WEIGHT (lbs)	FEED EFFICIENCY FACTOR
1948	84	3.57	3.17
1951	84	4.27	2.86
1955	70	4.39	2.63
1965	63	4.62	2.15
1972	56	4.50	1.99
1976	53	4.40	1.90

James Bell, president of Cobb-Vantress, described his company as "a research and development company, engaged in the production, improvement, and sale of broiler breeding stock, committed to integrity, quality, and progress through involvement with our team members, customers, suppliers, and community."

Poultry science and production technology methods have given the chicken industry not only a completive edge over the other proteins, they have given consumers a safe, affordable, and healthy variety of versatile food products for all meal occasions—at home or wherever they are when hungry.

This writer remembers his grandmother "wringing the neck" of a chicken in the backyard on their Kansas farm for chicken dinner on Sunday. Today a million chickens can be processed in federally inspected plants in one week, converted to finished food products available for dinner from a supermarket or a restaurant.

Consider that efficiency improvements have reduced the time to grow a mature broiler from sixteen weeks to five or six weeks depending on bird size desired, combined with feed conversion improvements from four or five pounds of grain to produce a pound of chicken—and that is without growth hormones! Dr. John Hardiman, VP, Research & Development at Cobb, said both the time required to produce a broiler and feed conversion rates would come down each year for the foreseeable future. Listening to Hardiman explain genetics is like listening to a conversation between noted dress designer Louis Vuitton and a lady of fashion. Hardiman says, "Tell me what you want your chicken to look like, I will design it for you and have that chicken ready in a relatively short time."

Michael Porter, in his landmark research, *Competitive Strategy* writes, *"Forward integrations can often allow the firm to differentiate its product more successfully because the firm can control more elements of the productions process."* [100]

THE UNIVERSITY OF ARKANSAS AND TYSON FOODS

As a leader in the poultry industry, Don Tyson's actions demonstrated his belief that making the pie bigger was key to earning a bigger piece of a bigger pie. He made the pie bigger by listening to customer and consumer needs and satisfying those needs. He earned the right to a bigger piece of the pie by outperforming his competitors in product development, financial and information management, efficient distribution methods, and hiring the best and the brightest—full utilization of all the resources available.

The partnership he built with the University of Arkansas was like all productive partnerships: mutually beneficial. Contributions from the Tyson Family Foundation and other Tyson entities at the university are in the millions. One of those gifts in 2004 endowed a chair at the Dale Bumpers College of Agricultural, Food, and Life Sciences. "Named for the retired President and COO of Tyson, the Donald 'Buddy' Wray Chair in Food Safety will support areas key to Arkansas' economy, including food processing and poultry processing. Research sponsored through this endowment will help ensure the quality of future processes and products. The chair holder will provide the additional faculty capacity needed to bring the University's food microbiology program to national and international prominence."

U of A Chancellor John A. White said:

We are extremely grateful to Tyson Foods for their ongoing support of the Bumpers College. Endowing and naming a chair for Buddy Wray not only honors him, but it also honors us by permanently associating his name with the University of Arkansas...Tyson Foods' participation in the Campaign for the Twenty-First Century fuels our vision of a nationally competitive, student-centered research university serving Arkansas and the world... John Tyson, chairman and CEO of Tyson Foods and chairman of the Campaign for the Twenty-First Century Corporate and Foundation Committee, said Tyson Foods is proud to be able to support the University of Arkansas by endowing this chair in the critically important discipline of food safety. We're also extremely pleased this endowment will honor

Buddy Wray, who, as part of the Tyson Foods family, spent his career devoted to the excellence for which our brand has become known. [101]

WHATEVER AND WHENEVER WE NEEDED SOMETHING, DON TYSON'S GENEROSITY WAS EVER PRESENT.

These sentiments were expressed as living testimonials about Don's lifelong generosity. I interviewed Dr. James Denton, Dr. Lionel Barton, Dr. Diane Bisbee, Dr. Richard Forsythe and Dr. E.L Stephenson.

LEADERSHIP INSIGHTS

- Tyson's investment in science and technology was driven by the leaders' need to prioritize and concentrate resources required to meet their long-term business goals, and to avoid the high costs of wasting limited resources.

- "Concentration of power is the ability to focus on and accomplish your most vital priorities to achieve optimum effect."
  Dr. Charles R. Hobbs, *Time Power*
  Harper & Row, © 1987

- A caveat: "Science alone of all subjects contains within itself the lesson of the danger of belief in the infallibility of the greatest teachers in the preceding generations...As a matter of fact, I can define science another way: Science is the belief in the ignorance of experts." [102]
  Richard Feynman, American and Nobel Prize Winner

CHAPTER 8
Politics, Government, and the Media

Summarizing Arkansas politics is, as Abraham Lincoln once said of running a democracy, about as easy as shoveling fleas. For every generalization, there are obvious exceptions. Every characterization must be qualified, and every label must be modified. [103]

The election of William Jefferson Clinton to the U.S. presidency in 1996 introduced a new dynamic to the management team at Tyson Foods. Don Tyson tells about a 1974 conversation he had with Bill Clinton, professor of law at the University of Arkansas, just down the road from Tyson headquarters. Professor Bill Clinton has just lost his first political campaign—his attempt to unseat Republican Congressman John Paul Hammerschmidt, a hard-working, thirteen-term congressman from the third district of Arkansas. When the election results were known, Don spoke to Professor Clinton, and said, "Bill, if you ever need a job, call me, you'd make a great sales manager."

Bill never called. He had other plans. As a high school boy, active in the Boys Nation program, he campaigned and won a trip to Washington, DC. He and his buddy Larry Taunton had lunch with two powerful U.S. senators from Arkansas, J. William Fulbright, chairman of the Foreign Relations Committee, and John McClellan, chairman of the

Appropriations Committee. The next day, the group toured the White House, meeting President Kennedy in the Rose Garden. Clinton's goal-seeking mechanism kicked in; his plans were made.

Don Tyson's goals were already well defined. By 1974, he had already acquired nine poultry companies in pursuit of his goal. Little did either man realize they would be the objects of a media blitzkrieg twenty years later. The stories ranged from the acerbic to the absurd.

A May 1994 *Wall Street Journal* article implied that the poultry industry might be getting preferential treatment by the Clinton administration, given the first family's close ties to chicken mogul Don Tyson. When that edition of the *Journal* reached the desks of Tyson execs in the high-carpet area, it triggered something of a debate—should Tyson respond, and if so, how? Those opposed to responding talked about cheap ink of the print media; the danger of TV news sound bites and Don's "Don't poke a skunk" theory; the need for the press to sell papers using salacious and sensational bylines. Don wrote a letter to the *Journal* saying, "Neither I personally, nor Tyson Foods, Inc., has in any way asked or received special or preferential [treatment] from any Clinton administration." He went on to say that his company works very closely with government agencies in seventeen states to ensure a safe poultry supply. "Our own quality standards are generally much higher than those required by government." [104]

The day after the story broke, Mike Wallace of the CBS program *60 Minutes* called Tyson and suggested he appear on the show and talk about his relationship with President Bill Clinton. Tyson said he would think about it. The senior management team, including Bob Keyser III, [105] a longtime Tyson friend and media relations consultant, met to make a decision about Don going on *60 Minutes* with Mike Wallace. Some warned of cheap ink in the print media and their need to sell papers using salacious and sensational bylines. Others warned of the dangers of TV sound bites. Then there was Don's theory about kicking a skunk. Those who thought that Don's appearance would be beneficial were Don and John Tyson, Archie Schaffer, and Bob Keyser. The decision was made to go on *60 Minutes*, and Don called Wallace accepting his invitation.

60 Minutes was near the end of its season, which gave Don time to prepare, and prepare he did. One of his leadership strengths was his commitment to learning. During that summer Tyson had a major corporate meeting of about four hundred Tyson folks at Colorado's Ski Resort at Keystone. They were in the middle of another very good year and used the Keystone meeting to celebrate current performance and identify ways to take Tyson to the next level. Don Legge, at Tyson's management center, created a twenty-foot mountain, outfitted senior managers with climbing gear, and choreographed their climbing to the summit! Each Tyson participant received a bronzed rooster, under glass, a model of "Big Red," Tyson's first corporate symbol.

Two other events of note: David Purtle, in operations, was teaching the operations people to enjoy the Chinese culinary delight, chicken paws. Don was learning how to manage the upcoming *60 Minutes* interview, working at Bob Keyser's Keystone cabin. He learned and performed well.

The show aired September 25, 1994. A few of the highlights: Wallace opened the interview asking Tyson about the national press reporting that he was a good FOB—Friend of Bill—asking Bill Clinton for favors for his company.

Tyson responded, "Asking a reporter to correct a mistake is like kicking a skunk; it just makes it smell worse." Tyson told Wallace he had seen Bill twice in two years; once in Arkansas at a social occasion and once in the White House during a Saturday group tour and he didn't have an appointment.

Wallace: "Have you talked to him on the phone?"
Tyson: "No, sir, not in two years."
Wallace: "You seem to go to great pains to minimize your clout with Bill Clinton, why?"
Tyson: "Because I don't have any."
Wallace: "A lot of people say, 'I know Bill Clinton.'"

Tyson: "I do know him. I know the governor of Texas, the governor of Oklahoma, the governor of Tennessee. That is part of my job." Continuing the interview Wallace, looking into the camera, said, "To keep his company growing Tyson acknowledges that he courts politicians who can pass laws either to help him or hurt him. He woos politicians with his wallet…why?"

Tyson: "If there's a race on, a political race, and there are two different views, and one of them we think would be better for our company and our people, we try to support that view."

Wallace: "Is there anything wrong with that?"

Tyson: "I don't think so. It's part of our system, and I see it as part of my responsibility."

Mr. John Tyson, the founder, also believed he had a responsibility for protecting his business from politicians who proposed or supported legislation that was unfair to farmers and farm agricultural companies. In 1953, Francis Cherry, Arkansas' Democratic governor, vetoed a bill repealing the 2 percent sales tax on feed. The tax had been in effect a couple of years, cutting into the already narrow profits in growing chickens and driving some growers to move to Missouri.

Cherry suffered the same fate as Clinton. Mr. John and Arkansas chicken farmers and producers supported Orval Faubus from Greasy Creek, Madison County, in northwest Arkansas.

As a young businessman, Don was active in Democratic Party politics, especially in western Arkansas. David Pryor, at the Clinton School of Public Service, adjacent to the Clinton Presidential Library in Little Rock, tells an endearing story about Don's involvement. Pryor knew Don for forty years—the years Pryor served in the U.S. Senate for four terms, the U.S. House for three terms, and one term as Arkansas governor. Pryor tells a story about Don coming to his campaign headquarters in Little Rock for a meeting. Someone had spray painted an obscenity on the building wall. Don volunteered to find someone to clean it up. A few days later, Don, with a case of spray paint, a tall ladder, and another campaign worker, Billie Schneider from Fayetteville, cleaned it up.

Billie Schneider is described in Clinton's book, *My Life:* [106]

> The local political hangout was Billie Schneider's Steakhouse on Highway 71, north of town. Billie was a hard-boiled, gravel-voiced, tough-talking woman who'd seen it all but never lost her consuming, idealistic passion for politics. All the local politicos hung out at her place, including Don Tyson, the chicken magnate whose operation would become

the largest agricultural company in the world, and Don's lawyer, Jim Blair, a 6'5" idiosyncratic genius who would become one of my closest friends. A few months after I moved to Fayetteville, Billie closed the steakhouse and opened a bar and disco in the basement of a hotel (Mountain Inn) across from the courthouse.

Back to Senator Pryor's endearing story—Billie Schneider lost her life to cancer in 1985. On Don's last hospital visit with Billie Schneider, Don asked her what he could do for her. She asked him if he would have a memorial plaque made for her burial site in the Fayetteville Cemetery on Mission Boulevard. He said yes and asked her what she wanted on the plaque. Billie Schneider said:

BILLIE SCHNEIDER
DEC. 15, 1925 "MAMA" SEPT. 14, 1985
"A YELLOW DOG DEMOCRAT"

Billie Schneider, "yellow dog Democrat," rests in the Garden of the Last Supper on a hillside facing the rising Arkansas sun. It is a contemplative place that encourages quiet meditation about lifelong friendships, shared ideals, and having fun along the way.

JIM BLAIR, Esq., "ONE OF CLINTON'S CLOSEST FRIENDS" [107]

Jim Blair was the "closest friend" of Bill Clinton, not Don Tyson. Blair's connection with Tyson Food goes back to the time Blair, as a young and struggling lawyer joined the law firm Crouch, Blair, Cypert & Walters. They had represented Mr. John Tyson beginning in 1935. Crouch provided counsel when Tyson went public in 1963. When Mr. Crouch died and his other partner was named a federal judge, Blair signed on as Tyson Foods' corporate lawyer. When Blair showed up for work, Don told him to see Howard Baird, VP, Industrial Relations, to complete the new employee paperwork. As Howard was walking Blair through the new employee orientation, Blair interrupted Howard and said, "I can't work with all these restrictions," and headed for Don's office. They worked out an in-house consulting contract that was in place until Blair retired in 2000.

In my interview with Blair, [108] at the end of the employment story, he smiled broadly and made this confession, "I have a defect which I discovered when I was three—I don't tolerate authority very well!" Blair is a kind of Hemingway adventurer. He finds adventure in building and maintaining strong relationships, and enjoys adventures in art, architecture, music, literature, archaeology (his office looks like that of a paleoanthropologist), philosophy, fast cars (he and Bill Jaycox at Tyson raced each other down the Pig Trail from Fayetteville to Tyson's Management Development Center near Russellville—Corvette vs. Mercedes Coupe), politics, making lots of money, philanthropy (e.g., the Blair Library at the U of A), physical fitness, and food. During the interview, his executive assistant Nancy Williams buzzed him. He graciously apologized for the interruption saying the call was important. The caller told him that morel mushrooms would be served at lunch; a lunch date was arranged.

Not to give the media a pass they haven't earned, but to explain the confusion about the Friends of Bill—who were they? Some of them were "Red Bone," a manager at Tyson Foods who introduced a twenty-year-old Blair to the futures market.

Bone "made and lost four or five fortunes," but remembered his good friend Blair when he was on top. The two started trading together, and the rest is a well-chronicled story that landed Blair spots on the front page of *The New York* Times and on *Good Morning America*. "I made a dozen or so of my friends a lot of money," says Blair. "Unfortunately, one of them was Hillary." Blair oversaw trades for then first lady Hillary Clinton that garnered her $100,000 return on a $1,000 dollar investment in cattle futures and other commodities. It got a lot of publicity, but it was really innocent. [109]

Another Friend of Bill's was Diane Kincaid, a professor at the University of Arkansas law school. She met Blair when they were wrangling over control of a county caucus meeting in 1972. They were married September 1, 1979, at the Fayetteville home of Dr. Morriss and Ann Henry. Governor Bill Clinton performed the ceremony.

Professor Diane Kincaid taught political science at the university and became good friends with Bill and Hillary when Bill was teaching there. The Clinton-Blair Camelot-like relationship was and is a story of profound friendship. Diane lost her life to lung cancer June 26, 2000. President Clinton, speaking at her memorial at the Walton Arts Center in Fayetteville, describes the depths of their friendship.

> 'It doesn't take long to live a life. And I guess what I would like to say today is that somehow, I felt about her as I have rarely felt about any human being, that she had this peculiar blend. She was beautiful and good. She was serious and funny. She was completely ambitious to do good and be good but fundamentally selfless. Sometime in our mid-thirties when Hillary and I were living in the governor's mansion we woke up one day and realized we might not live forever and that something could happen to us, and we actually made out a will. And I called Diane and Jim and said, "You know, we're making out this will. Would you raise Chelsea if anything happens to us?"

DON TYSON, ARCHIE SCHAFFER, SENATOR DALE BUMPERS, JIM BLAIR, SENATOR J.W. FULBRIGHT

This story is about how things work in a small, rural state, 2.7 million folks, similar to the population of Chicago. The population density of Arkansas is 51.3 persons per sq. mile; Chicago, 12,300 per sq. mile. The business and political environment in small, rural states is one that enables business and political leaders to work together to solve problems and achieve mutual goals. Everybody who wants access to influence political and business decisions knows who, where, and how to do it. Little Rock is the banking and political center of the state. From any corner of the state one can drive there in three or four hours, conduct business and drive home the same day.

Exhibit A: In 1974, Dale Bumpers, Democratic governor of Arkansas, from Charleston, Arkansas, challenged J.W. Fulbright for his U.S. Senate seat. Archie Schaffer from Charleston managed the campaign for Bumpers, Archie's uncle by marriage. Jim Blair, Tyson's legal council, managed Senator Fulbright's campaign. Bumpers and Schaffer won. Fulbright and Blair lost.

In Bumpers' 1970 campaign to defeat Governor Winthrop Rockefeller, Schaffer tells about "Uncle Dale" coming to Springdale to solicit Don's support for his gubernatorial campaign. As the two talked, Don told Bumpers his hair was a little long for the times. Don called his barber, invited him to his office to cut "Uncle Dale's" hair. Now, that is political correctness and political clout! Schaffer managed the campaign and Bumpers, a virtual unknown in the state, won.

Archie worked for "Uncle Dale" until 1977 when he became the administrator of the family owned nursing home in Charleston. Bumpers' first political office was on the Charleston School Board. Charleston was the first school district of the eleven-state Confederacy to integrate its public schools after the U.S. Supreme Court's Brown vs. Board of Education ruling in 1954. The handwritten entry in the Charleston School Board minutes says simply, "Motion by H.E. Shumate, seconded by A.R. Schaffer [Archie's dad], that we disband the colored school and admit the colored children into grade and high school. It passed unanimously." [110]

Eight years later Archie opened a public and government relations firm in Little Rock, Schaffer & Associates. In 1987, he was hired as executive director of the Arkansas Business Council, a position he held until he joined Tyson Foods in 1991, where he was once again associated with Jim Blair, Tyson's general counsel.

The Arkansas Business Council, better known as "The Good Suit Club," was formed by Don Tyson, Sam Walton, Charles Murphy of Murphy Oil, and other corporate leaders whose purpose was to improve the lives of Arkansas through school reform. Archie did the work of the council until Bob Justice retired as Tyson's director of media affairs in 1991. "Don Tyson pegged Schaffer as Justice's successor. Archie said, "At the time, I thought I was leaving a hot seat in Little Rock for a cushy corporate job in the pastoral quiet of the Ozarks. It hasn't quite worked out that way, largely because our governor decided to run for president about six months after I got here. Our alleged connections with Clinton, which have been greatly exaggerated, caused a media blitz for Tyson; it's an onslaught that will probably continue until Clinton is out of office. Still, I am tickled to death that Don gave me the opportunity to join this company." [111]

Archie Schaffer's contribution to the state of Arkansas, to the Arkansas Poultry Federation, and to Tyson Foods is extraordinary, and he is still contributing today as Tyson's senior VP, External Relations. Hired in 1991, Don invited Archie to come to Springdale and talk to Leland Tollett about how he viewed his job. This is the way the interview developed:

> I told Leland, I thought the company needed to be more aggressive in telling the public what Tyson Foods is all about. He suggested that I tour our

operations to see if this approach would work. I spent the next three months visiting forty-seven of our then fifty-four plants and decided that we did indeed have a great story to tell. That's about when Bill Clinton got elected to the presidency. Since then, it's been an ongoing challenge to get our story told. If we can ever get this political nonsense behind us, we can make a concerted effort to get the Tyson story out. I'm of the firm belief that we need to be open in dealing with all the attention this company is currently receiving. Had we not been open and honest during the past two or three years, the news accounts would have been far worse than they have been...An example of this attitude is the recent interview Don Tyson held with Mike Wallace for the *60 Minutes* TV news program. That show was our biggest recent success. ...A lot of people thought we were crazy to even consider doing an interview with Mike Wallace. [112]

Following the 60 Minutes program, Archie and Bob Keyser received a spectacular Lalique crystal rooster from Don, the leader who always had time to say "thank you."

ARCHIE SCHAFFER

Of the many knights of Don Tyson's roundtable, none were more courageous, loyal, competent, articulate, patient, tough, professional or gentle or endured so much personal pain doing his job. He lived out Don's principle of having fun at work and that meant having fun, day after day after day when you–know-what was hitting the fan. The last time the writer had coffee with Archie he was going shopping for cowboy boots to attend President George W. Bush's Black Tie and Boots Ball!

LEADERSHIP INSIGHTS

- Leaders are truth tellers
- Leaders, as they aggressively pursue the goals of the organization, understand they operate in the context of local, regional, national, and international communities and wisely guide policy decisions by behaving responsibly.
- Their first responsibility is to the success of the organization. Their second responsibility is to the communities where they operate.
- Accountability is the act of behaving responsibility.
- Leaders manage relationship with the media, and governments by applying the tools of truth telling forthrightness, and effective communications.

0

CHAPTER 9
PACKAGING AND TRANSMITTING THE SPIRIT OF DON TYSON—TRAINING AND DEVELOPMENT

London, Arkansas, 1985—A Place for People to Grow

Following Tyson's 1984 acquisition of Valmac/ Tastybird, Leland Tollett, president and CEO, announced a reorganization plan in 1985 designed to build on the strengths of the two companies. One of the items in his announcement was, "The appointment of Paul Whitley, formerly of ConAgra and Tastybird Foods, to a new position as director of Strategic Planning and Development for Tyson Foods. Beginning in late August, Whitley assumed primary responsibility for developing strategies for long-term management development to meet the needs of the company as it reaches its $2 billion goal. A management training agenda is now in preparation for mid-April start-up...Whitley will be based at the Tyson's Management Development Center (TMDC) in London, Arkansas (seven miles west of Russellville, one hundred miles southeast of Springdale, eighty miles west of Little Rock), where he will direct operations. In addition to his primary responsibilities, Whitley will also be in charge of development of the broker sales force. Such training plays a key role in the effectiveness of broker salespeople in the field. He will report to Buddy Wray, senior VP, Sales and Marketing. [113]

DOING THE WORK OF THE TRAINING AND DEVELOPMENT MISSION STATEMENT

The mission statement that was formulated in Buddy Wray's office in his first meeting with Whitley was typical of Tyson's history of making work more productive by organizing work around the people closest to the work. They had observed and acquired several companies who had become bloated with layer upon layer of supervision and management that effectively transferred the work of decision making from people closest to the work to a class of patriarchal authorities located in central offices far removed from where the work was done. It was clear from the writer's interview meeting with Tollett and his mission formulation meeting with Wray that they had developed a habit of agreeing on the work to be done and leaving the implementation to those closest to the work. They had been using this leadership principle successfully for twenty-five years. Please note, they never used the word "empowerment," a word that was becoming a buzzword in some management circles at the time. When you were assigned a task at Tyson Foods, you were empowered. There was no need to restate what had been obvious for years. It was inherent in the culture of having fun at work. In the mission statement formulation meeting, Buddy used two words, two behavioral principles that guided the implementation of our mission: responsibility and accountability. Responsibility for the work implied commensurate authority to do the work. When the people doing the work behaved responsibly and developed a habit of being accountable to themselves for their work, workers were free to grow, and to have fun at work.

This way of doing work, for those accustomed to hierarchical work structures, was not an easy adjustment. At best, they were uncomfortable doing work the same old way. At worst, they couldn't make the adjustment and chose to leave. Most chose to stay, clinging to the status quo like nonswimmers clinging to flotation devices in fast-moving water. This group presented the biggest challenge to the training and development staff. These were the folks who had learned how to work in a corporate environment where managers walk the halls and attend endless meetings at a central office where generals, popes, and assistants to assistants report to the lesser gods who report to the god who sits high and lifted up, whose job was to divide up the dividends of loyalty at the end of the year—the pomposity of egocentric hierarchies!

The eight-word mission statement was another example of Tyson's aptitude for simplicity—reducing perceptions of complexity. Was Don Tyson's idea of simplicity relevant to our work of creating a curriculum and building the facilities for training and development? We knew the answer was yes.

Implicit in the mission statement was the idea that we didn't have to invent or create something new—our task was to develop an experiential learning environment that would be most conducive for adults to learn the Tyson way of doing work.

A. SITUATIONAL ANALYSIS

1. Tyson had a workforce of eight thousand.
2. Tyson's newly acquired Valmac/Tastybird workforce of eight thousand doubled the workforce to sixteen thousand! The number of production plants grew from eight to sixteen; sales doubled from $750 million in 1984 to $1.5 billion in 1986. The work of training and development was complicated by the need to "Tysonize" the newly acquired workforce. "Tysonize" was the term we used to describe the work of influencing eight thousand newly acquired folks to do their work the Tyson way. It was the work of understanding the strengths of both work cultures and ensuring Tyson's work culture would be dominant. We discovered early on some

resistance from the "old-timers" at Tyson to accept the reality of the newly arrived competitive talent—performance trumped tenure!

3. Both companies had a direct foodservice sales force and both companies used regional brokers (commission agents). Valmac/Tastybird had been training their foodservice sales force at a facility designed to train twelve people every other week.

4. Key external customers were part of the training assignment. Foodservice distributors and foodservice operators i.e., hospital and university groups, fast-food chains—virtually anyone who would benefit from learning how to push or pull Tyson products through the channels of distribution.

5. The retail sales group was an occasional customer for special services. Selling supermarket customers was a process influenced less by "personal selling" and more by computer-driven category/volume data.

6. Hosting events for various professional and technical groups such as veterinarians, influential educational groups, health professionals, and food safety organizations.

7. Tyson was an active partner with local, state, and national educators who were also occasional customers at TMDC.

B. Values Scanning—Identify key management practices and behaviors embedded in Tyson's work culture.

1. Organizational integrity and trust.
2. Reliance on the power of workers' sense of personal responsibility.
3. Personal accountability.
4. A work environment that encourages folks to have fun doing their work. Compensate, promote, and reward performance.
6. Share company success by enabling all workers to become shareholders.
7. Encourage risk taking, and innovative and entrepreneurial thinking by honoring the principle that failure, when properly processed, is a profound teacher.
8. Avoid the corrosive effects of reliance on yesterday's successes.9. Elevate customer satisfaction to the highest-top-of-mind awareness
9. Be a good neighbor in the community where you live.

C. Action Planning Assumptions—What we knew for sure.

1. We had commitment from the triumvirate. Don Tyson had told us he wanted every supervisor in the company to have the Tyson experience at the TMDC twice a year. Buddy gave us the mission and the responsibility to do the work.

2. We had current basic resources and access to all the resources we needed to implement the mission. Leland, when asked how much money we had access to, answered, "I have never built one of these before. I know how much it costs to build plants, feed mills, hatcheries, and offices. We can afford to build what is needed to do the job. I don't like surprises so keep me informed." He added an interesting caveat. "If Don comes down to look over what you are building and suggests spending a bunch of money on something, call me first." It happened. I called him first.

3. We had an ideal training property and an experienced staff located in a resort setting with lots of expansion potential. The current training staff had a proven track record using adult learning principles and methods.

4. Perhaps our most valuable resource was the universal sense of confidence that permeated

Tyson's workforce, which cultivated a fertile learning environment.

Action Plans

1. Complete a skills assessment at all sixteen production locations.
2. Complete a work climate survey at all sixteen production locations.
3. Correlate the results of the skills assessment and the work climate survey with the principles identified in values scanning.
4. Do a gap analysis to develop and prioritize training tasks.
5. Design the curriculum with a feedback mechanism to ensure relevancy to the ten embedded practices and behaviors noted in the values scan.

The Role and Value of Behavioral Symbols in Training

Kaleel Johnson in her insightful book *The Nibble Theory* describes the negative results of pompous behavior. [114] She tells us that we come into the world a perfect circle. As we grow there are those who "nibble" on our perfect circle to make their circle bigger by diminishing our circle. It was

Don's sensitivity to the personhood of others that didn't allow some of the traditional symbols of position power. Business suits were replaced with khakis; no reserved parking except for visitors and the USDA; the use of first names; absence of org charts, formal job descriptions, and the egocentric use of titles. I think it was semanticist S.I.Don Hayakawa who suggested that words have little intrinsic meaning. They point the way to meaning and understanding when behaviors authenticate the symbols. The absence of the reserved parking places symbol was described in the *Tyson Update*, August 1989: "When you drive up to the corporate offices of Tyson Foods in Springdale, you won't find a parking place reserved for Don Tyson or any other executive. Don wants it that way. Vice president or groundskeeper, the first one on the job earns the best spot. This respect for accomplishments rather than ranks and titles goes back a long way." That issue of the *Update* was the issue welcoming newly acquired Holly Farms. It sent a clear message to all readers that Don's parking policy was more than symbolic—it was a leadership behavior he had practiced for thirty-seven years!

THE PROCESSES OF PACKAGING AND TRANSMITING THE SPIRIT OF DON TYSON

Our work was that of a supplier of adult learning to internal and external customers. For twelve years, 1985–1997, Tyson folks came to TMDC from Tyson operations in North Carolina, Alabama, Alaska, Florida, Maryland, Georgia, Illinois, Iowa, Indiana, Michigan, Minnesota, Mississippi, Missouri, Oklahoma, Pennsylvania, Tennessee, Texas, Virginia, Washington, Arkansas, and Mexico. External customers included distributors, chain operators, health care industry folks, veterinary medicine groups, educators, retail grocers; local, state, national and international groups. They came as adult learners to have a learning experience that combined traditional adult skills and behavioral training in an environment based on the adult learning assumptions developed by *University Associates'* William Pfeiffer[115]:

1. Learning is a process as opposed to a series of finite, unrelated steps that last throughout the life span of most people.

2. For optimum transfer of learning, the learner must be actively involved in the learning experience, not a passive recipient of information.

3. Each learner must be responsible for his or her own learning.

4. The learning process has an affective (emotional) as well as an intellectual component.

5. Adults learn by doing; they want to be involved. Regardless of the benefits of coaching, one should never merely demonstrate how to do something if an adult learner actually can perform the task, even if it takes longer that way.

6. Problems and examples must be realistic and relevant to the learners.

7. Adults relate their learning to what they already know. It is wise to learn something about the backgrounds of the learners and to provide examples that they can understand in their own frames of reference.

8. An informal environment works best. Trying to intimidate adults causes resentment and tension, and these inhibit learning.

9. Variety stimulates. It is a good idea to try to appeal to all five of the learner's senses, particularly to those identified by neurolinguistic programming: the visual, the kinesthetic, and the auditory. A change of pace and a variety of learning techniques help to mitigate boredom and fatigue.

10. Learning flourishes in a win-win, nonjudgmental environment. The norms of the training setting are violated by tests and grading procedures. Checking learning objectives is far more effective.

11. The training facilitator is a change agent. The trainer's role is to present information, skills and to create an environment in which exploration can take place. The participant's role is to take what is offered and apply it in a way that is relevant and best for them. The trainer's responsibility is to facilitate. The participant's responsibility is to learn.

My connection with University Associates began in the mid-seventies as sales manager for an Idaho potato processor. At a University Associates conference in San Francisco I met Dr. Paul Hersey, ED.D. Behavioral scientist and Founder and Chairman of the Board, Center for Leadership Studies, inc. in San Diego.

Dr. Hersey, Ken Blanchard Ph.D., Dewey Johnson Ph.D., and Spencer Johnson, authored or co-authored such business books as: *Management of Organizational Behavior; Situational Leadership; The One Minute Manager; Self Leadership* and other titles.

EXPERIENTIAL LEARNING

Experiential learning defined the work of training and development—packaging and transmitting the spirit of Don Tyson. Education theorists are a bit like economists in that they don't all agree. Our research into adult learning gave us vital insights into how Don Tyson's leadership behaviors influenced his people—neurolinguistic programming (NLP). "The most well know dimension of this component language is representational systems. This is the dimension that is most applicable to human resource development..."the basic premise of NLP is that people's perceptions of the world (what they perceive as information) are filtered through their sensory systems (Bandle & Grinder, 1975). Data is first processed at an unconscious level, experienced internally, and then manifested in external behavior. Language patterns are one method that people use to communicate their internal responses."

TYSON MANAGEMENT DEVELOPMENT CENTER (TMDC)

London, Arkansas is a small town, 1984 population 952, located on the sprawling, 34,000 acre Lake Dardanelle on the Arkansas River. Lake Dardanelle is part of the McClellan-Kerr Arkansas River navigation system that created a navigable waterway from Port Catoosa, Tulsa, Oklahoma to the

Mississippi River. The waterway is 445 river miles long, made possible by eighteen locks and dams. The nearest large town to London is Russellville, seven miles east of London.

TMDC's origin goes back to Valmac/Tastybird Foods, a Tyson acquisition in 1984. Competing with Tyson Foods prompted Valmac's president, Blake Lovette, Shelby Massey and Dick Hill to increase the selling skills and product knowledge of their field sales personnel and key customers. They purchased 1.75 acre property located on a peninsula jutting into Lake Dardanelle.

Tyson's Triumvirate wanted a facility that would communicate to those who came to the Center Tyson's work culture of satisfying workers, customers and shareholders. They wanted a first class facility without opulence.

From the time guests were picked up at the Little Rock airport until they were transported back to Little Rock, guests were treated as VIPs. From executives at customer companies to newly appointed Tyson supervisors, they all experienced great food prepared by Chef Barry Barnes and his staff; beautifully groomed grounds created by Joe Williams and his staff; fifty-four single occupancy bedrooms, full baths with milled soap ands plush towels; central atriums equipped with piano, billiards, a big screen TV, and game tables to bring folks together; a jogging trail; an exercise room; fishing gear; competent trainers led by Don Legge, Peggy Carta and

John Altland; the office staff led by Jimmie Elzy—a five-star staff dedicated to guest satisfaction.

Of the staff trainers, only one brought in from the outside. John Altland, PhD, joined the team to add academic experience to our experience based strengths. Dr. Altland was recruited from General Motors staff of professional educators. Peggy Carta fit the Tyson model of growing its own. At the time Tyson acquired Tastybird Foods, she was assistant to the president. When her position was eliminated, she asked to join the training staff with the condition that we arrange her schedule so she could return to the university and complete her education, which was interrupted by marriage and raising a family. We agreed. What a joy to be in the audience when she was awarded her college degree. Her story is about the power of a personal vision that refuses to accept mediocrity as a way of life. Whatever growing up a coal miner's daughter meant to some, to Peggy Carta it was not sufficient to deny her the knowledge and wisdom provided by an education. Supervisors who attended her seminars were inspired by another success story made possible when highly motivated folks work for a company that believes in its people.

THE MILLED SOAP TEST

A cost accountant at corporate compared the cost of milled bath soap to the tiny bars of soap offered at budget motels and concluded we weren't committed to being a low-cost operation. In defending the use of milled soap at the highest levels, we argued in favor of the principle that right cost trumped low cost, based on our mission statement to "package and transmit the spirit of Don Tyson." All smiled and agreed. Milled soap stays!

An example of their generosity and commitment occurred when we wanted to expand the center by acquiring the entire peninsula, building another lodge giving us a lodging capacity for fifty-four guests and a third training facility, and adding a first class dining facility. Leland came down to visit about the request. As we walked among the tall loblolly pine trees, he said, "Well, I suppose a $5 billion company could spend a little money for expansion. Send me your plans. Now, if Don comes down to look over the project and recommends spending a bunch of money, call me before you spend the money." Don came down. I called Leland—another example of the power of a relationship based on trust, not hierarchical power.

Don's passionate belief that "satisfied workers satisfied customers who satisfied shareholders" determined how we did our work of growing people. In the process we learned that growing people was more complex than growing chickens. Tyson Foods' historic performance in both areas set a high standard for our work. The next task was to measure worker satisfaction and to analyze the causes. This was accomplished empirically by completing a work climate and a worker skills survey, and anecdotally, by doing "listening visits" at all sixteen Tyson processing plants and support facilities like hatcheries, feed mills, grow out farms, plus Tyson's corporate offices.

With these tasks completed, the data were analyzed, and a core curriculum was developed and presented to the senior management team for their approval and buy-in. Initial approval and buy-in were relatively easy. Over the long term, buy-in was a continual challenge. One of the challenges was resistance of some managers to granting time for their folks to attend the seminars. Don had told me he wanted every supervisor in the company to have the TMDC experience twice a year. One frustrating challenge came from a couple of myopic managers, fearful that involving their folks in a corporate-wide development program would expose them to opportunities within the company, or in some cases, competitors, refused to let their folks attend. Over time, this changed as the mushroom theory never had worked very well. When we introduced computer-based maintenance training, one manager who refused to enroll his maintenance people told me he knew that if his folks gained new skills and more pay, our competitors would hire them. Our response was that if that did occur, perhaps they should review pay policies.

The curricula were behavioral based. Using adult experiential learning methods, we supplemented the behavioral data with relevant theoretical material and models. We resisted so called "canned" materials, preferring to "Tysonize" proven models we could contextualize. For example, Bob Love's department was responsible for developing new product labels and formulas had to be submitted to the USDA Foods Safety and Inspection Service for label approval. When a bunch of new products came along, the process began to bog down in our system. Folks were working long hours to satisfy sales and production needs. When lead times didn't improve, blaming and justifying behaviors began. We were invited in to work on conflict resolution that was symptomatic, not causal. When symptoms are treated as problems, the cost of problem solving creates a big black hole into which profits disappear and consultants prosper.

Our task was to create a situation that would allow the folks from each of the groups working in label and product research to solve their own problem. The model we used was David Marion's open systems vs. closed systems. [116] These folks were using what Marion called mechanical systems, in which parts were fixed; the whole always equaled the sum of the parts, and the same physical parts always produced the same whole or result. As soon as they were able to focus on process rather than personalities, they adopted Marion's open systems in which parts are flexible; the whole does not have to equal the sum of the parts; and when physical parts do not change, whole can vary depending on intangibles such as mood, style of communication, etc. Solution: change the process of moving documents from desk to desk to desk and back again, to a team process whereby one team composed of one person from each working group originated and completed the process. Two departments were consolidated; non-productive tasks were eliminated; costs went down and so did inventories. This is contextualized training.

Dr. Paul Heresy's research on managing organizational behavior influenced this work, as he influenced the writer's career, specifically his work on situational leadership. In *Managing Organizational Behavior* [117] the authors write in the preface, "As the inventory of empirical studies expands, making comparisons and contrasts possible, management theory will continue to emerge. Common elements will be isolated and important variables brought to light...Our belief is that an organization is a unique living organism whose basic component is the individual, and this individual is our fundamental unit of study. Thus, our concentration is on the interaction of people, motivation, and leadership."

The work of training and development can't be divorced from organizational development. Sociologist Amitai Etzioni wrote, "Our society is an organizational society. We are born in organizations, educated in organizations, and most of us spend much of our lives working for organizations. We spend much of our leisure time playing and praying in organizations. Most of us will die in an organization, and when the time comes for burial, the largest organization of all—the state must grant official permission. [118]

Measuring training and development results is not easy. We placed high value on seminars that were in highest demand. They were:

* MANAGING RELATIONSHIPS AT WORK
Major resource: Aubrey Sanford and Hyler Bracey
* TASK ORIENTED TEAM TRAINING
Major resource: Bob Fisher and Bethel "Bo" Thomas
* TIME AND RESOURCE MANAGEMENT
Major resource: Charles and Chris Hobbs
* STATISTICAL PROCESS CONTROL
Major resource: Ron Cristofono and Scott Stillwell
* Foodservice Sales Training
Major resource: Paul Whitley, Don Legge, John Altland

Other seminars: First-Line Leadership; Grower Communications Training; Negotiating Skills; Language and Cultural Immersion; Personal Safety--physical and emotional; Food Safety; Conflict Resolution; Computer Skills and Grower Communications. We also responded to special needs training for our internal customers including plant nurses, human resources, refrigeration, general maintenance, veterinary medicine and the senior executive group.

THE MULTIPLICATION OF SHARED RESOURCES BY PARTNERING WITH EDUCATORS

Tyson Foods understood its role in communities where Tyson plants were located. Budgets and guidelines were created to satisfy accounting and public relations requirements. Land was donated for schools and recreational facilities. Products and cash were contributed to sponsor school athletic teams, bowling leagues, food banks, disaster relief organizations, matching funds for United Way contributions, etc.

Tyson's president and COO Buddy Wray wrote an open letter of commitment to a working partnership with Arkansas Education. Excerpts from his letter:

Tyson Foods' expectation of Arkansas education is very high. You are the largest "supplier" of talent for the Tyson team. As an agri-based food company, we expect you to prepare all students of all ages to live productive lives. Our team members have credentials from the Ph.D., M.D., D.V.M., to the GED level. Every job is important to our company and to every team member...This partnership requires no legislation, no regulation, no appropriations, and no red tape. It does require vision, commitment, and the will to get "our" work of education done. In a letter to Thomas Jefferson after years of feuding, John Adams wrote, "We ought not to die before we have explained ourselves to teach other."

Our doors are open, come on in, and let's work together for the betterment of our children's futures. [119]

WORKING PARTNERSHIPS WITH EDUCATION

Several partnerships evolved following Buddy's letter. One partnership that became a systemwide model was with Green Forest Elementary School.

• Lyle Sparkman, principal of the elementary school at Green Forest, Arkansas, called me requesting an appointment. I didn't inquire as to why he wanted to drive to Springdale for a visit. Tyson has a processing plant in Green Forest employing more than a thousand people in a community with a total population of less than three thousand. Lyle's school is located adjacent to the plant, so I assumed we would be visiting about something related to plant operations or perhaps he would be looking to fund a school project.

Sitting in my office, Lyle said, "What I need from Tyson Foods, the largest employer in my school district is parental involvement!" There was a long pause in our conversation. That kind of request wasn't in our donation guidelines policy. If he had asked for chicken for a special school function, we could handle that. If he had asked for funds to buy band uniforms, we could handle that. If he had asked for support for a school bond election, we could handle that. But parental involvement—I needed time to think.

At the time Lyle was working on a specialist program at the university. His advisor, Dr. Beverly Elliott, was the founder of the Arkansas Leadership Academy, a Tyson partner. Being a renaissance man who thought outside the box, he envisioned the resource adjacent to his school that would satisfy a very large unmet need at his school—involvement of parents who worked at Tyson's plant. Lyle Sparkman, an entrepreneurial leader in public education!

Taking advantage of the culture of candor at Tyson, I walked Lyle to the high-carpet area, otherwise known as Oak Row, and introduced him to Buddy Wray, our president and COO. Lyle presented his need for parental involvement and described how it could be met. Would Buddy grant him permission to present the idea to the plant manager, Chris Graves? Lyle later described Buddy's action as the "power of permission." Buddy agreed to the partnership, which set in motion systemwide partnerships with local school districts to form working partnerships to help children.

Three years later, Lyle Sparkman came to Springdale to meet with Buddy Wray. Lyle opened a large manila envelope, placing dozens of handwritten thank-you notes from Green Forest Elementary on Buddy's desk. Not a word was spoken until Buddy read every note. When he did speak, with a bit of a quiver in his voice, "Do you know how rare it is to be thanked for doing what is right?" One of those notes was from a hearing-impaired third-grader who received a hearing aid when his mother came to a parent-teacher meeting at the plant, during night shift in the plant conference room, to learn her child would receive all the benefits of a public education, just like all the other children! What a paradigm— a schoolteacher coming to a processing plant at midnight to meet with the mother of one of her students! That is a working partnership! That is what Lyle Sparkman called parental involvement! One-on-one parent teacher meetings in the plant conference room at the convenience of the parent in the interest of the child's education!

The Green Forest Elementary School/Tyson Foods story is more than corporate altruism and public relations. It is what Peter Drucker calls "the third task of management— managing the social impacts and the social responsibilities of the enterprise." In the section titled Purpose and Mission, Drucker writes:

> An institution exists for a specific purpose and mission, a specific social function. In the business enterprise, this means economic performance. With respect to this first task, the task of specific performance, business and non-business institutions differ. In respect to every other task, they are similar. But only business has economic performance as its specific mission. In all other institutions, hospital, church, university, or armed service, economics

is a restraint. In a business enterprise, economic performance is the rationale and purpose...The first definition of business management is that it is an economic organ, the specifically economic organ of an industrial society. Every act, every decision, every deliberation of management, has economic performance as its firs dimension...The second task of management is to make work productive and the worker achieving. [120]

The phrase "power of permission" comes from Lyle Sparkman. It is about power—the power of a leadership action that improved the lives of Tyson workers and their children; action that multiplied the resources of hundreds of school districts in eleven states. Lyle Sparkman says it best:

In the years since, I have talked with other educators about that experience. There is a list of identified lessons that are reproducible by anybody seeking to improve the lot of migrant families, but none more powerful than taking that first step and communicating the deepest need to those who can help. Assuming walls of indifference are defeating. Assuming that permission awaits those who ask is empowering. If you want to improve circumstances for many, first gain permission for that improvement from highest level. The very hierarchy that seems an obstacle can become the key to success. It simply requires bringing a good idea to someone who can say, "Yes!"

With Buddy Wray's power of permission, the courage of plant manager Chris Graves, and the entrepreneurial leadership of school Principal Lyle Sparkman, Tyson Foods behaved responsibly.

Chris Graves was not only courageous; he was a wise and consequential thinker. He, like Don Tyson, acknowledged the fact that his success was dependent on how the thousand folks in his plant felt about their work at the Green Forest plant. Remembering what Don had said to a group of plant managers, "Go to your plant on Sunday morning and see how much work gets done when only you are there." Chris Graves, by his actions, had the effect of affirming the value of all the parents working in the plant. His actions became the model used in not only Tyson plants, but in the plants of many agri-employers "related to the production or processing of crops, dairy products, poultry, or livestock for initial commercial sale or as a principal means of personal subsistence." [121]

- ## ARKANSAS STATE DEPARTMENT OF EDUCATION ESL ACADEMY

During a three-year period, Arkansas public schools experienced a 300 percent increase of language minority enrollments. The state Department of Education did not have an endorsement program for English as Second Language (ESL) teachers. This situation made it very difficult for local schools, especially small, rural schools to meet federal requirements to educate all children in Arkansas schools.

Seeking a remedy, Barbara Berry, human services manager at Tyson Foods, championed the project. As an experienced educator and advocate for children, Barbara formed a working partnership with Dr. Andre Guerrero at the Arkansas Department of Education. At the time she was conducting Hispanic immersion classes for plant managers and senior execs at corporate. Having lived and worked outside the country for sixteen years, she was fluent in Spanish, conversant in French and Italian, and was a certified simultaneous UN translator. Barbara had a passion for language/cultural learning. She met with Dr. Guerrero over lunch and outlined on a napkin the idea of an ESL language academy for teachers and administrators. She used the model created by Dr. Beverly Elliott of the Arkansas Leadership Academy, a Tyson partner.

Dr. Ursula Chandler, chair, foreign languages, at Arkansas Tech University, joined the partnership. Berry and Chandler had "bonded" years earlier when working on a number of education projects. "Bonding" took on new meaning for this writer, observing the kinetic energy of these women as they broke through went over, under, or around, bureaucratic barriers that got in the way of meeting the learning needs of children.

Berry's Irish blood combined with Chandler's aggressive style, earning them gold medals in pursuit of their goals. Dr. Chandler is an inner-directed academic, driven by a passion for building learning bridges between cultures in modern civil societies. Her style is a kind of Germanic, loving, thumb-in-the-back pursuit of truth!

With the strong personalities of these two emancipated female educators, those attending the academies that may have had a provincial view left their classes with a twenty-twenty view of the world that is populated by people who needed to learn to communicate with each other.

According to Dr. Guerrero, the academies' curricula parallels the content areas required for certification in English as a second language. A graduate academy followed with a two-week, in-depth, advanced training as a follow-up to the five-day academies. Persons completing both academies were awarded twelve credit hours.

The burden for schools was both financial and academic. This working partnership with Dr. Andre Guerrero at the Arkansas Department of Education shared vital corporate resources to develop a program of endorsement for Arkansas teachers and administrators to teach English as a second language. Tyson also gave the state Department of Education access to the Management Development Center for the initial series of classes. According to Dr. Guerrero, the ESL Academy has endorsed more than three thousand teachers—administrators serving thousands of minority students!

• THE ARKANSAS LEADERSHIP ACADEMY
Dr. BEVERLY ELLIOTT, Director & Springfield Professor of Educational Administration in the College of Education at the University of Arkansas, Fayetteville.

Established in 1991, the Arkansas Leadership Academy is a nationally recognized statewide partnership of thirteen universities; nine professional associations; fifteen educational cooperatives; the Arkansas Department of Education, Higher Education, and Workforce Education; the Arkansas Educational Television Network, Tyson Foods, Inc., Wal-Mart Stores, Inc., and the Walton Family Foundation—a total of forty-four partners.

Purpose

The Academy, through the use of research and best practices, designs creative and innovative approaches to establish learning communities in public schools by developing human resources and by modeling and advocating collaboration, support, shared decision making, team learning, risk taking, and problem solving. Partners commit to changing their organizations to support improvement.

Vision

An innovative academy preparing educational leaders who develop high performing learning communities throughout Arkansas.

Mission

To develop and sustain a cadre of leaders in public education in Arkansas through collaborative governance by Academy partners resulting in an expanded vision, statewide system change initiatives, synergy among stakeholders, and leadership development institutes.

Beliefs

— People support what they help create
— Diversity is embraced and valued
— To change others, change yourself
— The greatest leaders are known by the number of leaders they create

I first met Dr. Beverly Elliott, Ed.D, when Archie Schaffer, Tyson's executive VP, External Relations, brought her into my office to discuss her vision for improving and reforming education in Arkansas. Bev Elliott is one of those unique visionaries who have mastered both the process of visioning and the process of enrolling others in her vision. Her manner is gentle, her speech is precise, and she listens for understanding, and leads her audience to a point of agreement and support of her vision, values and goals.

She has earned the right to talk about education, having twenty-two years' real work as a classroom teacher, assistant school superintendent, school superintendent, assistant to the State of Arkansas director of education, and college professor. Add to her credentials a list of publishing achievements.

She had an ally in Archie Schaffer in that prior to his employment at Tyson Foods, he directed the work of the Arkansas Business Council/Good Suit Club. In 1987, several prominent Arkansas business leaders organized the Good Suit Club. Their goal was better education and economic development in Arkansas. The group was made up of Sam Walton, Don Tyson, J.B. Hunt of Hunt Trucking, Charles Murphy of Murphy Oil, Thomas F. "Mack" McLarty of Arkla Gas, Charles Morgan of Axiom, and others.

Archie and I listened as Bev Elliott painted a striking word picture of how the Arkansas Leadership Academy would improve education in Arkansas and benefit Tyson Foods, directly and indirectly. Directly, in that she didn't have funding to support a training facility. Would Tyson consider making the Management Development Center available for lodging, meals, and classes? The other corporate partner, Wal-Mart, would fund materials and subject matter expertise and other related costs. After securing the commitment of Buddy

Wray, we became a corporate partner with the Arkansas Leadership Academy.

During the course of the first year, several hundred educators would experience a five-day immersion in Tyson's culture, eat elegantly prepared Tyson food products, and be pampered by the outstanding guest services of the center. Indirectly, Tyson would benefit by improving the education of Arkansas students, some of whom would be employed by Tyson Foods.

The academy is making a difference in how educators think and behave. Exhibit A is the Master Principal Program that builds on the academy's Principal Institute that has trained three hundred practicing principals in its five-year history. The Master Principal Program grew out of then state Senator, now the governor of Arkansas, Mike Beebe's wish to offer incentives to principals who lead low-performing schools. He proposed Act 44 to fund the Master Principal Program, a rigorous three-year training curriculum that provides bonuses upon successful completion. Master Principals will receive a bonus of $9,000 per year for five years upon earning the designation. They are eligible for an additional $25,000 per year for five years, if they are selected to serve in a low-performing school.

Kathy Morledge, leader of the Master Principal Group, noted that "the role of the principal, who works at the building level and sees students and teachers each day, is key to improving school performance. A good principal is always asking, 'Who is not learning? Why are they not learning? And what are we doing about it?' When the principal fosters a strong collaborative relationship at the building level, everyone is able to focus on helping children learn." [122]

Dr. Elliott, a complete visionary had the ability to inspire funding for her vision. She knew her way around the halls of the state capitol in Little Rock. From FY 1995 to FY 2006, the Legislature has supported her vision with $10,997,435!

In Buddy Wray's open letter to educators, he wrote, "I believe the process of improving education is simple, but not easy...We must hold each other accountable. We must behave responsibly as partners...It does require vision, commitment, and the will to get 'our' work of education done."

• WORKING PARTNERSHIP WITH THE U.S. DEPARTMENT OF EDUCATION'S OFFICE OF MIGRANT EDUCATION AND THE CAIR CONSORTIUM

U.S. Department of Education Press Release—July 29, 1997: U.S. Secretary of Education Richard W. Riley today announced that the Education Department will participate in six summer pilot projects aimed at back- to-school efforts for migrant workers and their families. The new initiative is called Agriculture + Industry + Migrant Families = AIM for Success in Schools and Communities...Aim for Success is a collaborative effort with the department's Office of Migrant Education, states in the Consortium Arrangement for Identification and Recruitment (CAIR), and four of the nations' top producers of meat and vegetable products...The four businesses participating are: Tyson Foods, poultry production and processing; IBP, Inc., beef and pork production and processing; Seneca Foods, fruit and vegetable harvest and processing; and Curtice-Burns Foods, vegetable harvest and processing...The corporations already have participated in activities with migrant families whose first language is Spanish, Vietnamese, Laotian and English...Tyson Foods Manager of Human Services Barbara Berry added: "It is in the best interests of Tyson Foods to develop the skills of our workers and to support their efforts to be involved in the education of their children. Our partnership with migrant education has benefited us as an employer, the families of our workers, and the communities in which they live. We look forward to being able to extend these pilots to all the communities served by our company.

Bayla White, director of the Office of Migrant Education in the U.S. Department of Education, was a pragmatic visionary who understood the learning needs of migrant children. She used her highly developed skills of partnering to access the resources of agri-employers and community infrastructure to meet the learning needs of children.

Bayla was not one of those ivory tower leaders who operated by fiat from a federal building in Washington, DC. She walked through fields of migrant workers harvesting crops, processing plants, classrooms, local school administration offices, and of course, knew her way around the U.S. Department of Education offices of Secretary Riley and his staff.

Jack Perry, executive director of the Interstate Migrant Education Council, organized for the purpose of "advocating policies that ensure the highest quality of education and other services for the migrant children," was an invaluable partner in working with key members and committees of the U.S. Congress. The law that was the basis for these activities was:

THE ELEMENTARY AND SECONDARY EDUCATION ACT OF 1965

President Lyndon Johnson enacted the Elementary and Secondary Education Act (ESEA) of 1965. This act was the first and largest comprehensive federal education law that provided substantial monetary funds for K–12 education. According to President Johnson, "Congress had been trying to pass a school bill for all America's children since 1870 and had finally taken the most significant step of this century to provide help to all school children." The act was reauthorized every five years.

• The organizing motive force that moved all the partners toward a common goal was the CAIR CONSORTIUM. My counterpart at Iowa Beef Processors (IBP) Ken Milbrodt, whom I had met in 1985, called to invite me to a meeting of the CAIR Consortium in Kansas City. I had not heard about the Consortium. Ken piqued my interest when he described how CAIR was facilitating partnerships between agri-based employers, state departments of education, local school districts, the U.S. Department of Education, the Office of Migrant Education, and other federal, state, and local agencies. "The aim of CAIR is to share resources and expertise with the purpose of reducing administrative and program function costs so that state programs can make more funds available for the direct services to migrant students." [123]

Several agri-employers arrived for the meeting during one of Kansas City's miserable ice storms. The meeting was facilitated by two academic types: Dr. John Farrell, executive director of CAIR, and Dr. Betty Alfred, Title I Migrant Education at the Nebraska Department of Education. Farrell presented the mission and purpose of the Consortium in his rapid, shorthand style. As we all learned later, Farrell was always in hurry, preferring to speed up the communications process by omitting unnecessary words. Dr. Alfred, an avid University of Nebraska Big Red football fan who idolized Coach Tom Osborne had earned a doctorate in educational psychology, was a private pilot, never missed early Catholic Mass, and was a passionate advocate for the education of migrant children.

The four employers at that meeting (Seneca Foods, harvester and processor of fruits and vegetables; Curtice-Burns Foods, vegetable harvester and processor; IBP, beef and pork processor; and Tyson Foods, a poultry grower and processor) left convinced our companies would benefit by becoming partners with CAIR. As partners we could lend a corporate hand assisting local school districts to meet their commitments to educate all children.

Congress had authorized and appropriated dollars for schools. For schools to receive these funds, the law required that they complete certificates of eligibility for each child. It was a tedious, cumbersome, and inefficient process. Dollar amounts ranged from a few dollars up to three hundred dollars plus for each child for a three-year period. The CAIR Consortium developed a system that was more accurate and efficient for local schools. The various state departments of education partnered with CAIR via their offices of migrant education. CAIR was the central partner collaborating with local schools, agri-employers, community infrastructures, local, state, and federal agencies, and other interested and influential organizations.

The collaborative work of CAIR and its partners had the effect of Pascal's Principle of Hydraulics, which allows for forces to be multiplied—a small force using a large volume of hydraulic fluid to move a larger force. Three to four hundred million dollars each year, authorized and appropriated by Congress, flowed into cash-starved school districts.

One of the rapidly growing costs in schools was teaching English. For example, the 2000–2001 annual report of the North Carolina State Board of Education reports that 150 languages were spoken in North Carolina classrooms. In a 1995 survey in Arkansas, eighty-seven languages or dialects were spoken. The same year, in school districts in northwest Arkansas, thirty-four languages were spoken in classrooms.

In my experience with educators, as student, teacher, commencement speaker, and citizen taxpayer campaigning for school bonds, I have not seen a more passionate work ethic than what I observed among migrant educators. They don't have the structure and/or comfort of a classroom schedule. They pursue parents in their homes; their churches; in plants and farms where parents work. Their work week far exceeds the traditional forty-plus hours with two days off each week. They wear out automobiles driving parents and students to appointments with doctors, hospitals, schools, funerals, employers, and charitable groups. They spend their own money assisting families. Today, the children they advocated for have graduated from high school. Some have gone to college. They have become good citizens in their communities, living out the family values their parents brought from Vietnam, Guatemala, Mexico, the Sudan, Asia, the Hmong—an ancient Asian tribe, and several other lands.

Buddy Wray said it best. Speaking about migrant workers, he said, "They are teaching and living the family values many Americans have lost."

LEADERSHIP INSIGHTS

- Leaders understand their success is influenced to a great degree by their behaviors, policies, and the work climate they create for their workers—from new hires to the executive suite.
- Leaders encourage, get involved with, and invest in the growth and development of the workforce.
- The most effective antidotes to ignorance and the negative effects of ignorance on the success of the organization are pragmatic, proven, adult learning experiences delivered in the context of organizational realities.

CHAPTER 10
Don Tyson Retires

El gallo, se va, The Rooster is going
El gallo, se va, The Rooster is going
El simper dice, He always says
Co cocori, cocora, Cock a doodle do.

On April 21, 1995, Don Tyson stepped down as Tyson's chairman of the board. Leland Tollett was elected chairman and CEO. Buddy Wray became president and COO. Don assumed the newly created position of senior chairman. He retained control of the business by holding 99 percent of Class B stock, which had ten votes to one for Class A stock.

Sales had grown from $1 million when Don joined his dad in 1952 to $5.5 billion in 1995. His retirement initiated a series of leadership changes that would break up the triumvirate, which had been together nearly forty years. Leland Tollett retired in 1997. He remained on the board. John Tyson, Don's son, was elected chairman of the board, with Wayne Britt becoming CEO. Buddy Wray retired in 2000. Britt also retired in 2000.

THE "ROOSTERS" RETIREMENT PARTY
April 28-29, 1995

Cleta Selman, Don's administrative assistant, asked Barbara Berry, Tyson's human services manager, to organize and choreograph an international theme as part of Don's retirement party, held at Tyson's Management and Development Center on Lake Dardanelle, near Russellville. The mission was to have fun, Don Tyson style. Picture this— Don, swinging a baseball bat trying to break open a huge, rooster-shaped piñata, surrounded by ninety invited guests. All the while they are singing, in Spanish, a song Ms. Berry had taught them titled, *El Gallo*, the rooster. After several swings of the bat and help from Jim Blair, the piñata yields its sweets. As they enjoy the sweets, Ms. Berry is teaching Buddy Wray, the bull rider, to do the Macarena!

The guest list of ninety of his friends included: Barbara Tyson, John and Kim Tyson, Carla Tyson, Cheryl Tyson, Steve Thomason, Jim and Diane Blair, Joe Fred and Billie Starr, Woody Bassett, Jim Stephens, Chuck and Terri Erwin, Clark and Georgi Irwin, Gerald and Charlotte Johnston, Jerry and Jean Jones, Barry Switzer, Larry and Chris Lacewell, Hayden and Mary Jo McIlroy, Archie and Beverly Schaffer, Jim and Cleta Selman, Billy Ray and Jenny Smith, Leland and Betty Tollett, Buddy and Linda Wray, Herman and Irene Tuck, and Hayden and Mary Joe McIlroy.

The food and beverage service provided by Foodservice Manager Barry Barnes and his staff at the Training Center lived up to Barry's reputation as a gastronomist. Thousands of Tyson folks had been enjoying Barry's epicurean delights for several years.

The large pavilion, built on the shores of Lake Dardanelle, was an ideal setting for guests to enjoy Don's music performed by his musical friends—Willie Nelson, Waylon Jennings, The Cate Brothers, Ronnie Hawkins and The Hawks, and Jed Clampit. When the amplified sound of guitars wafted across the lake, even though the event was not made public, residents living on the lakeshore anchored their boats near the pavilion to enjoy the party—a fitting tribute to the man having fun, celebrating his sixty-fifth birthday, and ready to begin the second half of his life.

"I REFUSE to HAVE a BAD DAY" -Don Tyson

TYSON MANAGEMENT DEVELOPMENT CENTER
RUSSELLVILLE, ARKANSAS

FRIDAY, APRIL 28th

2:00 pm - 5:00 pm	Check In & Get Acquainted	
5:00 pm - 6:30 pm	Cocktails & Clampit	Patio
6:30 pm	Waylon Jennings Show	Pavilion
8:00 pm	Dinner	Dining Room
9:00 pm	Willie Nelson & Family	Pavilion
After Willie	Late with The Cates	Dining Room

SATURDAY, APRIL 29th

7:30 am - 9:00 am	Breakfast	Dining Room
9:00 am-10:00 am	Culinary Team USA Chefs	Conference Rm. "C"
10:00 am-10:45 am	Planning Your Financial Future	Conference Rm. "C"
11:00 am-12:00 noon	Planning Your Tax Future	Conference Rm. "C"
12:00 noon - 1:30 pm	Lunch	Dining Room
1:30 pm - 2:45 pm	Hispanic Immersion	Conference Rm. "C"
3:00 pm - 5:30 pm	Downtime	
5:30 pm - 7:00 pm	Cocktails & Clampit	Patio
7:00 pm	Dinner	Dining Room
8:00 pm	Ronnie Hawkins & The Hawks	Pavilion
9:30 pm	The Band	Pavilion
After the Band	Late with The Cates	Dining Room

SUNDAY, APRIL 30th

8:00 am - 11:00 am	Breakfast	Dining Room
Departures at Leisure		

TOURS WILL BE AVAILABLE OF TYSON FARMS & PLANTS

The party was over. Change was in the wind. Leadership legacies were nearing completion. The Tyson Foods culture created by Mr. John Tyson, Don Tyson, Leland Tollett, Buddy Wray, and thousands of followers was giving way to a new and different culture to be created over time by a new management team.

A year before being elected our sixteenth president, Abraham Lincoln, an up-and-coming Republican, best known for debating Stephen Douglas, gave a speech at the Wisconsin State Fair on September 3, 1859. He was speaking to the Wisconsin State Agricultural Society covering current farmer interests. After speaking about the successful and unsuccessful farmer, he said:

> Let it be remembered, that while occasions like the present, bring their sober and durable benefits, the exultations and mortifications of them, are but temporary; that the victor shall soon be vanquished, if he relax his exertion; and that the vanquished this year, may be victor the next, in spite of all competition. It is said an Eastern monarch once charged his wise men to invent him a sentence, to be ever in view, and which should be true and appropriate in all times and situations. They presented him the words; "And this, too, shall pass away." How much it expresses! How chastening in the hour of pride!—how consoling in the depths of affliction! "And this, too, shall pass away." And yet let us hope it is not quite true. Let us hope, rather, that by the best cultivation of the physical world, beneath and around us, and the intellectual and moral world within us, we shall secure an individual, social, and political prosperity and happiness, whose course shall

be onward and upward, and which, while the earth endures, shall not pass away. [124]

Just as President Lincoln pursued his goal of preserving the Union to a successful conclusion, so did Don Tyson pursue his goal to become number one in the industry by being the best.

Don Tyson did for the poultry-based food industry what Clarence Birdseye did for frozen foods, John Harvey Kellogg did for cereal, James Harvey Kraft did for cheese products, and George Hormel did for meat. These visionaries led the way to adding value to commodity products by their commitment to satisfying customer demands for innovative, affordable food products.

Don's legacy is assured in the lives of thousands of folks whose lives were made better by his goodness as a their leader; by his integrity as a leader; by his humility as a person; by his commitment to customer, worker and shareholder satisfaction; by his commitment to communities at local, state, national and levels; by his and his family's generosity to educational and other institutions.

As he said to me as I was leaving his office, "Whitley, you can publish this, 'I REFUSE TO HAVE A BAD DAY.'"

LEADERSHIP INSIGHTS

Leaders are visionary people who influence others by behaviors that reveal:

- **competency and the skill to use those competencies effectively**
- **honesty**
- **integrity**
- **trust**
- **fair mindedness**
- **inspiring behaviors**
- **all the goodness of servant leadership**

ENDNOTES

Chapter 1

1   Peter Drucker, *The Effective Executive* (Harper & Row 1966)

2   James Kouzes, *The Leadership Challenge* **(Jossey-Bass 1987)**

3   Marvin Schwartz, *From Farm To Market* **(University of Arkansas Press 1991)**

4   Stephen Strausburg, *From Hills And Hollers (Arkansas Agricultural Extension Station Special Report, University of Arkansas 1995)*

5   E.L.Deci, *Intrinsic Motivation* **(Deci Publications 1975)**

6   A Warren Buffet quote, (The Conference Board's 'Across The Board' October, 1991)

7   Frederick Reichheld, *The Loyalty Effect* (Harvard Business School Press 1996)

8   Alfred P. Sloan Jr., *(My Years With General Motors* (Doubleday 1963)

9   Detroit News quote *www.info.detnews, com/history/story/index*

10   Peter Block, *The Empowered Manager* (Jossey-Bass Inc. 1987)

11   Dale Carnegie, *How To Win Friends And People* (Simon & Shuster 1936)

12   Stephen Strausburg, *From Hills And Hollers* (Arkansas Agricultural Experiment Station Special Report, University of Arkansas 1995)

13   Roy Reed, *Faubus, The Life And Times Of An American Prodigal* (University of Arkansas Press 1997)

14   Peter Drucker, *The Effective Executive* (Harper & Row 1966)

15   Studs Terkel, *Working* (Ballantine Books 1985)

16   Daniel Goleman, *Emotional Intelligence*, (Bantam Books 1995)

17   Quote from www.missionpossibleinc.com/emotion

18   Murray Gell-Mann, Distinguished Fellow Santa Fe Institute & The R.A. Millikan Professor Emeritus At Cal Tech University. Nobel Prize Winner In Physics, 1969 *Quark and the Jaguar* (Hold Paperbacks 1994)

19   Oliver Wendell Holmes, Jr., Associate Justice on the United States Supreme Court. b.1841, d.1935

20   James O'Toole, The Executive Compass:Business and the Good Society (Oxford University Press)

21   Thomas Kuhn, *The Structure Of Scientific Revolutions* (University of Chicago Press 1970)

22   How People Learn: Brain, Mind, Experiences and Schools; The United States National Research

23   Council Study

Chapter 2

24   Dr. Stephenson passed away in February of 1997

25   www.arkansastraveler.typepad.com/history

26   The writer's brother-in-law

27   Malcolm Gladwell, *Blink and The Tipping Point* (Little, Brown and Company 2005)

28   Steven C. Brandt, *Strategic Planning In Emerging Companies* (Addison-Wesley 1981)

29   Daniel Goleman, *Working With Emotional Intelligence* (Bantam Books 1998)

30   Theodore Schultz, From an article in *American Economic Review titled Investment In Human Capital*

31   Paul Hersey, Kenneth Blanchard, Dewey Johnson, *Management of Organizational Behavior 8th edition* (Prentice Hall Business Publishing 2001)

32   Colonel John Torres, United State Air Force, Commander, 15th Airlift Wing Hickam Air Force Base Hawaii

33   Dewey Johnson, Professor of Management Sid Craig School of Business, Cal State University Fresno, CA

34   Kaleel Johnson, *The Nibble Theory and the Kernel of Power*, (Paulist Press 1984)

35   JOANNES PAULUS PP., II Laborem Exercens, September 14, 1981

36   David McCullough, *1776* (Simon & Shuster 2005)

37   Ibid.

Chapter 3

38   Frederick F. Reichheld, *They Loyalty Effect* (Harvard Business Business Press 1996)

39   The Sassy Chick, Pine Bluff Complex Newsletter, Editor, Vicki Hilliard

40   Arkansas Democrat Newpaper, December 17, 1989

41   Pine Bluff Commercial Appeal Newspager, may 1989

42   Warren Bennis, *Why Leaders Can't Lead* (Training & Development Journal April1, 1989)

43   Frederick F. Reichheld, *The Loyalty Effect* (Harvard Business Press 1996

44   Tyson New Release, April 1, 2004

45   Tyson Annual Report, 1983

46   T.A.Harris, *I'm OK—You're OK A practical guide to Transactional Analysis* (Harper & Row 1969)

47   Ron Cristofono, *Process Improvement Guide Book* (Ron Cristofono 1984)

48   Kurt Lewin, *The Planning Of Change* (Holt, Rinehart and Winston 1969)

49   Memo from Paul Vinson, Director of Sales & Support Tyson Mexican Original

50   Peter Drucker, *Management: Tasks, Responsibilities, Practices* (Harper & Row 1974)

51   From the Torah, Genesis Chapter 2

52   Gloria Steinem, *Moving Beyond Words* (Simon & Shuster 1994)

53   Thomas Kuhn, *Structure of Scientific Revolutions* (University of Chicago Press 1970)

54   Frederick F. Reichheld, *The Loyalty Effect* (Harvard Business Press 1996)

55   Peter Drucker, *Management: Tasks, Practices,* (Harper & Row 1974)

Chapter 4

56   Wm. A. Tiller, *Science and Human Transformation: Subtle Energies, Intentionality and Consciousness.* Pavior Publishing 1997

57   www.fdic.gov/bank/historical

58   Ibid.

59   Tyson Tribal Stories, Tyson Lake House October 11, 1988

60   Richard Bach, *Jonathan Livingston Seagull* (Harper & Collins 1973)

61   Margaret Wheatley, *Leadership and the New Science* (Berrett-Kochler Publishers Inc. 1999)

62   www.inspirall.com.au/coherence

63   Senator David Prior, Dean of President Clinton's School for Public Service Interview June 21, 2002

64   Arthur K. Robertson, *Language Of Effective Listening,* (Scott Foresman 1991)

65   Warren Bennis, *Why Leaders Can't Lead* (Jossey-Bass Inc. 1987)

66   Robert Keyser III, The Keyser Group Denver, Colorado

67   Daniel Goleman, *Emotional Intelligence* (Bantam Books 1995)

68   W. Edwards Deming, *Out Of The Crisis* (Massachusetts Institute of Technology 1982)

69   Ruby K. Payne and Don L. Krabill *The Hidden Rules Of Class At Work aha*! Process 2002

70   www.intertwingly.net/stories

Chapter 5

71   Alfred P. Sloan Jr., *My Years With General Motors* (Doubleday 1963)

72   Max DePree, *Leadership Jazz* (Dell Publishing 1992)

73   National Chicken Council Data

74   Stephen F. Strausburg, *From Hills and Hollers* (Arkansas Agricultural Experiment Station report University of Arkansas 1995)

75   United States Department of Agriculture Research Service, www.ars.usda.gov/research/publications

76   David Merrill and Roger Reid, *Personal Styles & Effective Performance* (The TRACOM Corporation 1981)

77   David Pryor interview June 21, 2005 at the Office of the Dean of President Clinton's School for Public Service, Little Rock

78   Buckminster Fuller, *Synergetics* (Macmillan Publishing 1982)

79   Tyson Tribal Stories told at Tyson's lake house October 11, 1988

80   Peter Block, *The Empowered Manager* (Jossey-Bass Publishers 1987)

81   Con Agra Foods, Inc. www.wikipedia.org/wiki/ConAgra-Foods,Inc

Chapter 6

82   Marvin Schwartz, *From Farm To Market* (University of Arkansas Press 1991)

83   Orlena Miller, *Insider Racing News, A Fairly Successful Legend*

84   Ibid.

85   The Evolution of Eating Timeline, Rudd Center at Yale University

86   Charles R. Hobbs, *Time Power,* (Perennial Library, Harper & Row 1987)

87   Bryan Burrough and John Helyar, *Barbarians At The Gate* (Harper & Row 1990

88   www.themandajournal.com/sample_issue_Tysonv3_ asp

89   William MacPhee, *The Rare Breed* (Probus Publishing Company 1987)

90   David Matassoni, *Point B Consulting,*

91   The Wall Street Journal, October 13, 1988

Chapter 7

92   Stephen F. Strausburg, *From Hills and Hollers,* (university of Arkansas Press 1995)

93   Caduceus Newsletter, June, 2003

94   Bill Clinton, *My Life,* (Alfred Knopf 2004)

95   Journal of Agricultural Education, Texas A&M, Volume 41, Issue 4, 2000

96   Stephen R. Covey, *The 7 Habits of Highly Effective People* (Simon & Shuster 1989)

97   J.L.Adams, *Conceptual Blockbusting: A guide to better ideas,* (W.W.Norton, 1979)

98   Peter M Sense, *The Fifth Discipline: The Art and Practice of the Learning Organization,* (Doubleday 1990)

99   Dennis W. Bakke, *Joy At Work,* (Penguin Group Canada 2005)

100   Michael Porter, *Competitive Strategy* (The Free Press, A division of Macmillan Publishing 1980)

101   Tyson News Release, April 15, 2004

102   Richard Feynman, *The Pleasure of Finding Things Out*, (American Scientist, 1999)

Chapter 8

103   Diane Blair and Jay Barth, *Arkansas Politics and Government, Second Edition,* (University of Nebraska Press 2005)

104   www.sare.org/sanet-mg/archives

105   Bob Keyser III, Keyser & Associates

106   Bill Clinton, *My Life,* (Alfred Knopf 2004

107   Ibid

108   James Blair Interview, April 12, 2005

109   www.nwanews.com/story.php/paper

110   Senator Dale Bumpers, *The Best Lawyer in a One Lawyer Town,* (Random House 2003)

111   The Tyson Vision Magazine, March/April 1995, written by Curt Goeetsch

112   Ibid.

Chapter 9

113   Tyson Update Magazine, November/December, 1985

114   Kaleel Johnson, *The NibbleTheory,* (Paulist Press 1984)

115   C.A. Pfeiffer & Company, *Theories and Models in Applied Behavioral Science, volume II*

116   D.J. Marion, 1975 Handbook for Group Facilitators, University Associates

117   Paul Hersey—"godfather", Ken Blanchard, Dewey Johnson *Managing Organizational Behavior, 7th edition,* (Prentice-Hall, Inc. A Simon & Shuster Company 1969)

118   Amati Etzioni, *Modern Organizations,* (Prentice-Hall 1964)

119   Tyson Vision Magazine April-May 1997

120   Peter C. Drucker, *Management: Tasks, Responsibilities, Practices.* (Harper & Row 1973)

121   Title I, Part C, Education of Migratory children, United States Department of Education, October 23, 2003

122   The Arkansas Leadership Academy Web Site:www. arkansasleadershipacademy.org

123   CAIR: Executive Director, Dr. John Farrell, Program Specialist Dr. C.J.Heaton, State Liason & Special Projects Coordinator Laila Brownlee.

Chapter 10

124   Benjamin Graham, *The Intelligent Investor,* (Collins Business Essentials 1973)

Paul's Retirement, 1997

VITA

Paul Whitley was born into the food business where he worked most of his life. His father, G.P. Whitley borrowed fifty dollars during the great depression to open a combination grocery store, cream, egg and hide buying station in the tiny Texas-Oklahoma border town, Texhoma, Oklahoma

He was educated in elementary school in the Texas Panhandle town of Booker, Texas population 389. When his parents retired from the food business they moved to Ft. Collins, Colorado where he was educated at Lambkin High

School, the only high school in town, in 1950. His college work was at Pasadena College in Southern California where he supported himself working as a meat cutter.

Paul began his management career in Denver, Colorado managing a retail meat market in a neighborhood grocery store in North Denver. As the retail business shifted from small, neighborhood stores to supermarkets he opted for a career in sales with Sigman Meat Company serving retail and foodservice markets in Colorado. His career path followed a traditional growth pattern moving from local to regional to national and on to international sales. During his tenure as sales manager for Rogers Food, an Idaho based potato company, he traveled to and and worked with industrial customers in the U.K., France, Germany and Japan.

Whitley said the most influential persons in his life long learning were Mabel Hixson, Latin Teacher at Lambkin High School; Claude Herbst who taught him how to work at age fourteen at the Safeway Store Meat Market in Ft. Collins; Dr. Henry Ernst, Professor of History and German at Pasadena College; Dr. Paul Hersey, "godfather" and founder of The Center for Leadership Studies in Escondido, California; and the Dale Carnegie Sales Training Organization where he worked as a Certified Sales Course Instructor in the mid-sixties with Lowell Weiss & Associates.

He and his wife Barbara live in Carrollton, Texas. Barbara has two adult children, Melisa and John. Paul has two adult children, Connie and Mark. Barbara and Paul own PBW Insights LLC, a consulting, writing and publishing company. E-mail: pbwinsightsllc@gmail.com

His community and civic work includes a long list of activities from his years managing Tyson's Management Development Center in Russellville, Arkansas. His work on the Board of Friendship Services, a non-profit dedicated to meeting the needs of developmentally handicapped children and adults in the Arkansas River Valley of Central Arkansas, was a rich learning and most gratifying experience. Cindy Mahan, Founder and CEO possessed the rare combination of a passion for service and all the competencies of leadership validated over many years of success, continuing to this day.

In 1997 Whitley was asked to deliver the commencement address at the College of Education at the University of Arkansas at Fayetteville. He remembers asking himself as he sat on the podium, "what is a depression born boy from the Panhandle of Texas doing alongside these brilliant academics, luminous in their caps and gowns?" The theme of his address was Having Fun at Work. He told the story of how Ella Fitzgerald, The First Lady of Song, discovered her unique niche in life and the value of having fun at work.